RETHINKING RESTRUCTURING:
Gender and Change in Canada

During the past decade Canadian policy-makers have been forced to re-examine familiar forms of government and established programs in the face of growing budget deficits, economic instability, and a rapidly changing global economy. This collection of eighteen original essays presents a critical exploration of the question of political and economic restructuring from the vantage point of gender.

The authors argue that the present shift in the global order is revealing the contradictory effects of what is a dual process of both gender erosion and intensification. With the convergence of male and female job experiences in polarized labour markets, gender appears to be less important in understanding the global political economy; at the same time, gender becomes more of a determining factor in the transformation of politics and markets owing to the changing role of women as workers, care givers, and consumers.

The decline of the Keynesian welfare state has made claims-based politics less viable as a site of struggle for the women's movement. Not only has claims-based politics been replaced by a trend towards community and individual reliance, the women's movement itself has undergone a transformation that precludes a unitary, homogeneous approach to policy and politics.

ISABELLA BAKKER is an associate professor in the Department of Political Science at York University. She is editor of *The Strategic Silence: Gender and Economic Policy*.

ISABELLA BAKKER, Editor

Rethinking Restructuring: Gender and Change in Canada

UNIVERSITY OF TORONTO PRESS

Toronto Buffalo London

© University of Toronto Press Incorporated 1996
Toronto Buffalo London
Printed in Canada

ISBN 0-8020-0702-3 (cloth)
ISBN 0-8020-7651-3 (paper)

Printed on acid-free paper

Canadian Cataloguing in Publication Data

Main entry under title:

Rethinking restructuring

Includes bibliographical references.
ISBN 0-8020-0702-3 (bound)
ISBN 0-8020-7651-3 (pbk.)

1. Canada – Economic policy – 1991 –
2. Economic stabilization – Canada.   3. Women –
Canada – Economic conditions.   I. Bakker, Isabella C.

HQ1381.R48 1996   339.5'082   C95-932866-1

University of Toronto Press acknowledges the financial assistance to its
publishing program of the Canada Council and the Ontario Arts Council.

Contents

Contributors

Pat Armstrong, *Professor, School of Canadian Studies, Carleton University*

Abigail B. Bakan, *Associate Professor, Department of Political Studies, Queen's University*

Isabella Bakker, *Associate Professor, Political Science, York University*

Suzanne Bergeron, *Doctoral candidate, Economics, University of Notre Dame*

Janine Brodie, *Professor, Political Science, York University*

Barbara Cameron, *Associate Professor, Political Science, Atkinson College, York University*

Marjorie Griffin Cohen, *Professor, Political Science / Women's Studies, Simon Fraser University*

M. Patricia Connelly, *Professor, Sociology, St Mary's University*

Christina Gabriel, *Doctoral candidate, Political Science, York University*

Jane Jenson, *Professor, Political Science, Université de Montréal*

Joanna Kerr, *Senior Researcher, The North-South Institute, Ottawa*

Belinda Leach, *Assistant Professor, Sociology and Anthropology, University of Guelph*

Laura Macdonald, *Assistant Professor, Political Science, Carleton University*

Martha MacDonald, *Professor, Economics, St Mary's University, Halifax*

Lisa Philipps, *Assistant Professor, Faculty of Law, University of Victoria*

Daiva K. Stasiulis, *Professor, Sociology and Anthropology, Carleton University*

Acknowledgments

Thanks go out to many people for helping with this volume. Maureen O'Neil's leadership and vision provided the initial spark for this research project. Others at the North-South Institute were also instrumental in providing the intellectual and organizational support that went into the conference that brought the contributors to this volume together (Structural Change and Gender Relations in the Era of Globalization, Toronto, 1–2 October 1993). In particular, I would like to thank Joanna Kerr for her personal support and clear vision. Thanks also go to Lynn Hately.

I would like to thank the University of Toronto Press for their enthusiasm and careful shepherding of this project. Particular thanks go to Virgil Duff and Agnes Ambrus. I have also benefited a great deal from the thoughtful interventions of two anonymous reviewers of this manuscript. The care with which they and the editors handled the volume is greatly appreciated.

I would like to thank my family and friends for their sustenance. Without them I would not have been able to ride the storm during a very difficult time. Finally, I would like to acknowledge the support of the Canadian International Development Agency (CIDA), which provided funding support for this project under the Canada-India Applied Economic and Business Policy Linkage Program, managed by the Conference Board of Canada. In addition, funding from the Social Sciences and Humanities Research Council Strategic Research Grants Division supported vital research on women and restructuring in the form of a network of scholars and activists.

RETHINKING RESTRUCTURING

Introduction: The Gendered Foundations of Restructuring in Canada

In the last few years, the term restructuring has been used as a 'buzzword' referring to a necessary but painful process of change for Canadians. In general, restructuring has been presented as a response to the inevitable pressures of global liberalization. The new global economy, we have been told, requires increased international competition between countries for investment and production, a greater emphasis on trade, and less government spending and regulation of the economy. In other words, governments have no choice but to adapt their domestic economies, particularly the fiscal side, to the new demands of an increasingly global economy. Treaties and international trade agreements such as NAFTA reflect governments' intentions to create a favourable investment climate for foreign capital. Firms, industries, and workers are also being challenged to be more 'flexible' and 'competitive' in an effort to stem the outflow of manufacturing operations to countries of the South.

The internationalization of production is the most obvious manifestation of the forces driving restructuring. Broadly referred to as globalization, what it signals is a transformation of the methods and locations of production. Technological and managerial changes are taking place that allow firms to divide the different aspects of their operations globally in order to take advantage of the lowest-cost raw materials, the best research and development, the highest-quality assembly, and the most effective marketing. An oft-cited example of this new flexible international division of labour is Benetton, the Italian clothing company. While its marketing activities are highly centralized at the family headquarters in northern Italy, the production side is decentralized, with the skilled parts of the process – designing, dyeing, cutting, and final ironing – taking place at Benetton's main plants, but most of the weaving and assembly being done outside the company's plants by subcontractors in Italy and abroad (Mitter 1986b: 112–15).

Nation states' responses to transnational production are increasingly circumscribed by a neo-liberal consensus that imposes the same demands on all governments: the need to reduce state spending and regulation, maximize exports, and enable market forces to restructure national economies as part of transnational or regional trading blocs. The economic becomes self-regulating and depoliticized in the sense that the imperatives of efficiency and competition become inevitable, imposed by some external force over which people have no control. As Marjorie Cohen writes, 'its presentation as a universal force makes "restructuring" appear apolitical and, in conjunction with this, gender, race, and class neutral' (1995: 274).

The neo-liberal approach in economics rests on several premises:

– that institutions such as the state and the market should reflect the motivation of individual self-interest;
– that states provide a minimum of public goods along the lines of the nineteenth-century 'night-watchman' state;
– and that the most efficient allocation of resources and maximization of utility occurs through markets.

The shift in governing practices that is currently under way is mirrored in a parallel shift in how we understand citizenship rights. Canada's postwar experience was lodged in a Keynesian notion of social citizenship that assumed the public could and should enforce certain limits on the market. However, the new order is reshaping these ideals towards market-oriented values based on self-reliance and competition. The new 'ordinary' citizen does not make 'special' impositional claims on the state based on difference or systemic discrimination because one should be able to take care of oneself (Brodie 1994: 35).

Hence, part of restructuring involves 'reprivatizing' many maintenance and caring activities that, through Keynesian Welfare State (KWS) interventions, had become public, state-sector responsibilities. Activities within the public sector are also being reshaped to conform to private-sector rules and criteria. Program delivery, for example, is frequently based on a more individualized notion of dependency, with the social and structural foundations of dependency increasingly being cast aside in favour of *individual* solutions to what are perceived to be *individually determined* problems (Fraser and Gordon 1994). These responses to public-sector restructuring are driven by a number of structural forces and constraints that have put increasing pressures on state finances.

In terms of macroeconomic policies and state finance, several pressures are shaping the responses to structural change within many countries. The increased structural power and mobility of transnational capital has created pressure on nation-states to be tax-competitive and has sharply eroded national governments' power to tax owing to the spread of offshore tax havens. Traditional welfare-state expenditures in health, education, and pensions were fuelled by the demographic pressures of a growing and aging population. Aside from coverage extensions, increases in service and benefit levels have also been a contributing factor to rising social spending. Yet over the last decade, increases on the spending side appear to have played less of a role in contributing to chronic deficits than have changes on the revenue side and escalating debt-servicing costs. Revenue decisions such as a series of tax expenditures or tax breaks for individuals and corporations were reported to have cost the Canadian federal treasury at least $30 billion by the late 1980s. By using tax expenditures, governments could give the appearance of being fiscally responsible while still offering fiscal advantages to specific industries and individuals. A significant reduction in corporate taxes since the 1950s and the concomitant rise in the individual income-tax burden also places limits on the threshold of taxes Canadians are willing to pay. Higher interest rates, reflecting both a response to rising American interest rates and the Bank of Canada's preoccupation with zero inflation, had the effect of becoming a growing burden on government finances. By the early 1990s, interest payments on the public debt took up some thirty-odd cents of every dollar (Bakker 1994b).

These conditions created a skewed response to the challenges of restructuring and adjustment. Thus far, governments have pursued a strategy of adjustment that facilitates capital mobility through, on the one hand, a reduction in fiscal and regulatory burdens on industry and, on the other hand, a lowering of expectations about social-welfare, labour, and environmental standards. In a domestic context, this strategy involves promoting the politics of scarcity: the viewpoint that we can no longer afford the welfare state as it is a costly drain on our scarce resources. In an internationally competitive environment, the argument goes, we have no choice but to divest ourselves of these costs. In particular, this means decreasing the debt load through cuts in KWS services and a roll-back of some of the egalitarian gains that have been part of the rise of the welfare state (such as income redistribution and equal access to services like schools and health). It also has meant providing less funding for many of the transfers that were shared-cost programs between the provinces and the federal government (Bakker and Scott 1996).

Those involved in the debate about the future of the KWS agree that significant changes in the economy and the domestic sphere have eroded the ability of the state to underwrite economic and social reproduction. Neo-liberals have seized the occasion to advocate for a welfare state that subordinates 'social policy to the demands of labour market flexibility and structural competitiveness' (Jessop 1993: 9). This subordination entails a move away from redistributive concerns based on expanding welfare rights towards more cost-saving concerns. Proponents of neo-liberalism support continued emphasis on the elevation of the market and family in welfare provision, increased targeting of remaining public resources to the subsistence needs of the 'poorest,' in addition to measures to ease the transition from income-security programs to the low-wage labour market, often in the form of subsidies to low-wage employers (Myles et al. 1988). The new global order seeks to limit the terrain of government intervention and to valorize the market over politics, the private over the public. These elements of state restructuring are contributing to the reshaping of the economic and political identities of citizens.

The Gender Paradox of Restructuring

Despite the far-reaching implications of changing state forms, most restructuring discourse remains abstract and generic, treating 'global competitiveness,' 'flexibility,' and 'deficit reduction' as embodying both common sacrifice and benefit. In a sense, the old Keynesian order rested on a shared assumption of the inclusiveness of national policies and continuous growth – all citizens, male and female, within the boundaries of the nation-state would, by definition, achieve the highest possible well-being. This narrative of inclusivity mirrors economists' treatments of the household as a black box, a natural and obvious social entity that yields mutually agreeable rewards and trade-offs (see Bergeron, this volume). Some economists have challenged this view of the household as a harmonious unit of income-pooling individuals and suggest that a more realistic approach might be to characterize the household as a site both of cooperation and of conflict. The cooperative bargaining models suggested by Sen (1990) and Folbre (1986) go a long way towards recognizing that decision-making outcomes in households are a reflection of the differential bargaining power of the various household members, often determined by their gender and/or age.

Postwar Keynesian macro policies rested on the above model of the household as a single unit and, more broadly, on a gender order of a stable working class and nuclear family supported by a male breadwinner and women's domestic labour (McDowell 1991). For some women, such as those from the working class and the majority of women in the South, there are continuities in the current transition because of the centrality of their labour to household survival. Nevertheless, in both the old and the newly emerging orders the gender model described above underpinned the Keynesian economic and welfare policies of the industrialized countries, and was the basis for the state's construction of identities and division of resources along gender lines (Orloff 1993).

The present shift in the global order is, however, revealing the contradictory effects of what is a dual process of both gender erosion and intensification (Haraway 1991). In other words, gender appears to be less important in understanding the global political economy and, at the same time, more of a determining factor in its transformation. On the one hand, it is widely recognized that restructuring means a relative increase in the proportion of women exposed to direct market forces (whether as workers, traders, or consumers). As part 1 ('Labour-Market Restructuring and the State') of this volume illustrates, the feminization of work has been one consequence for some countries of the re-regulation of their political economy (Standing 1989). Feminization of the labour force is a process whereby women, often paid lower wages, take jobs formerly filled by men. The increasing share of service-sector employment in many OECD countries also shifts employment towards job categories dominated by women. In addition, the informal sector is also responsible for an increased share of female economic activity.

The lines between the informal sector and the formal sector are becoming more blurred with deregulation, casualization, and the growth of subcontracting and self-employment in both the North and the South (International Institute for Labour Studies 1994). In general, as several chapters in part 3 ('Globalization(s): Challenges and Alternative Strategies') reveal, the informal sector appears to expand and contract according to economic conditions – during recession formal enterprises rely on subcontracting (such as homeworkers) or may deregulate and partially enter the informal sector, whilst periods of expansion encourage regularization of economic activities in the formal sector to obtain loans and benefits (Baden, 1993). These trends suggest the increasing importance of a gender-based analysis of restructuring.

On the other hand, the process of labour-market polarization appears to be de-emphasizing the dominance of gender. As labour markets restructure, there is increasing evidence of a polarization of 'good' jobs and 'bad' jobs in the industrialized countries (OECD 1993). This process is revealing emerging class and race differences among women and is, as Armstrong illustrates in her chapter, causing more men to move into what were traditionally female jobs as manufacturing jobs are disappearing and labour-market standards are being lowered through explicit and implicit deregulation.[1] Rubery (1988) has argued that, in the reverse case, where women are entering previously male-dominated spheres, there is evidence that the status and rewards for such employment also tend to decline. Both shifts seem to suggest a convergence of male and female labour-market experiences within what are increasingly polarized labour markets.

Gender as an Interactive Category of Analysis

What these trends suggest is the need to consider gender as an interactive category of analysis in a complete account of the transforming global order. This should not imply that gender is always the most important factor but, rather, that a political-economy framework must incorporate its interaction with other agents (other groups or individuals), structural factors (assets, norms), processes (production, exchange, coordination, coercion), and sites (firms, states, markets, families).[2] Feminist economists increasingly emphasize the matrix of identities and factors that determine people's abilities and responses to economic change. 'The point is not,' as Nancy Folbre has stated, 'that conventional political economy fails to put gender first but rather that it understates its importance within the larger picture' (1994: 50).

Feminist interventions on globalization do not call for an exclusive or even primary focus on women; rather, the goal is to reveal the networks of power that are formed by the web of social relations. As Spike Peterson has noted, such an approach 'argues that (gendered) power itself is relational and operates downward, upward, and multi-laterally but *not* homogeneously. Because multiple oppressions are at work – sometimes overlapping, sometimes contradictory – emancipatory politics can rely on no single formula, universal subject, or utopian state but must engage a politics of difference' (1994: 15). Grewal and Kaplan (1994) refer to this reality as one of 'scattered hegemonies.' All of these authors are embedded in current feminist critiques of positivism that challenge our understandings of agents and subjectivity. Such critiques emphasize that subjects have multiple identifications (class, gender, race, ethnicity, sexuality, nationality) and that they interact with historically specific social contexts. Hence, feminists increasingly argue that an analysis of globalization must be locally contextualized rather than based on universal abstracts; such a situated knowledge is simultaneously recognized as a partial knowledge – in other words, a partial way of seeing the world (see Haraway 1991; Kabeer 1994).

This emphasis on contextualized knowledge has led for calls to 'rewrite' the process of globalization from the margins – from the vantage point of those who are outside of the privileged elites of western academia and transnational capital. Understanding and writing about globalization then becomes a process of revealing the silences of current renderings of globalization that contribute to the continued marginalization of non-Western women (Said's notion of contrapuntal reading [1993] or hooks's use of double marginality [1984], are both examples of such an approach). This epistemological break with modernism need not preclude white, Western academics from exposing the hegemonic understandings of globalization. bell hooks's distinction between a marginality that is imposed and one that one chooses as a site of resistance (1991: 153) can serve as a guide to a feminist politics of restructuring that spans alliances across gender, races, class, and nation. This does not imply a reaffirmation of the 'Sisterhood is Global' view of the women's movement. Such an approach, as Gabriel and Macdonald point out in their contribution, is untenable given that restructuring has created both women who are benefiting from and women who are being victimized by this process (see Bakan and Stasiulis, Armstrong in this volume).

All of these discussions may seem to be far away from the concerns of policy makers and analysts, who are generally guided by practical rather than strategic gender needs in the planning process.[3] However, the above epistemological discussion can be linked to attempts by policy analysts to include gender in accounts of restructuring, since they frequently encounter analytical frameworks that reinforce a unitary rational actor ('rational economic man') as the subject of policy and generally obscure the interrelatedness of economics with the political, social, and cultural (Harder 1993).[4]

Most attempts to move beyond gender neutrality are circumscribed by several factors: one is the global expansion of neo-liberal economic orthodoxy, which privileges a market-based accountability over social or political accountability; second, this neo-liberal world-view is super-imposed on a body of economic thought that does not 'address the unpaid process of production of human resources as well as the paid production of the gross national product; and explicitly consider the way the two are integrated. It must be prepared to consider as problem-atic relations within households, as well as relations between house-holds. It must extend the scope of what is defined as "the economy" and understand the functioning of the economy in terms of conflict as well as co-operation' (Elson 1994).[5]

A fundamental weakness in neoclassical economics (as well as critical perspectives such as the Keynesian or the Marxian), according to femi-nist writers, is that need and production are not situated within an anal-ysis of systemic reproduction *that includes* human reproduction and sustenance. This leads to a limited view of restructuring. For example, those who care for others become dependent on income transfers or must take on employment income that creates a double burden in terms of paid and unpaid work. Cutbacks in government spending, however, create a more precarious economic situation for many recipients of transfer payments (see Bakker 1994 for a detailed discussion of these issues). Also, cuts are off-loading many of the human caring services to the private sector and the household (see Connelly and MacDonald, this volume). This can have negative-feedback effects ranging from women's delayed re-entry into the labour market (and a subsequent downgrading of their seniority and skills) to greater stress and poorer health for women. In addition, a combination of some of these pressures appears to be contributing to the greater incidence of unregulated forms of homeworking, as is discussed by Leach in her chapter.

These then are some of the broader issues raised by a discussion of restructuring. But how do they relate to Canada? What is the nature of economic, political, and social restructuring in Canada? How is the gen-der order being transformed? Are gender disparities getting better or are they intensifying? This volume begins the attempt to address some of these important questions.

Gender and Restructuring in Canada – Policy Impacts and Women's Agency

During the past decade, Canadian policy makers have been forced to examine familiar governing instruments and established programs in the face of growing budget deficits, economic instability, and a rapidly changing global economy. Canada, like its international counterparts, has been forced to 'adjust' to these new realities through stabilization and structural-adjustment policies aimed at reducing governmental expenditures, promoting economic reorganization, and expanding international trade. Together, these policies have shifted patterns of paid labour, strained existing social programs, inhibited the development of new ones, and increased the role of the market in resource allocation.

What these policy shifts suggest is a very different environment from that of twenty-five years ago when the report of the Royal Commission on the Status of Women (Canada 1970) was released. This report had a far-reaching impact in highlighting issues of equality as well as providing impetus for the creation of an institutional framework ranging from various governmental women's bureaux to the establishment of the National Action Committee for the Status of Women (NAC) in 1972. The feminist policy agenda that emerged from this period was largely galvanized by equal-opportunity concerns such as labour-market justice, child care, legal rights, and reproductive rights (see Vickers et al. 1992 for a detailed discussion).

The current policy environment has served to marginalize the organized women's movement[6] at the same time as it has fostered a greater awareness on the part of women's groups of the importance of macro issues of restructuring. In particular, feminists have been quick to identify economic decline and fiscal restraint as circumscribing the extension of equity policies (Fudge and McDermott 1991). However, there is nothing within the sphere of public finance that prevents governments from pursuing a strategy of growth as well as equity through the patterning of revenues and more effective targeting of expenditure allocations (see Bakker 1994b; Palmer 1992). As Philipps points out in her chapter, the imposition of personal-wealth taxes on those with significant assets is a powerful tool for government to effect distributive change. This could in turn counteract some of the 'harmonizing down' that is currently occurring in the Canadian labour market, as is discussed by Pat Armstrong in her chapter.

It was the free-trade debate from 1985 to 1988 that broadened the terrain of so-called women's issues from a status-of-women approach towards a feminist politics (MacDonald 1995). The issue of free trade forced the women's movement to grapple with broader macroeconomic questions and changed its focus to an analysis of restructuring that emphasized that the adjustment process was not a gender-neutral one when it came to potential gains and losses. Through analyses of job changes in manufacturing and services, several conclusions emerged that allowed the women's movement to forge coalitions with other popular-sector groups. As Martha MacDonald has summarized, NAC's opposition to free trade was based on four main points: 'First, that the costs of free trade would be disproportionately borne by the most disadvantaged in the labor force, namely women; second, in the manufacturing sector women were most likely to lose their jobs due to their concentration in vulnerable industries; third, women's prospects for re-employment are less than men, given their more restructured access to training and other programs; and fourth, free trade in services would displace Canadian labor and threaten public services' (1995: 18–19). Despite the defeat of oppositional forces in the election of 1988, the intervention and leadership of NAC and other social movements set the stage for future participation by feminists in debates on issues as wide-ranging as the Constitution, the deficit, and the erosion of the public sector and of social programs.

What the authors in this volume set out to do is to sketch the parameters of the current restructuring process through a consideration of some of the concerns raised by the new feminist politics. By focusing on specific policy areas (the labour market, fiscal policy, trade, citizenship), the authors highlight recent trends as well as the often gender-blind policies of 'adjustment' advocated by governments at all levels. Whilst the mapping of differential impacts on women and men and, indeed, among different groups of women is important, the authors also focus on women's agency through a consideration of responses by women to the new global order.

Part 1: Labour-Market Restructuring and the State

Much of traditional equity policy has focused on the labour market through such state measures as pay equity, training, and affirmative action. However, the restructuring of labour markets is now presenting a set of broader issues for policy makers that require new approaches to a set of rapidly changing conditions spurred on by globalization. The emergence of the global assembly line and, in particular, the growth in the number of informal-sector workers and the rise in women's paid work is one of the centre-pieces of global restructuring (Feldman 1992: 1–2).

The feminization of work has been one key explanation offered for the changing picture of labour markets across countries. Feminization of work refers to both the notable rise in female labour-force participation and the transformation or feminization of many jobs traditionally held by men. This thesis has been interpreted in different ways. Some authors see women's increased economic activity as an important step forward in establishing greater economic independence for them-selves. Others are less optimistic, suggesting that a series of changes in women's economic roles has taken place, 'increasing their use as workers but weakening their income and employment security in both low-income industrializing and industrialized countries' (Standing 1989: 1077). This change has been due to *explicit* deregulation, an erosion or abandonment of formal labour-market regulations by legislative means, and *implicit* deregulation, through which remaining regulations have been made less effective through inadequate implementation or systematic bypassing.

Pat Armstrong argues that women's increasing similarity to men in paid-employment patterns does not necessarily mean improvement for women. For Armstrong, the feminization of the labour force has not pri-marily meant 'good jobs' for most women; it has meant more women's work for some men. By simultaneously examining changes in men's and women's patterns of employment, she concludes that using a male stan-dard to evaluate women's progress 'often exaggerates women's gains and hides harmonizing down for some men.' Restructuring of labour markets away from full-time jobs in all but non-commercial services and services to business has led to a decline in men's overall position. This deterioration in men's work may lead to the appearance of false gains for women in terms of a narrowing of the wage and labour-force-participation gaps. Women and men's work is becoming more similar mainly because fewer people of both sexes have a choice of 'good jobs' (that is, secure, with relatively high wages, full-time, and unionized).

In addition, Armstrong finds that men were generally more success-ful than women in capturing new full-time employment in those very areas where women traditionally found their best jobs, such as in the commercial and non-commercial services. While much attention has been paid to the latest figures on what appears to be a narrowing wage gap between women and men (70 per cent for full-time, full-year work-ers in 1991), Armstrong suggests that this shift was due in part to a decline in male average wages. Women's average earnings did not rise primarily because they took high-paying jobs away from men; women who made it into the top ten paying occupations averaged 61 per cent of male earnings. Armstrong cautions that any sign of women's progress reflects a decline in men's position as a result of restructuring rather than gains for women. For her, globalization leads to a harmonizing down for many (bad jobs) and an improvement for a few (good jobs).

Training initiatives have frequently been held up as programs responsive to women's needs in the newly globalizing economy. **Barbara Cameron** uncovers the uneven record of the Canadian federal government from 1972 to the present in accommodating the interests of women in overall federal training policy. Cameron argues that pressure by women's organizations has been sufficient to ensure that the interests of women were accommodated within the general policy of the day, but have not been enough to win policies designed specifically to address the training needs of women.

In the early 1970s, accommodating women's needs took the form of first removing discriminatory barriers and adopting an equal-opportunity approach. Women's participation rates in some training programs did improve as a result of more gender-sensitive government policy, and women fared best in those programs over which government had the greatest control (such as non-apprenticeship institutional training). In the late 1970s, a more proactive positive-action approach was incorporated into some of the training programs, with the government's shift to training for higher-skilled jobs reflected in the National Training Program. Cameron concludes that the special measures directed at women's participation in training for non-traditional occupations had some positive effects but that these were not sufficient to offset the negative impact on women of cuts in the overall number of trainees in employer-based programs.

After the mid-1980s, training programs reflected a targeted employment-equity approach that may continue under the current Liberal government, although the federal review of social programs seems to reflect a gender-neutral approach to policy that does not recognize women as a separate policy group. The Canadian Jobs Strategy (1985) represented a break from the past – training was to be more directly related to market demand by using government spending to encourage a larger role for employers in training. The CJS also adopted the Commission on Equity in Employment's recommendations of four targeted equity groups that face systemic discrimination in labour markets (women, people with disabilities, visible minorities, and aboriginal peoples). The equity focus of CJS, combined with its primarily low-skill orientation, had contradictory effects for women: on the one hand, they had greater access to federal training programs; on the other hand, they were concentrated in programs that trained them for low-paid sex-stereotyped jobs. Greater flexibility in the labour supply at the bottom end of the labour market fit into the government's overall strategy of a dual labour market, whereby the majority of women were in the emerging, poorly protected and remunerated, service industries.

In order to contextualize further the discussion of labour-market restructuring, **M. Patricia Connelly** and **Martha MacDonald** offer a case-study in the public sector in Nova Scotia. The example of home-care workers highlights the issues of the casualization of work, subcontracting, and the effects of government restraint. In addition, the case confirms what studies of Structural Adjustment in the South have revealed: that it is women who bear the brunt of these changes both as workers and as primary care givers in the home. Situating their research within the broader context of flexibility strategies in the labour market, Connelly and MacDonald conclude that these strategies, whether they target wages or the allocation of tasks, create marginalization for the majority of women.

Through their case-study of new forms of health-care delivery that emphasize privatization, de-institutionalization, and keeping people in the community, the authors explore the nature of home care, the workers, and the actual labour process. They conclude that the change from full-time to part-time work and the extension of tasks in the workload of home-care workers has increased the employers' flexibility and cut costs. For the employees, flexibility has decreased as wages and benefits have been lowered, and autonomy and discretionary use of time have been lessened. At the same time, women who are single parents appreciate the flexibility of their work hours and some of the relative autonomy that remains over tasks. However, Connelly and MacDonald are concerned about the long-term impact of these changes in the labour market and the increase on the number of such jobs as the economy continues to undergo restructuring. Any new policy initiatives must, they urge, take into account the shifting of economic activity across paid and unpaid work.

The theme of gendered employment relations as being at the heart of restructuring is extended by **Jane Jenson**, who focuses on the rise in part-time employment in her chapter. She argues that the postwar 'worker model' of the male breadwinner supporting a dependent wife and family is eroding with women's rise in employment and the restructuring of jobs towards non-standard employment such as part-time work and limited-term contracts. These shifts are gendered in nature, as women are disproportionately found among non-standard workers and are concentrated in the growing service-sector, so-called bad, jobs. Jenson maps a form of employment and a time schedule that is overwhelmingly female in all 'postindustrial' societies. The shift in the distribution of employment in the direction of the service sector has been characterized by a reliance on part-time employment, an employer- and state-driven strategy directed at unemployment, Jenson argues, that is heavily gendered.

How these new structures of employment and inequality are being created can vary depending on how choices are made about *how* and *whether* to employ part-time, with some choices being more likely to promote gender equality over others. Jenson is careful not to paint part-time employment as a functional necessity, whether economic or familial; instead, she offers a series of contrasting patterns of responses to part-time employment and evaluates them from the vantage point of gender equality. She concludes that part-time employment is largely an employer-driven strategy that gives them flexibility in the management of their labour forces and saves on wage bills. States have also promoted part-time work through neo-liberal strategies of cost cutting and privatization. In addition, part-time workers relieve some of the pressure of overall levels of unemployment. The result may be new structures of gender inequality, as part-time work is often seen to be a 'choice' by women to meet other family obligations, thereby relieving governments of spending on services such as child care and parental leaves. Jenson reviews the range of responses by states, unions, and women to rising rates of part-time employment: doing nothing; accepting, but bringing in measures to improve the benefits and protections of part-time workers; encouraging part-time employment as a solution to the employment crisis; and developing alternatives that would make part-time employment an equal choice for both women and men. She suggests that a different way to achieve flexibility and reduce unemployment may be a reduction of working time for all.

Part 2: National Policies and Social Citizenship

The postwar period in Canada brought with it a new understanding of the relationships between states, markets, and individuals. In particular, the state, through the Keynesian mechanisms of fiscal and monetary policy, played an important role in meeting the needs of its citizenry. Thus developed an expanded notion of citizenship that encompassed some public provision of basic needs such as health care and education. The Keynesian notion of citizenship shifted the focus away from the individual when it came to such issues as poverty and unemployment, placing them squarely on the shoulders of a national community. As Janine Brodie writes in her contribution, it is this Keynesian ideal that is currently being displaced through the dismantling of the KWS. From the vantage point of gender equity, there is no doubt a great deal to be concerned about in this shift towards self-reliance and greater private provision of welfare services. Yet, as Bergeron suggests in her chapter, a state-centred perspective that harkens back to the Keynesian era should also not go unproblematized. Its gendered construction of the workplace and the home presumed a stable working class, a nuclear family, and a dependent wife and children supported by a male breadwinner (McDowell 1991). It is the state's very construction of women as wives and mothers that 'enabled women to organize, to make political claims, to lobby the state for better services for the family, and eventually, to demand state actions to improve the condition of women in all aspects of social life' (Brodie 1994: 29). While liberal and social-democratic states have been instrumental in creating a space for the empowerment of women, Bergeron warns us that we should not idealize the state when it comes to its role as a producer of identities and as a regulator of certain identities to the margins.

Suzanne Bergeron provides a novel introduction to macroeconomics and macropolitical discourse. Through a careful discussion of how the concept of nation is integrated into classical, Keynesian, and post-Keynesian theory, Bergeron exposes the male bias of existing macroeconomics and offers a feminist alternative. The nation, she suggests, is treated as a natural and eternal entity that appears to include all of its citizens, male and female, within its boundaries. This construction of the nation is facilitated by the way the macro is conceived of in economics. The macro deals with aggregates and does not talk about men or women. Instead, discussion is about the nation, growth, GDP, employment, and so on. Such a conceptualization implies a 'horizontality' of interests, suggesting that the well-being of the nation is shared by all its members. In this sense, differential effects of policy are difficult to fit into the narrative of national economic well-being, because a decline in inflation rates or a rise in GDP is assumed to benefit all, even those at the margins of the nation.

Janine Brodie's chapter grounds Bergeron's discussion by tracing the definition of interests in the postwar gender order in Canada. She argues that the passing of the welfare state marks more than a series of state responses to the changing international economy or the 'debt crisis.' For her, it also signals a paradigm shift, that is, a new way of thinking about governing practices. Brodie explores two dimensions related to changing popular conceptions of citizenship resulting from this shift. First, she traces the implications for Canadian women of the notions of citizenship that inform the new thinking about social-welfare provision. Second, Brodie looks at the gendered implications of the targeting of social-service delivery. For Brodie, the neo-liberal state marks a distinct shift in what it means to be a citizen and what citizens can legitimately demand of the state.

She reviews current federal initiatives such as the social-security review (ISSC) and provincial pilot projects in New Brunswick and Alberta to illustrate the shift away from social citizenship. Gender, she argues, is central to the analysis of social assistance, dependency, and personal culpability. Targeting has been used as a way to divide citizens between those who are deserving and undeserving, between the normal and those with special needs. Brodie believes that 'targeting serves to pathologize and individualize difference as well as place the designated groups under increased state surveillance and administrative control.' By removing the possibility to make universal claims based on the social category of 'woman,' the 'hollowed out' welfare state is degendering citizens and stigmatizing the targeted as being outside of the norms of the new citizenship.

Lisa Philipps illustrates that the emphasis on new citizenship will only serve to accentuate inequalities in economic citizenship. She explores a dimension of women's economic position that is relatively invisible in policy debates – the unequal distribution of wealth (as opposed to income) between women and men. This habit of overlooking wealth distribution means that economic policies are formulated and assessed by reference to an incomplete picture of the nature and degree of inequality in Canadian society. Moreover, lack of access to wealth poses special problems for women that go beyond those of income poverty. This is of particular concern in the current context of restructuring. The ability to survive and 'adjust' to a shifting, contracting labour market may depend heavily on the availability of savings or other forms of capital. Without any capital base, it is difficult to obtain necessary credit or other financing for a new business, house, or other major investments.

Lack of wealth may also limit a worker's ability to leave paid employment in order to receive additional education or training aimed at enhancing her labour-market potential. Such a lack may also limit a person's capacity to relocate in search of new work (that is, mobility). Influence and status in both the public and private sectors are also related to the control of major assets, and Philipps illustrates how gender is implicated in such an analysis. She attempts to reveal the patterns of gendered wealth distribution in Canada through largely indirect evidence, given the lack of published data disaggregated by gender.

Philipps argues that taxation and other economic-policy reforms must take wealth disparities into account if we are serious about including women in all aspects of economic life. This means that wealth should be part of the calculation of ability to pay – using income as a proxy for ability to pay obscures the full nature and extent of gender bias in the tax system. Philipps links the failure to address wealth inequalities through the tax system to what she refers to as 'the privatization of women's economic lives within the family.' Tax policy assumes that women's lack of economic power will be balanced by private, family means whereby altruistic male breadwinners provide for economic needs whilst selfless wives and mothers provide the necessary 'care.' Philipps discusses the use of spousal exemptions in the tax system to underscore her argument.

Part 3: Globalization(s): Challenges and Alternative Strategies

Global restructuring, as is revealed in the following chapters, is an uneven and fractured process. This suggests that strategies need to be developed that are context-based, reflecting a specific region, country, or sector of workers. At the same time, globalization is integrating national and regional economies in such a way as to require a 'transnational' response. The chapters in this section reflect a range of possible responses to the challenges and opportunities posed by global restructuring. What becomes evident is the need to engage on many terrains if the desired goal is the advancement of women in all parts of the world.

Trade agreements are increasingly the facilitators of the new global-restructuring process, codifying the ideology and economic climate for global economic integration. In concert with the increasing fiscal pressures on nation-states, trade policies are reinforcing the increased privatization of what were previously collectively provided services. For **Christina Gabriel** and **Laura Macdonald**, trade liberalization also highlights the contradictory and complex interconnections that exist between women in Canada and Mexico. Such a reflection will enrich our understanding of restructuring, according to Gabriel and Macdonald, because it will go beyond the centre-periphery vision of the global economy and feminist organizing. Trade agreements can therefore also present opportunities for cross-national organizing of social-sector groups. Because NAFTA brings together two advanced industrialized countries with a developing country with high levels of poverty and inequality, NAFTA provides a valuable point of encounter between women within both the North and the South.

NAFTA presents the possibility of developing a socially located analysis and acknowledging the particular struggles and agency of Third World women. Macdonald and Gabriel employ Nesiah's term 'feminist internationality,' which confronts the notion of universality embodied in global sisterhood and speaks to a transnational political alliance of women whose differences are directly confronted. According to the authors, organizing around NAFTA can potentially present a new, more mature stage in international feminism that goes beyond seeing Western feminism as the bearer of a transformatory and liberatory politics and casting Third World women in the role of mere victims. Such an approach also forces feminists to examine differences among women within Canada based on race and class.

Marjorie Griffin Cohen, in her contribution, highlights the potential problems for democracy arising out of recent trade agreements such as NAFTA, arguing that such agreements may undermine both national institutions and market-correcting policies by subsuming these to international regulations. This has particularly profound implications for equity-seeking groups, who frequently rely on state regulation or intervention. She urges a broader focus on how the economic regulations inscribed within NAFTA will constrain government from acting on behalf of people's economic interests. This view links debates about trade effects to broader concerns about the changing nature of citizenship.

Cohen offers several examples from NAFTA that illustrate the breadth of trade policy in areas of national sovereignty. In particular, she examines how agreements in the areas of resources and the public sector remove public policy from the power of democratic institutions. Cohen sees the push for harmonizing conditions between trading nations as prohibiting substantial differentiation in economic policy between nations. This denies the historical, geographic, and social differences between Canada and the United States. In particular, economic policies in Canada were designed to deal with the country's unique conditions, such as climate and size. The public sector has played a different role in Canada because of inequality of resources between regions and the need for strong public transportation and communication systems. However, built into NAFTA, according to Cohen, is the requirement that the public sector be reshaped to reflect a commercial approach to the provision of goods and services. The reshaping of the public sector suggests important challenges for feminists, who have historically relied on the political responsiveness of the state and legislators. For Cohen, the current trade regime presents real concerns for the ability of women, minorities, and the disadvantaged to have their interests met in the public sphere.

Belinda Leach moves the discussion from the macro to the micro by highlighting the increasing amounts of paid work located in the home. She examines one trend in particular – public-sector homeworking. Leach suggests that the consequences of increasingly popular homework policies such the 'telework' policies of the federal government and the more traditional industrial homeworking are far-reaching, going beyond the problem of organizing homeworkers to improve their work conditions. While homework policies are intended to improve worker productivity, the social conditions that propel the majority of women into homework are likely to lead to their effective seclusion inside the household, making exposure to and consciousness of different political ideas extremely difficult.

Homework policies, according to Leach, are not gender-neutral because it is mainly women who adopt homework as an income strategy and because men and women adopt homework for very different reasons and under different circumstances. Traditionally, homeworking has been a private-sector strategy, but recent fiscal constraints and shifts in the perceived role of the state have led to the introduction of homework as a new public-sector strategy. Leach suggests that the federal government's telework strategy introduces a spectrum of homework, with public-sector workers at one privileged extreme, as employees with good benefits and status, and garment-industry workers at the other, with little protection or security. Aside from the collective-organizing implications of more and more work being off-loaded into the home, Leach discusses the limits to shifting the balance of power between men and women in the home (long a goal of feminism) when work is absorbed into the continuous workday of the home.

One of the results of structural adjustment and trade liberalization has been the migration of labour from the South to the North. Dislocated rural labour is often inadequately absorbed into the factories of the export processing zones. Also, debt-repayment policies encourage citizens of Third World countries such as the Philippines to seek employment abroad and to make remittances to families back home. One of the impacts of poverty and underdevelopment has been to produce an increasingly large pool of women workers in search of First World citizenship rights. A discussion of female domestic workers serves to accent various states' relationships to different paths of economic development, including the contemporary 'export-import' of migrant labour. How state and non-state actors construct female domestic workers as marginal citizens (or in some cases, lesser humans) through perceptions, beliefs, and attitudes that translate into policies is explored by **Abigail B. Bakan** and **Daiva K. Stasiulis**.

Bakan and Stasiulis examine the migration of Third World women to Canada through the foreign-domestic-worker policy (the Live-In Care-Giver Program). They argue, one, that structural forces such as the generalized conditions of global unevenness, exacerbated and amplified by imperialist structures and policies, tend to create conditions that force female citizens of poor states to seek citizenship on virtually any terms in richer states, and two, that countries in the North such as Canada are both able and willing to exploit this increased supply in order to advance their own policies of structural adjustment. They note: 'The example of domestic-worker policy is illustrative of how policies that are damaging to the interests of women as a whole, such as the reduction or elimination of public day care, is rendered palatable, and even beneficial, to women of selectively high income and status within the boundaries defined by First World citizenship.' Bakan and Stasiulis claim that Canada's domestic-worker policy is less abusive relative to the policies of some other countries, yet foreign domestic workers remain structurally subordinate to 'normal' immigration flows internationally. They illustrate how Canadian domestic-worker policy has been constructed to take advantage of the conditions of underdevelopment within the Philippines and the English Caribbean. In this sense, Canada is inextricably linked to the global pattern that benefits from and contributes to the structural exploitation of Third World women.

Given the diversity of issues and actors involved in considerations of globalization, how is one to come up with concrete policies and strategic alternatives? If power is interactive and multilayered and political identities are increasingly multiple, are there markers to guide feminist responses?

Joanna Kerr calls for the building of strategic alliances based on women's differences as well as common interests. Alliances between middle-class and working-class women, women from the North and South, and academics and community-level activists and policy makers need to be forged. Echoing Gabriel and Macdonald's conclusions about confronting and recognizing differences between women, Kerr believes that this broadening will allow for a truer picture to be presented to policy makers who need to regulate the negative impacts of restructuring. Second, Kerr argues for the development of concrete solutions to protect workers under the new economic paradigm. She offers three strategies to deal with the changes entailed by the emergence of new flexible production systems: redeployment, decentralization, and flexibilization. Developing standards for casualized workers, as well as international standards that include social clauses as part of trade agreements, are discussed. Third, a commitment to investing in social programs at the national and international level is a cornerstone for improving overall levels of human development. Fourth, the gender bias in economics needs to be tackled through the dual thrust of policy analysis and reform. Finally, the viability of the current economic system needs to be assessed in the context of not just increasing productivity and profit but also meeting overall levels of human development.

Conclusion

Several critical themes are developed by the authors in the following pages. The overriding concern is to obtain a clearer understanding of the current restructuring process through a gender-sensitive lens. Such an approach does not privilege gender, but situates it within what Haraway (1991) calls 'the webs of power' – the networks of political actors, structures, and processes that shape women's and men's experiences on a daily basis.

Many authors identify the changing role of nation-states and the state itself as a key to the restructuring process currently under way. Sovereignty of nation-states has been circumscribed by transnational economic and political forces that limit individual states' regulatory powers. Shifts in state forms are, in turn, altering the way in which politics is being done within the boundaries of individual nation-states. Increasingly, individual states are taking on a highly paradoxical role.

On the one hand, the Canadian state is recasting its role as a more mini-mal provider of traditional public goods, with the result, as revealed in this volume, that households become both sites for coping with economic hardship (see Connelly and MacDonald) and sites of production (see Leach). On the other hand, we are seeing an emerging role for the state in certain targeted areas that will re-situate the public/private division of resources through such measures as taxation, training, trade liberalization and immigration policies (see Philipps, Cameron, Cohen, Brodie, and Bakan and Stasiulis).

The reconfiguration of government has significant implications for the women's movement now and in the future. Some authors argue that with the decline of the Keynesian welfare state, the state has largely been displaced as a site of struggle for the women's movement (Brodie 1994). Not only has a claims-based politics been displaced by a trend towards community and individual reliance, the women's movement itself has undergone a transformation that precludes a unitary, homogeneous approach to policy and politics. While the latter point is generally accepted within the movement (Pierson and Cohen 1994), the former is the subject of a great deal of debate and contestation. In particular, some authors argue that state power is not being reduced as much as transformed in the context of these global dynamics and proliferating identities (ibid.: 11). Yet it remains a truism that the women's movement can no longer articulate claims that are solely directed at the state.

Perhaps an understanding of politics as a process of contestation not just claims-based outcomes is one answer to shifting state forms. Anna Yeatman, an Australian writer, has talked of politics as 'the space between established policy and an emancipatory movement's claims on equality' (1993). In this view, politics is treated as a process rather than an abstract set of principles, and policy is seen as informed 'by an ongoing and openly contested politics of voice and representation' (230). This process of contestation goes beyond demands imposed on the state by various marginalized or interest-based groups. Rather it is a dual process where 'equality exists only within the relationship of polit-ical contestation, where those who are excluded by established policy both show its bias and make a claim on a prospectively more inclusive policy' (ibid.: 235).' In a sense, restructuring is challenging the feminist movement, its thinkers and activists, to develop a new approach to the state. Part and parcel of such a process is to begin to think about the limitations of the old Keynesian state form and to develop alternative scenarios for the future organization and functioning of the state (Bakker and Miller 1996).

NOTES

1 Explicit deregulation refers to an erosion or abandonment of formal regulations by legislative means, while implicit deregulation is a process through which remaining regulations have been made less effective owing to inadequate implementation or systematic bypassing (Standing 1989).

2 See Nancy Folbre 1994, *Who Pays for the Kids?*, for a fully elaborated model of feminist political economy.

3 Policy responses to restructuring can be characterized as directed at problem solving or meeting *practical gender interests*. In Molyneux's words, the latter 'are usually in response to an immediate perceived need, and they do not generally entail a strategic goal such as women's emancipation or gender equality' (1985: 233). By contrast, *strategic gender interests* reflect a more critical approach that links women's subordination to a systemic analysis.

4 For detailed feminist critiques of neoclassical economics, see Pujol (1992), Ferber and Nelson (1993), and Kabeer (1994).

5 This conclusion applies to both neoclassical and various critical perspectives such as the Keynesian, Kaleckian, structuralist, and Marxist approaches. As Diane Elson writes: 'Although individuals are conceptualized as gendered in the critical economics of the family, markets and firms are not generally conceptualized as gendered in a comparable way, though they operate in ways that are particularly constraining and disadvantageous to women. At the macro level, gender is absent altogether: the discourse is all about monetary aggregates' (1994: 38).

6 For a discussion of this marginalization, see Brodie 1994.

PART 1: LABOUR-MARKET RESTRUCTURING AND THE STATE

1

The Feminization of the Labour Force: Harmonizing Down in a Global Economy

PAT ARMSTRONG

The United Nations' 1993 *Human Development Report* applauds the global tendency towards the privatization of state enterprises, the deregulation of national economies, the decentralization of governance, the removal of barriers to international trade, the shift to a service economy, and growth in the labour-force participation of women. It is concerned that these tendencies have been accompanied by jobless growth, deteriorating job security, and continuing inequality for women, minorities and indigenous peoples, those in rural areas, and the disabled. But the solutions offered are really more of the same; more liberal trade policies, more service work, more decentralization, and more self-employment. The bad tendencies are to be offset by more education and training, by employment safety nets provided through public-works projects introduced during bad economic times, by providing disadvantaged groups with access to paid work through affirmative-action programs, and by redefining work (United Nations Human Development Programme 1993).

However, increased competition, privatization, and a growing service sector, even when combined with extensive formal education and affirmative-action programs, have not served to improve significantly Canadian women's position in recent years. It is true that, if we look at such measures as participation rates, the proportion of women in traditional male work and in higher education, the gap in wages between women and men, and job tenure, female and male employment patterns have become increasingly similar. Indeed, it could be said that the labour force is being feminized now that women make up close to half of the Canadian labour force, that some women have moved into traditionally male areas of work, that equal pay for work of equal value is required by law, and that most women are in the labour force, even when their children are young.

But increasing similarity with men does not necessarily mean improvement for women. Undoubtedly, the growth of the service economy, increased competition, and legislative action have helped some women move into well-paid, satisfying work in the labour force. But women's and men's labour-force experiences have become increasingly similar not simply because some women now have the kinds of good jobs traditionally held predominantly by men, but also because the labour-force work of a growing number of men has become more like that traditionally done by women and because fewer women have alternatives to labour-force work. The restructuring that is part of globalization has created more women's work in the market. At the same time, it has eliminated some men's jobs and altered many of the jobs traditionally done by men in ways that make them more like women's work. This kind of feminization of the labour force does not mean that the position of most women has improved. Instead, it means that the position of some men has deteriorated, becoming more like that of women. While some women and men do have good labour-force jobs, many more women and men have bad jobs. And this tendency is unlikely to be halted by the kinds of strategies the United Nations document suggests.

At least part of the increasing similarity between women and men's work can be explained in terms of a harmonizing down for some men and greater economic pressure on many women. Most of the good jobs are still dominated by men, but fewer men have jobs that offer the kinds of rewards and opportunities many men became accustomed to after the Second World War. Some men are responding to this trend by moving into areas where women have traditionally found their best jobs.

This paper looks at the most recent period of labour-force restructuring in Canada. Relying primarily on Statistics Canada data, it documents changes in participation rates, occupations, wages, hours, and conditions of work for women and men. It focuses on the 1990–2 period, because this has been a period of rapid restructuring. However, the limited nature of the data available for the most recent years means that it is often necessary to look at data for earlier periods in order to develop a picture of overall trends. Even with these data, however, it is difficult to develop a picture of differences among women and men based on location, disability, and cultural difference.

The paper argues that the use of a male standard to evaluate women's progress often exaggerates women's gains and hides a harmonizing down for some men. Some women have improved their position in the market, but many more women do women's work at women's wages and, increasingly, so do some men. The patterns in Canada provide just one example of both the impact of globalization and the limited effectiveness of the kinds of strategies the United Nations suggests.

Labour-Force Participation

The dramatic rise in female labour-force participation has been amply documented and widely publicized. The rise was halted during the 1990s, however, and female labour-force participation rates declined between 1990 and 1992. While women's participation rates were rising rapidly, men's were falling slowly. But over the last two years, the rate of decline in male participation has increased. Although women's participation rates decreased by less than one percentage point between 1990 and 1992, men's rates declined by more than two percentage points. The combination of these trends means that the difference between male and female participation rates is decreasing more rapidly than would be the case if men's rates remained stable. Similarly, women's participation in higher education has been rising much more rapidly than that of men, virtually eliminating the difference between the sexes in terms of education. By 1992, almost six out of every ten women over the age of fifteen were counted as part of the labour force, and this was the case for just over seven out of ten men. In that year, 42 per cent of the female labour force and 41 per cent of the male labour force had completed post-secondary education at either the university or the college level.[1]

Labour-force figures include both all those with any kind of job in the market and those seeking paid work. This combination of employed and unemployed in one figure can obscure greater differences between the sexes in employment and unemployment experiences. It can also hide differences between the patterns of young people who are still in school and of those over age twenty-five who are more likely to seek full-time labour-force work. It is therefore useful to examine more specific patterns for women and men as well as for people of different ages. It is not possible from these data to explore patterns for those from different cultural or racial groups, with disabilities, or of different immigration status.

Employment patterns indicate a feminization of the labour force and a deterioration in men's position. By 1992, 46 per cent of the employed were female. Of those over 25 years of age, 51 per cent of the women and 68 per cent of the men were officially counted as employed. Just two years earlier, 53 per cent of the women and 72 per cent of the men in this age group had labour-force work. In this two-year period, the percentage of young people with employment declined even more. And the decrease was greater for males than for females.

Higher education did not guarantee a job for men or women. Employment declined for those with post-secondary education, regardless of sex or age. The largest drop was for men with post-secondary diplomas or certificates, with employment/population ratios for this group falling from 81 per cent to 75 per cent. In other words, between 1990 and 1992 the percentage employed declined for both sexes, but it declined more for men than for women and education provided little protection from job loss.

Not surprisingly, the unemployment rate rose significantly for both sexes during this two-year period. The largest increase was for young men. However, the unemployment rate rose faster for adult men than for adult women even though more men than women dropped out of the labour force altogether. Indeed, the number of men between the ages of twenty-five and sixty-five who left the labour force was five times the number of women. As a result, the number of women and men without paid work became more similar and more men had interrupted employment patterns that were similar to those of women.[2]

By 1992, there were 332,000 fewer people with labour-force work than was the case in 1990, and overall job loss was almost five times greater for men than for women. But the loss of full-time work was significantly higher than the figures on the net loss indicate. There were 458,000 fewer people with full-time work, but 126,000 more people had part-time jobs. The net figure camouflages the fact that much of the new work was part-time. Because men are more likely than women to have full-time jobs, more of them lost full-time work. And because more of women's work is part-time, women took more of the new part-time work. Women's overall loss seems so much less than that of men because many women found part-time work to replace full-time jobs (see table 1).

Part-time work has been, and continues to be, dominated by women. In 1990, 71 per cent of part-time workers were women. While there were 125,000 fewer full-time jobs for women in 1992 than was the case in 1990, there were 69,000 more part-time ones. The percentage of employed women with part-time work increased by over one point,

TABLE 1
Industrial employment changes in Canada, 1990–2

Industry	Full-time	Part-time
Both sexes	−458	+126
Goods-producing industries	−355	+37
Service-producing industries	−102	+90
Agriculture	−1	+5
Other primary industries	−28	+2
Manufacturing	−222	+9
Construction	−117	+20
Transportation	−38	+9
Trade	−86	−6
Finance, insurance, and real estate	+7	+2
Service	+23	+86
Public administration	+4	0
Unclassified	n/a	n/a

Calculated from Statistics Canada 1991 and 1993c.

leaving more than a quarter of employed women with part-time jobs.[3] Given the large loss in full time jobs, it is not surprising that the proportion of women employed part time because they did not want full-time work declined sharply, dropping from 39 per cent in 1990 to 31 per cent in 1992. Put another way, the majority of women in part-time jobs can be classified as 'involuntary' part-time workers and their numbers are growing. Fewer and fewer have a choice about taking part-time rather than full-time work.

Although part-time work was still women's work, a rapidly growing number of men could find only part-time employment. The proportion of men working part-time also grew by more than a percentage point during this two-year period, with the number of men employed part time increasing by 57,000. Half of this growth was for men in the 25-to-44-year age group; that is, among the men who have traditionally been the most likely to want and have full-time work. As is the case with women, the proportion employed part time who did not want full-time work dropped significantly, decreasing from 19 to 15 per cent of those employed part time. But the percentage of women who had little choice increased twice as fast as that of men. In short, more men and even more women found only part-time work and the majority of both sexes did so 'involuntarily.'

These figures on part-time work refer to all those who usually work less than thirty hours a week, unless they consider themselves full-time. They leave out all those who work for part of a year and thus overstate the number of people who have full-time work all year. Statistics Canada does not publish data on part-year work in the *Labour Force Survey*, so it is difficult to examine changes between 1990 and 1992. However, data from the Labour Market Activity Survey show both that large numbers of women and men do not have full-year work and that the differences between the sexes are not great. '61% of all women who worked in 1988 were employed the entire year, compared to 69% of the men.'[4] Some of these people work for only part of the week, and thus would be classified as part-time. Others work more than thirty hours a week and thus would be counted as full-time even though they are employed only part of the year. Census data indicate that in 1991 almost 40 per cent of the men between the ages of 25 and 65 did not work mostly full time for 49 weeks or more, and this was the case for 60 per cent of the women.[5] It is clear, then, that many women and quite a few men did not have full-time, full-year work in 1990. And there is every reason to believe that the figures for 1992 would show that the number of part-year workers of both sexes has increased in 1992 as more jobs involved short-term contract or temporary work.

In sum, unemployment and both part-time and part-year employment have been growing for both sexes. Women's job loss was smaller in part because women captured more of the new part-time work, even though most of the women taking the part-time jobs did not do so by choice. With men's labour-market position deteriorating more rapidly than that of women in some areas, women's and men's employment patterns became more similar. Another part of the explanation for women's smaller job loss can be found in the nature of the new jobs that did appear during this period, as will become evident in the next section.

Industrial Restructuring

Over the last three decades, employment in all industrialized countries has grown rapidly in service industries and declined in the others (Akyeampong and Winters 1993). Between 1990 and 1992, job loss in the Canadian goods-producing industries was twenty-five times that in the service-producing industries. Put another way, 96 per cent of the employment loss was in primary industries – in manufacturing, construction, and utilities.[6]

For the purposes of the analysis presented here, this restructuring in employment is important for two reasons. First, most of the jobs in the goods-producing industries are male jobs and most of those in the service-producing industries are female jobs. Second, many of the new jobs in the service sector are what the Economic Council of Canada (1990) terms 'bad jobs,' jobs that offer little security, little opportunity for promotion, and little economic reward and that require few recognized skills.

Goods-Producing Industries

Given that just over 75 per cent of those employed in the goods-producing industries are men, it is not surprising that three-quarters of the full-time jobs lost in the goods-producing industries were men's jobs. Nor is it surprising that most of the male job loss occurred in these sectors. More than four out of five full-time jobs lost to men were in the goods-producing industries. These jobs did not disappear for men because women entered the labour force and took male jobs. Their disappearance was part of a major reorganization of employment in the market, as some operations shut down and others introduced new technologies and work structures.

This is not to suggest that there was no impact on women's jobs in these industries. Almost two-thirds of the women employed in goods-producing industries were employed in manufacturing and women in these industries saw their unemployment rate rise by three percentage points between 1990 and 1992. Significantly more women than men lost jobs in the manufacturing industries (171,000 women, compared with 149,000 men), even though women accounted for less than a third of those employed in these industries. Moreover, men took just over half of the new part-time jobs, even though they accounted for only 44 per cent of the part-time workers in these industries. As a result, the proportion of men employed part time in these industries increased by a full percentage point.[7] Most of this female job loss would be among immigrant women, given that they account for more than two-fifths of the women working in product manufacturing (Badets and McLaughlin 1989: 40).

Rising male unemployment, then, is to a large extent explained by the decline in the goods-producing industries that men dominate rather than by competition from women. Indeed, when women and men do compete, it is women who are more likely to lose their jobs. Although many men's jobs in these sectors were not necessarily good jobs in the sense of requiring high levels of education, providing non-repetitive work, or offering significant opportunities for promotion, many were covered by strong unions and paid relatively high wages. In fact, most unionized men worked in industries in the goods-producing sector.

Service-Producing Industries

Even during the recession of the 1990s, employment continued to grow in the service-producing industries. The very large service sector, where more than 70 per cent of all labour-force workers are employed, includes a wide range of jobs, many of which may be considered good jobs according to several criteria (Economic Council of Canada 1991: chapter 2). But many of them fit the Economic Council's definition of 'bad jobs.' Within the service sector, employment is divided into three relatively equal parts: traditional service industries, non-commercial industries and 'dynamic' services. And within each of these sectors, there are both 'good' and 'bad' jobs, although the most attractive work is more concentrated in some industries.

Lower-Tier Industries: Traditional Services
In his study, the *Quality of Work in the Service Sector*, Krahn (1992: 15) shows that by 1989 a third of the service workers were employed in what he terms lower-tier services. Jobs in the lower tier were unlikely to have fringe benefits or to be unionized, and were most likely to be done by women and young men. A Statistics Canada survey found that 'workers in the lower-tier services, especially those in non-standard jobs, typically reported lower skill requirements and a greater mismatch between their education and job. They were also more likely to say they were overqualified for their job, and were less likely to agree that their job was good' (Krahn 1992: 15). In other words, they had 'bad jobs.'

What is meant by lower-tier industries are the retail trades and commercial personal-service industries. Although the kind of detailed data necessary to examine the changes in these industries between 1990 and 1992 are not published annually by Statistics Canada, it is possible to look at trends between 1976 and 1991 and, in this way, get some idea about what may be happening in the 1990s.

Employment grew in the retail trades over this fifteen-year period, but it fell by just over 50,000 jobs between 1990 and 1991. It declined because sales declined, because work was reorganized to make each employee work harder, and because new technologies replaced workers. In both

TABLE 2
Employment change for adult women and men, service-producing industries, 1990–1

	Full-time		Part-time	
Occupation	Men	Women	Men	Women
Total employment	−120	−14	+28	+36
Goods-producing industries	−105	−24	+10	+8
Service-producing industries	−16	+10	+18	+28
Traditional services				
Retail trade	−24	−3	+3	−5
Amusement and recreation	0	−2	+2	−2
Personal and household services	−1	−2	0	+1
Accommodation, food, and				
beverage services	+1	−6	+1	+7
Miscellaneous services	+3	−1	+2	+1
Non-commercial services				
Education	+4	+16	0	+8
Health and social services	+25	+21	+3	+12
Religious organizations	−3	−7	−	−2
Public administration	−5	+7	−1	−2
Dynamic services				
Transportation and communication	−19	−3	+3	+3
Wholesale trade	−18	0	+3	+1
Finance, insurance, and real estate	+10	−8	−1	+6
Services to business management	+10	−3	+5	+1

Calculated from Statistics Canada 1992c.

1976 and 1991, retail trade accounted for 13 per cent of labour-force workers (see table 2).

'In 1991, youth, adult men and women shared the number of jobs in Retail Trade almost equally,' although most of the youth and a third of the adult women had part-time work and this was the case for only 5 per cent of the adult men.[8] But these groups did not share equally in the jobs lost and gained. Between 1990 and 1991, 52,000 fewer people had full-time work, while 1000 more had part-time employment in retail. Adult men accounted for almost half of the full-time job loss, but they took far more than their share of new part-time work. Men's greater full-time job loss is largely explained by their domination of the full-time work force and by their distribution within the retail sector, rather than by competition from women. Men, for example, account for 80 per cent of those in automotive sales and close to 40 per cent of men employed in retail trades work in these trades. Men lost jobs here mainly as a result of restructuring and the recession.

Women were more likely to be found in food stores and in general-merchandise stores. Sales remained fairly strong in these retail sectors, although here too technology was beginning to have an impact and helped account for the loss of 3000 full-time jobs for adult women and 5000 part-time ones.[9]

Commercial personal-service industries provide a greater share of the labour-force employment than do the retail trades. Jobs in these industries increased from 14 per cent of the labour force in 1976 to 17 per cent in 1991. Overall employment did not decline in these industries between 1990 and 1991, although full-time employment decreased by 31,000. But all of this job loss was among youth and adult women. Full-time employment for adult men increased by 4000, while 10,000 full-time jobs for adult females disappeared. Part-time work increased for adults of both sexes, although almost twice as many women found only part-time work.[10] And these figures do not include the growing number of workers employed full time on temporary work contracts. Estimates indicate that 13 per cent of those working in these industries have jobs with a specific end date (Krahn 1991: 38). Here, too, the variations in patterns for women and men reflect the segregation and restructuring of the market more than they reflect competition between the sexes for jobs.

Employment, especially for women, has grown significantly in the lower-tier industries since 1976. However, between 1990 and 1991 full-time jobs disappeared and more part-time work appeared. And these were the sectors that already had the highest proportion of part-time work. Adult men's full-time job loss was greater than women's in retail trades, but adult men captured more of the new part-time work. In the growing commercial personal-service industries, however, more men found full-time work, while a large number of women lost full-time jobs. As a result, male and female employment patterns became more similar.

Upper-Tier Industries: Non-Commercial Services
Over this five-year period, employment grew more in the non-commercial services than it did in the commercial ones. By 1991, jobs in health, social services, and education accounted for almost a quarter of service-sector jobs. If jobs in public administration are included, these services employ a third of all those with service jobs in 1991. These jobs were

particularly important for women, given that adult women form the overwhelming majority of workers in these industries and that women have traditionally found many of their best jobs here. Many of the jobs require high levels of formal education and for this reason may be classified as highly skilled (Economic Council of Canada 1991: 93). Women who work in these industries are much more likely than other women to be unionized and are much more likely than other women to benefit from affirmative-action programs (National Union of Provincial Government Employees 1989). Many of the jobs here fit the Economic Council's criteria for 'good jobs.'

Of the new full-time jobs created in health, social services, and education between 1990 and 1991 for those over age twenty-five, 56 per cent went to women. However, women accounted for more than 70 per cent of the adult workforce in these industries. Men, then, captured much more than their share of new full-time work. The picture was different in public administration, however, where more adult women found full-time work and more adult men lost full-time jobs (table 2).

Women were much more successful than men in acquiring the new part-time jobs appearing in health and education. While 20,000 more adult women worked part time in these industries, this was the case for only 3000 more men. All of these part-time jobs for adult men were in health and social services. But adult women account for more than 90 per cent of the part-time workers, and therefore they got less than their share of new part-time work. In public administration, part-time jobs disappeared for both sexes, although twice as many women as men lost such work. In this industry, men experienced more part-time job loss than their numbers would suggest. And here, too, the figures on part-time work do not include those who work full time on temporary contracts. Estimates indicate that one in ten jobs in health, education, and social service is temporary (Krahn 1991: 38).

In sum, employment increased in health, social services, and education, and more of the jobs were full-time rather than part-time. More of the additional jobs went to women rather than to men. But there are at least two reasons to be cautious about assessing these trends as positive and permanent gains for women. First, men took a much greater share of the new jobs than their traditional numbers would warrant. Second, new state initiatives are threatening jobs in these industries, eliminating some, privatizing others, and transforming others into 'bad' jobs in terms of security, wages, responsibility, power, and skill. The trend towards privatization was evident between 1990 and 1991, when more than three-quarters of the additional work in health and social services did not result from an increase in those paid directly by a government agency. Two-thirds of them were for private paid workers and another 10 per cent were for self-employed workers. Only one in five new jobs were government paid. In education, a quarter of the new jobs were not for state employees. Private paid jobs are less likely to be unionized, secure, and well paid than are state-sector jobs. They are more likely to be 'bad jobs.' And so are many of the jobs for the self-employed, as we shall see in a later section. It should be noted, however, that the income of these private paid and self-employed workers may still come from tax dollars through state-purchased services. The impact of new government initiatives designed to reduce payrolls and increase state control is too recent to examine through labour-force data, but there is every reason to believe the impact will be greatest on women, given that they form the overwhelming majority of the workforce here.

Nor is there reason to be optimistic about jobs in public administration. Although women may have captured some of the new work as a result of affirmative-action programs, the segregation of the public-administration workforce suggests that male job loss is much more likely to be the result of reorganization than of competition from women. And female job gain is much more likely to be the result of new taxes that increased the need for clerical workers than of women taking male managerial work (Task Force on Barriers to Women in the Public Service 1990). Moreover, privatization may mean that men are receiving more public-sector work as private-sector consultants, a process that is impossible to monitor from labour force survey data. And, finally, further downsizing will doubtless eliminate more women's work and may reduce their opportunities for promotion.

Upper-Tier Industries: Dynamic Services
Industries involved with distribution (transportation and communications, and wholesale trade) and with servicing businesses (finance, insurance and real estate, and services to business management) make up the rest of the service sector. The Economic Council classifies them as 'dynamic' services because they 'are high-value-added industries that, for the most part, have become more and more involved in globally competitive markets' (Economic Council of Canada 1991: 8–9). High-value-added does not necessarily mean 'good jobs,' however. While there are certainly some well-paid and challenging jobs here, many of the jobs in distribution involve repetitive work with low educational

requirements and many of those who provide services to business do repetitive clerical work. Those who hold the good and bad jobs in distribution industries are mainly men and almost all those who do the clerical work are women. Together, these industries provide employment for almost a third of the labour force.

Being competitive and high-value-added does not necessarily mean creating more jobs either. Full-time employment in the distribution industries declined by 60,000 between 1990 and 1992. Men dominated these industries and over half of the full-time jobs lost were lost to adult men, although a significant number of adult women also lost full-time work. New part-time jobs did appear, and men over age twenty-five took the majority of new part-time work, even though women formed the majority of part-time workers (table 2).

Employment did increase between 1990 and 1991 in those industries providing services to business. All of the new full-time work went to men over age twenty-five. Both the number of young people and the number of women employed full time declined significantly. While 20,000 more adult men found full-time work, 11,000 fewer adult women and 6000 fewer young people had full-time jobs. The net gain in full-time jobs was very small.

Most of the new work in the 'dynamic industries' was part-time. Adult women counted for more than half of the new part-time workers. Adult men took a third of the new part-time jobs, but such men had accounted for less than 20 per cent of the part-time workers in 1991. In other words, men gained over adult women and young people of both sexes, although more adult men had only part-time work. The 'dynamic' services that are defined by the Economic Council as the leading edge in the global economy did provide a limited number of new full-time jobs for men, but many women and some men were left in a worse position in terms of full-time work.

These detailed data on industries indicate some clear patterns. Many full-time jobs disappeared in the goods-producing industries as well as in retail and the distributive trades, but new part-time work appeared. New full-time and part-time jobs were created in education, public administration, health and social services, and in those industries providing services to business. Only one of these industries is primarily in the private sector.

Although full-time job loss was greatest for young people, a much higher percentage of adult men than adult women lost work. These men lost work to a large extent because jobs disappeared in the goods-producing industries that men dominate. In some cases, full-time jobs were replaced by part-time ones and more of these new jobs went to men. As a result, male part-time employment became more similar to that of women. In the service-producing industries, adult men lost jobs in retail and in distributive trades, in areas that they dominate. In both industries, men took more than their share of new part-time work. Adult men also took more than their share of new full-time and part-time work in both commercial and non-commercial services, areas where many of the 'good jobs' are found.

So, then, while many men lost full-time jobs or replaced them with part-time work, men were more successful than women in capturing new full-time employment in areas where women traditionally found their best jobs. The only exception to this trend was public administration, where women gained and men lost full-time work and men did not acquire significantly more part-time work. This is the only area where significant numbers of women may be successfully competing with men for jobs, but the jobs in public administration are currently under threat. Most of the increasing similarity in men and women's labour-force work can be accounted for by losses to men that had nothing to do with women. The losses can be explained primarily by the restructuring of the labour force.

Occupational Restructuring

Men and women's jobs are also becoming more similar because many of the good jobs traditionally dominated by men are not so good any more. It is not possible to do a detailed analysis of changes in occupations for the 1990s because only the Census, carried out every five years, publishes information on very specific occupational categories. But by combining information from a variety of sources it is possible to offer an indication of trends in the managerial, administrative, professional, and technical occupations that are often considered the most highly skilled and, therefore, the best jobs (Economic Council of Canada 1991: 93). Between 1990 and 1992, this broad occupational category accounted for all the full-time job growth and a great deal of the new part-time work (see table 3).

The fact that women took the majority of new jobs in this broad occupational group is often understood to be a sign of real progress. But a more detailed analysis of the many occupations within this category suggests a more complicated trend. For example, the number of women

TABLE 3
Occupational employment changes in Canada, 1990–2

Occupation	Full-time	Part-time
Both sexes	−458	+126
Manufacturing and other professional	+80	+30
Clerical	−141	+26
Sales	−1	0
Service	−38	+44
Primary occupations	−19	+5
Processing, machining, and fabricating	−180	+4
Construction	−117	+2
Transport equipment operating	−33	+8
Material handling and other crafts	−8	−1
Unclassified	n/a	n/a

Calculated from Statistics Canada 1991 and 1993c.

in the managerial and administrative category that falls within the larger managerial group increased between 1990 and 1992, while the number of male managerial jobs decreased. But even this category contains a wide range of jobs, many of which are highly sex-segregated. And not all of them could be considered 'good jobs.' A third of the additional work was in what Statistics Canada classifies as 'other managers and administrators.' This category primarily covers managers in very small enterprises or at junior levels where jobs are the least secure and the least well paid. Many of the jobs in other management categories were not highly rewarded or full-time.

Census data indicate that the number of men employed as senior managers and other senior officials, another occupational group within the managerial and administrative category, dropped by more than 15,000 between 1985 and 1990. At the same time, the number of women grew by less than 10,000. Clearly, fewer men did this kind of work but they were not all being replaced by women. Much of the male job loss reflected the shut-downs and the flattened hierarchies that are part of the new global strategy. There is additional evidence that demonstrates women were not taking the top male jobs. The average salary for women in such jobs was only $40,633 in 1990, compared to an average of $71,349 for men in these jobs and of $38,648 for all men employed full time. Equally important, more than one in five of the women gaining new employment in this occupation did not have full-time, full-year work.[11]

Similarly, the largest group within the other managers and administrators category is sales and advertising management occupations.
Women took most of the new work here, but the average salary for full-
time female managers in this category was close to the average for all
women and more than $10,000 less than that for all men who work full
time. Women employed full time got only 60 per cent of what men in
the group earned and close to a third had only part-time work and part-
time pay. Obviously, with salaries averaging less than $27,000 a year in
1990 and much of the work part-time, these were not the 'good jobs'
often associated with the term management.[12]

In another group within the managerial and administrative category –
financial management occupations – jobs grew for both sexes, although
women took more of the additional work. However, over 60 per cent of
the men taking new work found full-time jobs, while this was the case
for less than 15 per cent of the women. And the salaries of women
employed full time in these occupations were, at $36,728, considerably
below that of both all men and of the men in these occupations who
averaged $59,416. Together, these figures suggest that the jobs women
got in management were not necessarily the good ones men used to
have; rather, they suggest there were fewer of the 'good jobs' men used
to have.

Research by Boyd, Mulvihill, and Myles (1991: 428) supports this
claim. They conclude that 'women rarely are supervisors or managers of
men although men rule over both men and women. Census data indicate that the inroads of women into management are primarily at the
lower rungs. Both census and survey results also show that gender differences in access to management and supervisory positions are largest
in those service industries where women are in a majority.' Growth in
the service industries has been concentrated in areas where women
work, so it is not surprising that women took more of the management
jobs.

In the other, professional jobs that make up this broad category,
employment increased between 1990 and 1992 for both women and men
in proportions that matched their share of jobs in these occupations. But
here too, greater detail in the data suggests more complex processes at
work. Men took all the new jobs in natural science and women's
employment declined in this male-dominated work. In the female-dominated social sciences, men gained almost as many new jobs as women,
taking more than their share of the jobs. In teaching, men took almost
half the new jobs, even though they made up just over a third of the

teachers. And while 80 per cent of those in medicine and health occupations are women, men took well over half of the new jobs. In short, more men were moving into women's occupations and more women were doing traditional women's work.

Within each of these professional categories, much of the growth was in the jobs at the bottom of the hierarchy, in jobs traditionally dominated by women. In health, for example, jobs for nursing supervisors and for registered nursing assistants and orderlies declined significantly between 1985 and 1990, while jobs for nursing attendants and for those in related assisting occupations accounted for more than two out of every five new jobs in nursing work. A third of the additional work in the entire health professional category went to technicians, opticians, denturists, and nutritionists, those in the 'other occupations related to medicine' category. So, for instance, there were eight times as many new jobs for dental hygienists as there were for dentists, but both jobs were counted as part of the growth in professional work. Together, the nursing attendants, the other assistants, and the various technician categories accounted for more than half of the overall job growth in health professions. Women account for over three-quarters of the workers in these jobs, although men took a significant share of the new work.

Of course, women increased their share of jobs in such professions as pharmacy, medicine, and law. But more women in these jobs did not necessarily put men out of work, given that the overwhelming majority of those working in these professions are self-employed. Moreover, women's movement into these professions has coincided with changes in the work that make it more like women's work. Take pharmacy, for example. By 1986, a majority of pharmacists were women. But the growing number of female pharmacists were employees, rather than employers or self-employed professionals as small drug stores were taken over by large corporations and as more hospitals hired their own druggists. Work became more repetitive as drug companies increasingly pre-packaged the required mix and dosage. Moreover, although there were 3600 more pharmacists in 1990 than there were in 1985, two-fifths of them did not have full-time, full-year work. Female pharmacists working full time, full year made little more than the overall average male wage and more than $14,000 less than male pharmacists, an income that reflects their status as employees.[13] Similar patterns are becoming evident in medicine and law (Armstrong and Armstrong 1992).

Certainly some of the new managerial and professional work provides 'good jobs.' But the growth in these occupations and the significant increases in women's employment here do not simply indicate absolute gains for women. They also reflect a restructuring that is eliminating many of the good managerial jobs men held and transforming some professional work in ways that make it more similar to traditional women's work. In the process, men's work has become more similar to women's work and more men are taking on jobs in areas traditionally dominated by women.

Hours of Work

Data on hours of work provide another indication of both how women's work and men's are becoming more similar and how some of this similarity reflects a deterioration in jobs for both sexes.

We have already seen that many more of the new jobs are part-time or part-year and that this is increasingly the case in what have often been classified as good jobs. More adult men and adult women found only part-time and part-year work and men's share of part-time work has been increasing in recent years. Not only does part-time work mean less pay and little security, it can also mean shift work. 'About 6 in 10 part-time employees are shift workers, and the majority of them do not have regular schedules' (Sunter 1993: 19). And even though the majority of part-time shift workers were young, adult women, they accounted for a third of all these workers and a growing number of adult men had such work. Women of all ages were less likely than men to have prearranged schedules. Shift work, especially when the hours are irregular, makes it more difficult to organize family and social life.

While more people have reduced hours per week and weeks per year, those with full-time jobs are working longer hours. Between 1975 and 1990, the percentage of full-time workers who worked long hours increased much faster than did the percentage who worked full time. Although three-quarters of those with long work weeks were men, the percentage with long work weeks rose much more rapidly for women than for men, thus reducing the gap between the sexes.

Traditionally, long work weeks have been most common for the men employed in primary industries, where work is very long in some seasons and quite short in others. But the men working in fishing, mining, logging, and farming cannot explain much of the recent increase in long work weeks, given that their jobs have been disappearing. What is happening is that more and more of those in the 'good jobs' are working long hours. According to Statistics Canada (Cohen 1992: 10), 'the incidence of long workweeks for workers with university degrees (19%) was double the rate recorded for workers with other levels of educational attainment' and 'climbed considerably for teachers (from 14% to 20%) as well as for managers and administrators (from 11% to 17%).' It is not surprising, then, that as the number of university-educated women, and of women teachers and managers, increases, so does the number of women's weekly work hours. And most of these women have another job at home or have had to give up marriage and children in order to accommodate their labour-force work (see Armstrong and Armstrong 1994: chapter 3).

Not only are those in the good jobs working more hours but more of them are working shifts. And the 'vast majority of both male and female full-time shift workers felt that they had no control over their work schedules' (Sunter 1993: 18). As Sunter (1993: 22) points out, the future is 'likely to hold more of the same' as the pressure to be more productive increases and as services are supplied more at the customer's convenience. The new technologies that make it possible to work around the clock, around the world also increase the likelihood that more of those in the good jobs will work both long hours and irregular shifts.

Self-Employment

Self-employment has grown significantly since 1975 and this, too, is often taken as a sign of an increase in good jobs (Crompton 1993: 24). But most of the self-employed are 'own-account' workers – 'that is, self-employed individuals who do not themselves have employees' (Economic Council of Canada 1991: 79). Such workers tend to have either very long or quite short hours and to have lower wages than paid workers. Many have little choice about the kind of work they take (Armstrong 1989 and Cohen 1988).

In the past, most self-employed workers were men in the primary sector or in construction and most worked full weeks. By the end of the 1980s, two-thirds of the self-employed, own-account workers were in service industries (Economic Council of Canada 1991: 80). A growing number were women, and many of them sewed or sold clothes in their own homes, did word-processing or gave massages, looked after other people's children or did housekeeping (Crompton 1993: 25). 'Among women, 40 per cent worked part-time, and almost two-thirds were in traditional services in 1989' (Cohen 1988: 80). Two out of five of them did clerical work (ibid.: 80). In 1991, women in unincorporated businesses averaged 55 per cent of men's income (Crompton 1993: 31).

It is not possible from published Labour Force Survey data to examine the detailed trends in the 1990s, but it is possible to get some idea of overall patterns. Between 1990 and 1992, self-employment grew by 56,000 and 57 per cent of this increase was in unincorporated businesses.[14] According to the Economic Council (1991: 79), about 90 per cent of own-account self-employed workers are unincorporated. This kind of self-employment declined in primary-sector industries and increased in manufacturing, finance, and services. Two-thirds of the increase was in the service industries and almost three-quarters of these additional self-employed were women.

While some of these women may be choosing to work for themselves, it seems likely that most of this increase is the result of contracting out to homeworkers or of the transformation of permanent jobs into contract jobs. By 1992, the percentage of women and men with self-employment became more similar to a large extent because women accounted for most of the new own-account self-employed. More women also incorporated businesses. However, the increase was much smaller than that for unincorporated businesses and much smaller for women than for men.

Multiple-Job Holding

The 1990s saw a reversal in the trend towards multiple-job holding (Krahn 1991: 40) and an increasing similarity between women and men in terms of holding more than one job. Between 1990 and 1992, the number of men holding more than one job decreased by 18,000 and the number of women multiple-job holders increased by 6000. The number of multiple-job holders decreased in manufacturing, construction, and transportation as jobs became more difficult to find. And they increased in service industries. In other words, they increased in female-dominated areas and decreased in male-dominated ones.[15] It seems likely that restructuring was making it more difficult for men to find extra work and more necessary for women to take on more than one job, given that more women found only part-time jobs.

Among occupations, multiple-job holding increased in the management and professional category, in sales, and in service. There may be many reasons for this increase, but certainly the fact that much of the job increase was concentrated in part-time employment would be a factor in both encouraging people to take more than one job and making more than one job available. Much of the growth in part-time work in these areas was for women, and this may explain why more of them took more than one job.

Wages

Wage data provide one of the clearest demonstrations of the central argument made in this paper: that women's gains are at least as much a result of the deterioration of men's jobs as they are the result of real improvements in women's position and that this deterioration is mainly the result of restructuring rather than of competition from women.

When the 1991 wage data were released in 1993, a great deal of attention was paid to the significant decline in the wage gap. Between 1990 and 1991, the female-to-male earnings ratio increased to 70 per cent from 68 per cent for full-time, full-year workers.[16] Women's wages were up 2 per cent, even after adjusting for inflation. But a closer examination of wage differences suggests both that women's gains were not made at the expense of men and that women's gains may be not only limited but temporary. Wage patterns over the last seven decades show major differences in male and female gains, suggesting that the wages for each sex often change independently. So, for example, while male average wages rose by 16 per cent between 1930 and 1940, women's average wages dropped by 6 per cent. In the 1950s, when men's wages grew by 44 per cent, women's rose by only 36 per cent (Rashid 1993: table 1). Unlike women's, men's real average annual wage fell for the first time between 1980 and 1990 (Rashid 1993: 18).

It is this drop in male average income that explains a great deal of the decline in the wage gap. Between 1990 and 1991, the average earnings of male full-time, full-year workers dropped by $370, while average earnings for females employed full year, full time rose by $517 in constant dollars. Wages fell in male-dominated occupations. Men's actual earnings dropped in materials handling and in forestry and logging, areas where very few women work. Women's average earnings fell in agriculture. In all other areas men's average actual annual earnings increased. And in teaching, social science, and health – all female-dominated areas – male dollar increases were significantly more than those of women. For example, males employed full time, full year in medicine gained $13,832 between 1990 and 1992, while women in health occupations added an average of $2109 to their income. Some of the decline in male averages is also explained by the disappearance of jobs for male senior managers, although in the managerial category as whole male average wages rose by $4538 and those of women by only $2683.[17] Overtime hours for hourly paid workers also declined between 1990 and 1991, and men are much more likely than women to have paid overtime (Perspectives on Labour and Income 1993: 64).

In occupations in the natural sciences, traditionally a male-dominated field, women did gain more than men in terms of dollar increases. However, as we have seen, between 1990 and 1992, men took all the new jobs in natural sciences and women's employment declined. Fewer women have these more highly paid jobs. Moreover, women's overall wage increases were largely accounted for by their jobs in the public sector, and these are precisely the jobs targeted for cutbacks in new state initiatives.

There are other indications that women's gains were not largely the result of women taking good jobs from men. Between 1990 and 1992, the largest decline in the wage gap was for those with zero to eight years of education. These are the people most likely to work in the primary and manufacturing industries; that is, in the areas where men's unionized jobs disappeared and where new part-time work for men appeared. At the same time, the wage gap increased among those with university degrees, that is, among those most likely to have the good jobs and among the women most likely to be directly competing with men for such jobs.[18]

The decline in male wages has an impact not only on the wage gap but also on women's choices about paid employment. Decreasing male wages, especially when combined with rising male unemployment, means there is even more pressure on women to provide economic support for their families. Even with most women in the labour force, family income went down between 1989 and 1990.[19] The largest decline was among young couples, female lone-parent families, and two-parent families with one earner. But families with two earners barely held their own, and those with more than two earners saw their incomes decline. Most women, like men, had little alternative to labour-force employment.

Women's average income increased relative to that of men in part because they did different jobs from those of men and in part because male average wages declined. In 1991, 80 per cent of those in the ten highest-paying jobs were men and three-quarters of those in the ten lowest-paying jobs were women. And those women who made it into the top ten paying occupations averaged 61 per cent of male earnings.[20] Clearly women's average earnings did not rise primarily because they took the high paying jobs away from men.

Total Quality Management

Along with globalization have come new managerial strategies that go by various names, the most common of which is Total Quality Management. They are billed as involving teamwork, flattened hierarchies, worker participation, and quality service or goods for the consumer. These strategies use the same kind of language that was popular in the women's movement. They speak to many of women's concerns about their work and reflect some practices that have been most common in women's work. For example, nurses have traditionally worked in teams and the overwhelming majority have worked as general-duty nurses, with very little room for promotion. They have stressed providing care for the patient and tailoring their work to patient needs, and discussed patient development with a variety of care givers. It is not surprising, then, that many women find the new language appealing and that managers are introducing the new strategies as more and more jobs come to resemble traditional women's work.

But, as these managerial strategies are practised, they often serve to transform these ways of doing work into means of intensifying labour, increasing insecurity, and reducing power, while eliminating promotion ladders that have provided routes to the top. Teamwork frequently becomes a means of getting more work out of fewer workers, especially when the team is expected to take up the extra work when a member is absent. Decision making is often reduced to such limited matters that workers have less opportunity to influence what happens, especially when flattened hierarchies mean there is a greater distance to the top where the major decisions are made. Workers usually get more responsibility, but less power and fewer resources to work with. Quality control frequently means greater surveillance, surveillance that is more and more often done through modern technologies and work formulas. Workers fearing job loss cannot fully participate and the many employed short term or part time have difficulty acquiring the knowledge that could help make meaningful participation possible. And these new strategies often serve to undermine old union practices that provided some protection and power for workers.

As these managerial strategies are introduced into both the goods-producing and the service-producing sectors, women's and men's jobs become more similar. Many of men's traditional managerial jobs disappear with flattened hierarchies, and both sexes find fewer routes to the top.

Conclusion

Women's progress is usually measured against a male standard. But what is happening is a deterioration in some men's work, and therefore measuring progress in relation to men does not necessarily indicate real gains for women. Many signs of women's progress reflect a decline in men's position rather than real gains for women. And the decline in men's position is primarily the result of restructuring, rather than of competition from women. The segregation of the labour force has protected some women's jobs and offered new work to others.

Restructuring for a global economy has meant the disappearance of full-time jobs in all but the non-commercial services and services to business. Jobs disappeared in the primary industries, in construction and manufacturing, in the distributive and wholesale trades – in the areas where men dominate. Almost all of the full-time job growth has been in the public sector, in areas where women dominate. Although men suffered more in terms of full-time-job loss, they took more than their share of new full-time and part-time work in the female-dominated areas. In other words, some men are moving into women's traditional areas and successfully competing with women there.

Restructuring is not only eliminating many men's jobs and creating many part-time or part-year ones, it is also transforming many of the full-time jobs that remain. Many of the 'good jobs' are not so good any more. Hours and shift work have increased, and so has insecurity. Work has intensified, whether or not people have full-time or part-time employment. Those women who have moved into traditional male work frequently find that it has become more like traditional women's work, and management strategies in all sectors frequently serve to reduce workers' power, though claiming the opposite. According to Boyd, Mulvihill, and Myles (1991: 428), the growth in the 'service economy not only represents the continuation of female subordination, but also represents its consolidation.' The feminization of the labour force has not primarily meant 'good jobs' for most women; it has meant more women's work for some men.

Moreover, new state strategies are designed to cut jobs in the non-commercial services, in the areas where women have found their best jobs and where affirmative action has been the most successful. Without new jobs in these areas, women's position would be worse than that of men. Once new policies are in place, this is likely to be the case. Privatization has primarily served to create part-time or short-term, non-union jobs. And any new jobs in the 'dynamic' industries are likely to be part-time or part-year and are likely to go to men.

Women's and men's work have become more similar mainly because fewer people of both sexes have a choice about the kinds of paid work they take and because more of the jobs are 'bad jobs.' Job insecurity, less union representation, less opportunity for promotion or skill development, lower wages, and more unemployment and underemployment have come with globalization. Education has not protected workers and affirmative-action policies are more and more difficult to implement in a declining economy and with more-liberal trade practices. Decentralization of decision making has much the same problem as total quality management: those at the local level have fewer and fewer decisions to make as those who control the global economy and those at the local level grow further and further apart. The locals too have more responsibility, but less power.

The Canadian example suggests that, instead of improving the lot of the disadvantaged, globalization leads to a harmonizing down for many and increasing control for a few, mostly white, men. It also suggests that the United Nations' solutions may exacerbate, more than alleviate, the problem.

NOTES

1 These labour-force data are calculated from Statistics Canada 1991 and 1993c: tables 1 and 5.
2 Ibid., table 1.
3 Calculated from ibid., table 18.
4 Statistics Canada 1992e: 9.
5 Calculated from Statistics Canada 1993d: table 2. In 1991, 60.5 per cent of men between the ages of 25 and 65 were employed mostly full time for 49 to 52 weeks and so were 38.8 per cent of women in this age group.
6 Statistics Canada 1993c: table A-16.
7 Calculated from ibid., table 10, and table 10 in Statistics Canada 1991.
8 Statistics Canada 1993c: A-6.

9 Calculated from ibid., tables 2, 3, and 4.
10 Calculated from ibid. Commercial personal service work includes amuse-
   ment and recreation, personal and household services, accommodation, food
   and beverage services, as well as miscellaneous services. Not included
   among the commercial services discussed here are services to business management. They are excluded because these are identified as dynamic services
   by the Economic Council (1990) and are not considered part of a third tier
   that provides 'bad' jobs.
11 The census data is calculated from Statistics Canada 1993e: table 1.
12 Ibid.
13 Ibid.
14 Calculated from Statistics Canada 1991 and 1993c, table 13.
15 Calculated from Statistics Canada 1991 and 1993c: table 25.
16 Statistics Canada 1993f: 7.
17 Calculated from Statistics Canada 1992d and 1993f: table 5.
18 Statistics Canada 1993f: text table 1.
19 Statistics Canada 1993g: 9.
20 Calculated from Statistics Canada 1993h: 11.

2

From Equal Opportunity to Symbolic Equity: Three Decades of Federal Training Policy for Women

BARBARA CAMERON

A growing body of research is demonstrating that labour-market policy in Canada has served historically to reinforce an unequal gender division of labour in society. Studies of such policy areas as unemployment insurance, collective bargaining, minimum-wage legislation, training, and social assistance have shown that they were organized around a paradigm of the male-breadwinner/dependent-wife family.[1] Within this paradigm, adult men were seen as the primary workers, single or otherwise husbandless women and young people comprised a secondary labour force, and women were expected to withdraw from the paid labour force upon marriage. These assumptions informed government policy and practices, but were also widely accepted at the time by influential women's organizations such as the National Council of Women. As more and more married women, including mothers of young children, entered the paid labour force in the 1960s and 1970s, this paradigm began to be challenged. An emerging movement for women's equality rejected the ideological distinction between the public and the private spheres and the assignment of married women to the household. Under the pressure of women's organizations, governments introduced policies with explicit gender-equality objectives.

Training is one area of federal-government policy where the shift from a male-breadwinner paradigm to an equality paradigm was evident. In their study of such programs before and after the Second World War, Ruth Pierson and Marjorie Cohen demonstrated that federal training policy was directed at preparing women for domestic work or for other 'occupations perceived to be appropriate for women' (Pierson and Cohen 1984: 233). Even during the Second World War, when women were actively recruited to replace men in industrial working-class jobs, the training for women was 'designed to fit them for specific jobs for the duration of the war, not for lifetime careers as skilled workers, much less skilled mechanics who might compete with men in the post war job market' (ibid.: 233). Beginning in 1972, federal training policies began to incorporate equality objectives initially in response to the recommendations of the 1970 Royal Commission on the Status of Women. Over the course of the next twenty years, the federal approach to women's labour-market equality progressed from an 'equality of opportunity' model to an acceptance of positive-action measures to a recognition of women as a key labour-market partner.

This chapter traces the evolution of federal training programs for women for the period 1972 to 1995. The central problem it addresses is the effect of the shift to an equality paradigm on the relationship between training programs and the gender division of labour. Did the recent training programs, like the earlier ones, reinforce the gender division of labour or did they contribute to decreasing sex segregation in the labour market? This chapter explores this question through an examination of women's access to training programs and of the nature of training that women received. It argues that, while women's access to training improved during the period, federally funded training programs continued to channel women into low-paid, sex-typed jobs. Thus, despite the shift to an equality paradigm, federal training programs for women continued to reflect and reinforce an unequal gender division of labour.

Equality of Opportunity in Basic Skills Training

The federal government historically has played a role in ensuring a supply of labour for business through immigration policy, special wartime measures, and short-term programs directed at unemployment. The adoption of a policy explicitly directed at managing the quantitative and qualitative supply of labour dates from 1960. In that year, the federal government enacted the Technical and Vocational Training Act, the key element of which was a 75 per cent federal financial contribution to the expansion of the provincial infrastructure of colleges and vocational training institutions. Recognition of the need for a more directive role for the federal government followed a few years later with the publication in 1964 of the first annual report of the Economic Council of Canada. This report advocated an active labour-market policy to facilitate an efficient flow of labour. The argument of the Council was that improved labour mobility would permit high levels of employment without the upward pressure on wages caused by labour shortages. Training was one way – along with government employment services and mobility incentives – to help match unemployed workers with jobs.[2] Convinced by the arguments advanced by the Economic Council in favour of an active labour-market policy, the Liberal government of Lester Pearson established the Department of Manpower and Immigration in 1966 with a mandate 'to facilitate the economic growth of Canada by ensuring that the supply of manpower matches the demand, qualitatively, quantitatively and geographically.'[3]

A new legislative framework was provided for training programs in 1967 with the passage of the Adult Occupational Training Act. Under the Act, the federal government undertook to cover the full cost of occupational training for adult members of the labour force, leaving the provinces the responsibility for education and training for the non-adult members of the population.[4] Federally funded training was divided into two main categories: institutional and industrial. Institutional training included all those courses provided by provincially run community colleges or vocational institutions, including the classroom portion of apprenticeship programs. The federal government funded institutional training courses by purchasing places or 'seats' in courses offered by the provincial institution. These came to be called 'general purchase courses.' Industrial training was provided at the workplace by the employer and the federal contribution took the form of a subsidy paid to the employer for all direct training costs and a portion of the wage of the trainee.[5]

The worker envisaged under the programs of the new Department of Manpower and Immigration was very definitely the male breadwinner. Young single people and most married women were excluded from receiving training allowances by the criterion that a worker either have been in the labour force for three years or have one or more dependents. Anyone living at home with an employed spouse or parent was excluded. The eligibility criterion effectively operated as a systemic barrier to the participation of married women: in 1967/68, 87% of single men and 84% of single women received training allowances, but 98% of married men and only 80% of married women did.[6] As the name of the department indicated, the target group for the programs of the Department of Manpower and Immigration was adult men with an established attachment to the labour force.

In the late 1960s, however, women began to emerge as an important political force and this was reflected in the policies of the department throughout the 1970s. A particularly influential event was the publication in 1970 of the report of the Royal Commission on the Status of Women. Noting that women made up only 22 per cent of trainees in the full-time general purchase courses in 1967/68 and 23 per cent in 1968/69, the royal commission recommended that the Adult Occupational Training Act be amended to recognize full-time household responsibility as equivalent to participation in the labour force for purposes of eligibility for training allowances.[7] It also stressed the importance of 'orientation to the world of work' programs for women seeking to re-enter the work force[8] and urged the Department of Manpower to 'set up a continuing programme of training for all its counsellors to ensure that they are kept fully aware of the changing life patterns of women and the problems that women face in relation to the labour force.'[9]

The government responded quickly to some of the recommendations of the royal commission. Effective 1 July 1972, the Adult Occupational Training Act was amended to eliminate the requirement of a three-year attachment to the labour market and to allow a $30 a week training allowance for adults living at home with an employed spouse or parent.[10] The next year, the department appointed a Senior Consultant on Women's Employment to identify the special needs of women and five Regional Women's Employment Coordinators to assess the quality of services offered to female clients.[11] Materials on the needs of women clients were prepared for use in training programs for staff at Canada Manpower Centres. Perhaps in response to the recommendations of the royal commission, the department also introduced in 1973/74 two new elements to its Basic Training for Skill Development program: Work Adjustment Training (WAT) and Job Readiness Training (JRT).[12] Both of these were directed at orientating unemployed workers to the world of work.

International Women's Year, celebrated in 1975, provided another occasion for the department to respond to the growing movement for women's equality. In preparation for IWY, Manpower and Immigration developed a policy statement which provided that 'female clients must be directed to the full range of placement and training opportunities ... all activities and programs must reflect the active promotion of equal opportunities for women.'[13] The policy was given effect by the work of Women's Employment Coordinators who organized preparation and orientation courses. The period leading up to IWY was also the time that women appeared as a separate category in the department's reporting.

A particularly strong focus of the department's efforts to promote equality of opportunity for women after 1975 was the development of an employment plan for women. In 1977, a reorganized department was given the gender-neutral name of Employment and Immigration Canada.

Women's participation rates in some, but not all, training programs did improve as a result of the more gender-sensitive government policy. The 1 July 1972 change in the eligibility criterion for training allowances and the introduction of a $30 a week allowance for trainees living with an employed spouse or parent resulted in a 35 per cent increase in the participation rates of women in institutional training between July and December 1972 compared to one year earlier.[14] Other government initiatives, in particular the expansion of the Basic Training for Skill Development program, led to some increase in women's participation rates in all institutional training courses after 1973/74, but these rates hovered around 33 per cent from 1976/77 through 1978/79 (Dale 1980: 43). These rates were depressed by the extremely low participation rate of 3 per cent for women in apprenticeship programs throughout the 1970s. When apprenticeship is removed from the calculation, women's participation rates in institutional programs during the 1970s fluctuated around 48 per cent (ibid.: 50), which compares with 23 per cent reported by the Royal Commission on the Status of Women for 1968/69. Women made little progress throughout the 1970s in industrial training courses, accounting for 27 per cent of trainees in 1972/73 and 29 per cent in 1978/79.

In both types of training – the institutional (including general purchase and apprenticeship courses) and the industrial – women faced problems regarding the kind of training they received. Within the general-purchase institutional courses, women had their highest levels of representation in language courses, where they comprised 55.5 per cent of the total in 1978/79, and in Basic Training for Skill Development courses, where they made up 55.2 per cent. In contrast, they accounted for only 38.4 per cent of the occupational-skills training courses that year.[15] Furthermore, women enrolled in occupational-skills training followed courses that led to sex-typed occupations. In 1978/79, fully 60 per cent of the women taking occupational training courses were being trained for clerical positions. Of the tiny group of women enrolled in apprenticeships, 74 per cent were being trained in personal-service occupations, mainly as cooks and hairdressers (Dale 1980: 57). Similarly, under the industrial-training component, eight out of the ten occupations with the highest number of women trainees were female dominated (ibid.: appendix II, table 15).

The removal of barriers to women's participation in training programs that was characteristic of an 'equal opportunities approach' did have a positive impact on women's access to training, particularly in the period immediately following the removal of overtly discriminatory measures. However, the improvements did not keep pace with women's changing relationship to the paid labour force. In the period between the 1971 and the 1981 census, women accounted for 63.9 per cent of the increase in the experienced labour force.[16] Since the general-purchase institutional courses were strongly oriented towards basic training for employment, the 48 per cent participation rate appears quite low. The picture with respect to industrial or employer-based training programs was even less remarkable in this period, rising only 2% from 27% in 1972/73 to 29% in 1978/79. These figures are not impressive when compared with the steady rise in women's share of the paid labour force, from 33.6% in 1970 to 40.8% in 1980.[17] Furthermore, the training that women were able to access channelled them into sex-segregated service and clerical occupations.

Positive Action within a High Skill Strategy

Beginning in 1978, the federal government began to shift its labour-market policies to place greater emphasis on training for more highly skilled jobs. The emphasis on more highly skilled occupations was reflected in the National Training Act, proclaimed in August 1982, which replaced the Adult Occupational Training Act.[18] The shift in focus to training to meet existing and future skills shortages characterized both the institutional and the industrial programs, but was most strongly reflected in employer-based or industrial courses funded under the two components of the National Industrial Training Program: the General Industrial Training (GIT) and Critical Trades Skills Training (CTST). CTST courses were directed at training for occupations such as tool-and-die maker, industrial maintenance mechanic, and others where there was a shortage of skilled labour. Employers offering training for occupations recognized under CTST could receive federal funding for up to two years. The GIT courses concentrated on training workers for other occupations in demand, retraining workers affected by new technology and industrial restructuring, training the unemployed, training women in non-traditional occupations, and training adults with special needs.

The focus on training for occupations experiencing skill shortages brought new initiatives for women. The positive-action measures began in 1978 as the shift in focus was introduced and were continued into the National Training Program. The 1978/79 annual report of Employment and Immigration Canada (EIC) noted that several regions had established pre-trades courses to train women for occupations in which they were traditionally underrepresented. In 1979/80, orientation courses to assist women in the selection of training that would lead to careers in non-traditional occupations were made available across Canada. Also in that year women's liaison counsellors were designated in Canada Employment Centres and targets were set for the number of women to be trained in non-traditional occupations.[19] In September 1980, Women in Non-Traditional Occupations was introduced as a new element of the employer-based Manpower Industrial Training Program then in place. Non-traditional occupations were defined as those in which 10 per cent or fewer of the workers were female.[20] This initiative continued under the National Training Act, and beginning in 1982 was carried out in both the GIT and CTST programs.[21]

The positive-action measures for women were implemented in the context of a major reallocation of resources within the employer-based training programs. Between 1980/81 and 1984/85, total expenditures for these programs increased from $113.6 million to $156.3 million. This global figure reflects an increase in CTST expenditures from $7.5 million to $71.1 million and a decline in GIT expenditures from $106.1 million to $85.2 million. The drop in the number of trainees enrolled in the GIT courses was even more dramatic than the decline in expenditures. In 1980/81, there were 79,863 GIT new starts; in 1982/83 the number dropped to 30,631, rising slightly to 30,714 in 1984/85. At the same time, the number of CTST new starts increased from 4102 in 1980/81 to 11,891 in 1984/85. In total, fewer workers received employer-based training, but more money was spent on those who did, allowing them to pursue the longer training required for more highly skilled jobs.[22]

As a result of the drop in the total number of trainees in employer-based programs under the National Training Program, two separate comparisons need to be made in evaluating the impact of the positive-action measures for women's training. One comparison is the number and participation rates of women in training programs during the last year of the NTP compared with its first year. A second comparison takes the number and participation rates of women at the end of the NTP and compares these with the situation before the introduction of the program.

TABLE 1
National Training Program, Women GIT Trainees

	1982/83	1984/85
Total new starts	30,631	30,715
Total women new starts	6965	7891
Women as a percentage	22.7%	25.7%

Source: Canada, EIC, *Annual Statistical Bulletin, 1982/83* and *1984/85*, tables 5.9 and 7.3

TABLE 2
National Training Program, Women CTST Trainees

	1982/83	1984/85
Total new starts	6,917	11,891
Total women new starts	138	708
Women as a percentage	2%	6%

Source: Canada, EIC, *Annual Statistical Bulletin, 1982/83* and *1984/85*, table 9.7

Using the first method of comparison, it is evident that women's participation in employer-based training programs improved in both absolute and percentage terms during the life of the NTP. Tables 1 and 2 show that the number of women beginning the employer-based GIT courses increased from 6965 in 1982/83 to 7891 in 1984/85, and from 138 to 708 in CTST training in the same period. This reflected an increase in women's share of the total number of trainees in these programs: for GIT from 22.7% in 1982/83 to 25.7% in 1984/85, and for CTST from 2% to 6%.

A different picture emerges, however, when the second method of comparison is used and the participation of women trainees in the final year of the NTP is compared with the situation before its introduction. A dramatic decline in the number of trainees, including women trainees, took place in all employer-based training programs during the first full year of the NTP, from 79,863 in 1980/81 to 37,548 in 1982/83.[23] For women, the decrease was from 21,883 new-start trainees in 1980/81 to 7103 in 1982/83.[24] This reflects a decline in women's share in the total number of trainees as well as in the number of women participants: from 26 per cent in 1980/81 to 18.9 per cent in 1982/83. By 1984/85, the total number of women trainees in employer-based programs had risen

TABLE 3

National Training Program, distribution by sex, employer-based
programs (%)

	1982/83		1984/85	
	Men	Women	Men	Women
GIT	78	98	67	92
CTST	22	2	33	8
Total	100	100	100	100

Source: Canada, EIC, *Annual Statistical Bulletin, 1982/83* and *1984/85*,
tables 5.9, 7.3 and 9.7

TABLE 4

Women trainees started in non-traditional occupations, employer-
based programs

	1982/83	1983/84	1984/85
GIT	1226	1422	1318
CTST	128	543	708
Total	1354	1965	2026

Source: Canada, EIC, *Annual Statistical Bulletin, 1982/83; 1983/84;
1984/85*, table 11.16

to 8599, far below the 1980/81 figure, and their share of the total had
increased to 20.2 per cent – again below the 1980/81 figure.

During the life of the National Training Program, the participation
in employer-based training of women as well as men shifted towards
the higher-skilled CTST programs. The shift, however, was more pronounced for men than for women. Table 3 shows the distribution by sex
of new-start trainees in employer-based programs in the first and the
last full years of the National Training Program. Under the NTP, the
expansion in employer-based training came from the CTST, with men
trainees accounting for 89 per cent of the CTST increase and women for
11 per cent. The decline of 842 in the number of men GIT trainees was
made up by an increase of 926 in the number of women trainees, resulting in a small total increase of 84 in the number of GIT trainee new starts
in 1984/85 compared with 1982/83.

During the life of the National Training Program, both the number

TABLE 5
National Training Program, institutional programs, women trainees as percentage of all new starts (%)

Program	1980/81	1982/83	1984/85
Occupational orientation	86.0	83.3	76.6
JRT	53.6	53.5	53.4
BTSD	51.3	44.8	49.6
WAT	43.4	40.7	41.2
Language	42.4	45.3	46.8
Skill	40.9	32.5	32.7
Apprentice	3.1	3.3	4.8
All institutional	30.8	25.7	30.6

Source: Canada, EIC, Annual Report, 1980/81, appendix 7; Annual Statistical Bulletin. NTP. 1982/83 and 1984/85, 6

and the percentage of women participants in training for non-traditional occupations increased. The improvement during the course of the National Training Program and the comparison with the situation a year earlier are shown in table 4. In percentage terms, the proportion of women trainees in GIT courses related to non-traditional occupations rose from 19 per cent in 1982/83 to 26 per cent in 1984/85. Close to 100 per cent of the women in CTST courses were pursuing training leading to non-traditional occupations. Yet, when the progress during the life of the NTP is compared with the situation in 1980/81, the year immediately preceding its introduction, a different picture emerges. In 1980/81 the total number of women trainees in non-traditional courses was 2191, compared with 2026 in the last year of the NTP.

Under the National Training Program institutional training courses, as well as the employer-based ones, were to be covered by the emphasis on higher-level skills and by the positive-action measures for women. The experience of women in institutional courses under the NTP is summarized in tables 5 and 6. As table 5 shows, women's participation in all institutional courses dropped to 25.7 per cent in 1982/83, the first full year of the NTP, from 30.8 per cent the previous year. By the last year of the NTP, the proportion of women had returned to 30.6 per cent. This pattern of an initial decline and then recovery is similar to that seen in the employer-based programs. In contrast to the employer-based programs, the total number of trainees in institutional programs did not register a significant decrease.

TABLE 6
National Training Program, institutional program,
distribution of women new-start trainees in skill courses by
occupation (%)

Occupational group	1982/83	1983/84
Managerial and related	3.0	3.5
Service	13.0	13.2
Clerical and related	46.0	43.0
Medicine and health	9.2	8.6
All other	28.8	31.7

Source: Canada, EIC, Annual Statistical Bulletin, 1982/83 and 1984/85,
table 4.4

Despite the decline in women's share of the total number of places in Skills courses during the life of the NTP, however, a larger proportion of women starting such courses pursued training in non-traditional occupations. In 1984/85, 18.7 per cent of all women beginning Skills courses (described by EIC as 'new starts') took training related to non-traditional occupations, compared with 11 per cent in 1982/83. This percentage increase was the combined result of a rise in the number of women in non-traditional training from 2280 to 3516 and a decline of 1832 in the total number of women beginning Skills courses.[25]

The increased proportion of women pursuing non-traditional occupations did little to alter the overall emphasis of federally funded training programs on training women for service and clerical occupations. Table 6 shows that the majority of women taking Skills courses under the NTP began their training in these sex-typed occupations; there was only a slight decline in the proportion of women entering clerical training courses between 1982/83 and 1984/85. Furthermore, within the Skills component, women did not fare well in training for Occupations of National Importance, which were occupations 'so designated because it is anticipated that there will be a regional shortage of workers sufficiently serious to justify special training action.'[26] In 1984/85, there were 15,493 new-start trainees pursuing Skills courses in Occupations of National Importance; of these only 11.7 per cent were women.[27]

The experience of women in apprenticeship programs confirms, rather than contradicts, the gendered character of women's training. The number of women trainees in apprenticeship courses increased from 1804 in 1980/81 to 2243 in 1984/85.[28] In percentage terms this was an increase in women's share of Apprentice new starts from 3.1 per cent in 1980/81 to 4.8 per cent in 1980/81.[29] However, this increase was not in non-traditional apprenticeships. The number of women new starts in non-traditional apprenticeships actually declined from 468 in 1982/83 to 424 in 1984/85.[30] In 1984/85, 9986 new-start trainees began apprenticeship courses in Occupations of National Importance, of which 1.3 per cent were women.[31]

From the perspective of women's equality, the record of the National Training Program is mixed. On the one hand, the shift in emphasis within the employer-based program to training for more highly skilled occupations or occupations experiencing a labour shortage resulted in fewer women having access to employer-based training, including training in non-traditional occupations. On the other hand, the combination of positive-action measures and the focus on higher-skilled training resulted in a larger number of women having access to employer-based training for the most highly skilled industrial occupations under the Critical Trades Skills Training program. Similarly, in the courses delivered in institutions, a smaller number of women had access to Skills courses; at the same time, a higher proportion of the women pursuing Skills courses pursued training related to non-traditional occupations. It appears that the women beneficiaries of the NTP were the small number of women who gained access to highly skilled trades training under the CTST and the somewhat larger group of women who took Skills courses leading to training in non-traditional occupations. For most women, the NTP made little difference, as they continued to be channelled into service and clerical occupations.

Back to Basics: Targeted Equity

The Conservative party came into office convinced that the private market is in a better position than government to create jobs and to deliver many programs. At the same time, their 1984 winning election campaign highlighted the theme 'jobs, jobs, jobs' after what was then the severest recession in the post–Second World War period. The 1984 campaign was also one in which the women's movement played a visible role through the televised leadership debate on women's issues. Just after the election, in October 1984, the Report of the Commission on Equity in Employment (the 'Abella Report') was released. The labour-market policy introduced in 1985 as the Canadian Jobs Strategy (CJS) reflected these influences.

The Canadian Jobs Strategy represented a departure from training policy under the Liberals in several ways. It moved away from the attempts by government to encourage training in specified areas of skills shortages, particularly high-level skills. Instead, training was to be more directly related to market demand by using government spending to encourage a larger role for employers in training. Private-sector involvement in the delivery of training was encouraged by a new policy of purchasing a certain portion of training seats from private-sector trainers, both commercial and non-profit training organizations. The administration of Employment Canada programs was decentralized, with regional (provincial) offices receiving block funding to be allocated in line with local priorities. Local Advisory Committees were set up to advise EIC on local needs. Finally, the Canadian Jobs Strategy had a more fully articulated affirmative-action component than any previous federal-government training initiative.

The Commission on Equity in Employment had designated four equity groups as those facing systemic discrimination in the labour market: women, people with disabilities, visible minorities, and aboriginal peoples.[32] While the CJS ignored the specific recommendations of the Commission with respect to training for women, it did adopt its definition of the target groups and provided for the integration of members of these groups into each component of the Canadian Jobs Strategy. With the signing of federal/provincial/territorial agreements on enhancing the employability of social-assistance recipients on 18 September 1984, social-assistance recipients were recognized as a fifth target group with participation targets established for the Job Entry and Job Development Programs. Funding for an increased number of training spaces for social-assistance recipients came through the diversion of funds under the Canada Assistance Plan.[33]

Table 7 presents information on the total number of participants in Canadian Job Strategy programs and the percentage of those participants who were women for the years 1985/86 and 1988/89. The table shows that the majority of trainees were enrolled in basic job-orientation courses under the Job Entry option or in subsidized work/training programs for the long-term unemployed under the Job Development program. (Participation rates here include both new starts and continuing trainees.) The table also shows that women were well represented in the Job Development and Job Entry programs, but made up a smaller proportion of the Skills Investment trainees and a very small proportion of the trainees in the Skills Shortages program, which was directed at

TABLE 7
Canadian Jobs Strategy, participation of women (new and continuing trainees), 1985/86

Program and year	Total trainees	Total women	% women
Job Development			
1985/86	96,100	35,461	36.9
1988/89	89,006	45,381	51.5
Job Entry: Challenge			
1985/86	88,100	45,460	51.6
1988/89	85,150	43,512	51.1
Job Entry: Other			
1985/86	23,400	14,859	63.5
1988/89	71,091	47,489	66.8
Skills Shortages			
1985/86	14,500	1,058	7.3
1988/89	109,595	10,631	9.7
Skills Investment			
1985/86	4,500	1,404	31.2
1988/89	37,739	14,341	38.0
Community Futures			
1985/86	9,100	2,839	31.2
1988/89	5,480	1,765	32.2
All programs			
1985/86	235,700	101,081	42.9
1988/89	398,061	163,119	41.0

Source: Canada, EIC, Annual Reports, 1985/86. 1988/89 figures
provided by EIC, Statistical Analysis Division. Number of women
participants was calculated from columns 2 and 4.

training in areas of critical skills shortages. In the Skills Shortages programs, the highest percentage of female participants was 9.7 per cent, achieved in 1988/89.

Research conducted by Terry Dance and Susan Witter on training received by CJS participants in 1986 and 1987 showed that in all programs, including Skills Shortages and Skills Investment, the very large majority of women were trained for traditional female occupations or lower-skilled manufacturing assembly work (Dance and Witter 1988: 10). This conclusion is supported by an analysis of the Canadian Jobs Strategy undertaken for the Canadian Advisory Council on the Status of Women. Using data on Job Entry/Re-entry projects obtained for several regions, Wendy McKeen found that all but one of the sixteen Re-entry projects in Toronto offered training in sales, clerical services, and health occupations. In Newfoundland, four of the eleven Re-entry projects were teaching office skills, despite the presence in the province of 4000 unemployed office workers at the time. Six of the ten Job Entry projects in Saint John were offering training in sales, food-services industries, and hospitality and the other four provided training courses in light manufacturing, warehousing in food industries, day-care cooks, and cooking. Of the twenty Re-entry projects in the British Columbia/Yukon region, all but a few were related to office skills and clerical occupations (McKeen 1987: 15).

The combination of the primarily low-skill orientation of the CJS programs and an equity focus had contradictory effects for women. On the one hand, women had greater access to federal training programs, with their 1988/89 participation rate in all CJS programs averaging 40.3 per cent compared with 31.9 per cent in institutional programs and 28.3 per cent of industrial programs under the Liberals in 1977/78. On the other hand, the women were concentrated in programs that provided few job skills or in occupational training leading to low-paid sex-typed jobs. The Job Entry programs provided a bridge into the labour market, but women were trained for clerical and other traditionally female occupations. Furthermore, once a woman had completed a job-orientation course, there were few opportunities for her to pursue training for higher-skilled occupations. Despite the existence on paper of targets for women's participation in all training programs, there were no measures in place to enforce equity targets in Skills Investment and Skills Development programs and little conception of a training continuum where the less skilled could move from the bridging courses into higher levels of training.

The privatization also had contradictory effects for women. In a submission on the Canadian Jobs Strategy presented to the minister of employment and immigration, Flora MacDonald, the National Action Committee on the Status of Women raised the concern that 'women are too often the victims of entrepreneurs who offer high-priced training of questionable value' (National Action Committee on the Status of Women 1985: 6). The quality of commercial training remained a concern for women's organizations. At the same time, public institutions had not demonstrated a particular sensitivity to the unique training needs of women before the introduction of the Canadian Jobs Strategy. The purchase of seats by Canada Employment Centres from private-sector trainers, including profit and non-profit organizations, allowed community-based training organizations for women to benefit from government support.

Under the Canadian Jobs Strategy, community-based training organizations for women became a stronger component of Canada's training system, particularly in Ontario. In the course of designing and delivering courses specifically to meet the needs of women, these trainers developed an expertise and a shared feminist conception of training. The weakness was that the community-based training organizations were seriously underfunded, with their staff receiving low wages and their programs precariously dependent on the whims of government funders. They also existed at the margins of the overall training system, with often poor links with public institutions. None the less, the community-based programs provided a grass-roots foundation for the work already under way at a national level through the Canadian Congress for Learning Opportunities for Women. They created a larger constituency of women politically interested in government training policy. In this period, coalitions involving community-based training organizations were created in two provinces: Advocates for Community Based Training and Education for Women (ACTEW) in Ontario and Women's Education and Training Coalition (WETC) in British Columbia.

The Canadian Jobs Strategy did not contain any measures to ensure that the decentralization of Employment and Immigration Canada would benefit women. In its 1985 brief to the minister of employment and immigration, the National Action Committee proposed that 'since the Local Advisory Councils will help to identify skill and training needs of communities, half of the Council members should be women, including native, immigrant and handicapped women' (NAC 1985: 11). In practice, the Local Advisory Councils proved to be poor reflections of the community generally, not only of women. Appointments were made by local members of Parliament, mainly from the ranks of their own supporters. The transfer of block funds to regional EIC offices also did not contain any advantages for women because no equity standards were attached to any of the funds dispersed under the CJS. Monitoring and reporting of participation rates of the targeted groups were the only enforcement mechanisms.

On balance, women were poorly served by the Canadian Jobs Strategy. On the positive side, the Job Entry component recognized the importance of bridging programs for women and the funding of the community-based training programs created space for a feminist approach to training to grow and provided a grass-roots constituency for women's training as a political issue. The reporting requirements also provided systematic data on the participation rates of women and other disadvantaged groups. But, on the negative side, these programs existed within the framework of a federal labour-market policy that emphasized deregulation and commercialization. Under the Canadian Jobs Strategy, the emphasis was on low-skilled jobs at the bottom of the labour market; there was little focus on training for the more highly skilled occupations. CJS courses did not include any 'ladders' that would allow women to move through job orientation to higher-skilled training programs and lacked enforcement measures to ensure that women gained access to higher-skilled training. The overall result was that the CJS reinforced the already existing inequalities between men and women on the labour market.

Symbolic Equity

In 1989 the Conservative government introduced, with much fanfare, a new Labour Force Development Strategy (LFDS) whose objective, as stated in the policy document *Success in the Works*,[34] was to transform Canada's unemployment-insurance system from a 'passive' income support program into an active labour-market policy. Despite the rhetoric, the LFDS initiatives appear to have been shaped to a great extent by the deficit-reduction agenda of the Conservative government. Unemployment Insurance was made more 'active' through the cutting of entitlements for unemployed workers and using the $1.29 billion saved to finance new programs. In addition, the federal government eliminated its annual contribution of approximately $2.7 billion to the UI Fund to cover the costs of maternity benefits, fishermen's benefits, and course costs.[35] From this perspective, the Canadian Labour Force Development Strategy represented an exercise in off-loading financial responsibility from the federal treasury to the Unemployment Insurance Fund, which henceforth would be financed entirely from premiums paid by employers and employees.

Initially, the training and employment programs under the LFDS were presented as extensions of the Canadian Jobs Strategy. However, once the new programs were in place it became clear that a new, bipolar model of training and adjustment programs was taking shape. One pole involved Employability Improvement Programs directed at ensuring a supply of labour for jobs at the lower end of the labour market, particularly in the services sector. These were directed at individual workers and included basic skills training, preparation for employment, language training, and occupational orientation courses. The other pole involved Labour Market Adjustment programs that were directed at subsidizing employers' training and adjustment needs. Included here were Human Resource Planning initiatives, training trusts, workplace-based retraining of workers, and adjustment services to allow employers and employees to implement joint action plans in situations of lay-offs due to industrial restructuring. These adjustment programs were directed at serving corporations in the manufacturing and resource-processing industries, particularly in unionized sectors.

Another element of the Labour Force Development Strategy was the establishment of a representative body to advise Employment and Immigration Canada about labour-market policy as it affects the private sector. This began as a proposal in *Success in the Works* for a National Skills Development Advisory Board, which would be created after discussions with business and labour. Consultations were organized through the Canadian Labour Market and Productivity Centre and resulted in the creation of the Canadian Labour Force Development Board (CLFDB). Representatives of 'labour market partners' sit on the board, including eight representatives of business, eight of labour, four from equity groups, and two from training and educational institutions. A women's representative is among the four equity representatives.[36] The recognition of women – and of other 'equity groups' – on such a labour-market body as one of the key 'labour market partners' is unique in the world. As the analysis below indicates, however, this representation was mainly symbolic and not reflective of the underlying realignment taking place in federal labour-market policy.

From the perspective of women's training, the most important change brought about by the Labour Force Development Strategy was increased reliance on the UI Fund for funding income-support and program costs for training. This shift affected women's training programs in three main ways. First, by making UI the main source of income support for training it excluded women entering or re-entering the workforce who had been targeted for training before. Second, it forced the community-based training organizations for women to either reorient their programs away from entry/re-entry women and towards women who were eligible for UI or face the prospect of losing their funding completely. Third, the various shifts and cuts in funding resulted in a decline in the amount of money targeted specifically to women's training. Table 8 shows that $205,455,000 in spending was cut from spending on women's training programs between 1987/88 and 1991/92. This amounts to a 30 per cent reduction, without including inflation. The table also shows that the proportion of training money going to women has decreased sharply at the same time that the percentage of women participants decreased much more gradually. This suggests that the training women are receiving might be more short term than was the case previously. While women are among those workers receiving training through the developmental-uses program under the UI Fund, their participation rate in 1992/93 was 30.8 per cent.[37] This is considerably lower than the participation rate of women under the Canadian Jobs Strategy.

The decreases for women are part of a general shift away from funding four of the five designated groups under the Canadian Jobs Strategy. A report prepared by Employment and Immigration Canada for the Canadian Labour Force Development Board showed the following declines in spending between 1989/90 and 1991/92 for the designated equity groups: 86% for visible minorities, 28.5% for persons with disabilities, 24% for women, and 19% for aboriginals. The sharp decline in spending for visible minorities was in part the result of a change in bookkeeping within Employment and Immigration Canada, as $80 million in language-training spending was transferred from employment programs to the Immigration Settlement Program.[38] This reveals the extent to which visible-minority participation had been concentrated in language-training programs. Spending for designated groups also declined as a proportion of total spending. Table 8 shows women's share of total CJS spending dropped from 53.8% in 1987/88 to 33.9% in 1991/92. The drop in the share of expenditures for visible minorities between 1989/90 and 1991/92 was from 7% to 5%; for persons with disabilities, from 3% to 2.4%; and for aboriginal people from 9% to 8%.

The decline in training expenditures targeted to equity groups contrasts sharply with an increase in funding for social-assistance recipients as a category. An April 1994 study by the Program Evaluation Branch of Human Resources Development Canada reported that expenditures on social-assistance recipients under the Canadian Jobs Strategy increased from $200 million to $295 million between 1986/87 and 1990/91. As a

TABLE 8
Training of women under Canadian Jobs Strategy, expenditures and participation rates ($000)

	1987/88	1988/89	1989/90	1990/91	1991/92
Amount spent on women	$687,969	$611,785	$638,269	$590,975	$482,514
Total amount	$1,278,557	$1,419,454	$1,482,669	$1,494,216	$1,422,848
Women as % of total	53.8	43.1	39.6	39.6	33.9
Women as % of participants	41.8	40.8	40.3	38.8	38.3

Sources: Unpublished Employment and Immigration Canada data on program expenditures (total and women) and participation rates of women; and estimated expenditures for women and participation rates of women for 1987/88, 1988/89, 1989/90, 1990/91, and 1991/92. Total expenditures for 1988/89, 1989/90, 1990/91, and 1991/92 were calculated from Employment and Immigration Canada, *Statistical Bulletin for the Canadian Jobs Strategy* (March 1992), table 2, pp. 11 and 12. Expenditure figures from 1987/88 to 1990/91 cover the following CJS programs: Job development, Challenge, Other Job Entry, Skills Investment and Community Futures. Due to reorganization of EIC programs, expenditures and participation rates for 1991/92 use different program categories.
Note: Figures for participation rates of women differ slightly from table 7 owing to different data source.

proportion of CJS expenditures, spending on social-assistance recipients increased from 13% in 1986/87 to 19% in 1990/91.[39]

While women's participation continued to be reported as a separate category, under the Labour Force Development Strategy women lost their previous status as a more or less undifferentiated 'equity target group.' The labour market for women as well as for men was becoming polarized. Although not officially acknowledged, women would be treated differently depending on their location within this emerging labour market. At the top end, increasingly well educated women were an important source of labour for the more highly skilled jobs. To the extent that equity objectives would be in place at all, they would be discussed in terms of increasing access of women to non-traditional employment. At the bottom end of the labour market, dominated by low-paid, insecure, and increasingly 'non-standard' jobs in the service sector, women would disappear as a separate category. Here women would be subsumed under the larger categories of 'workers with family responsibilities,' social-assistance recipients (particularly single parents), and older workers. Through cuts to entitlements, new rewards and punishments, and wage subsidies for employers, these workers would be forced to fill the growing number of poorly paid jobs in the services industries. In this context, the recognition women achieved as a 'labour market partner' with representation on the Canadian Labour Force Development Board could be little more than symbolic and did not reflect a serious commitment on the part of the federal government to equality.

Conclusion

The Canadian federal government officially embraced an active approach to labour-market policy with the establishment of the Department of Manpower and Immigration in 1966 and the passage of the Adult Occupational Training Act the following year. Initially, the design of training programs under this policy was informed by a 'male breadwinner paradigm,' resulting in barriers to women's participation. The report of the Royal Commission on the Status of Women and the growing strength of the women's movement brought about a shift to an 'equality paradigm' as the framework for federal training programs. This chapter has traced the implications of this shift for women's access to training and the nature of the training women received through four different policy periods: equal opportunity, positive action, targeted equity, and symbolic equity.

The analysis here has demonstrated that equality measures of various types did have a positive impact on women's access to training. The equal-opportunity period saw the removal of systemic barriers to women's access to training, and this change resulted in an increase in women's participation rates in institutional training. During the life of the National Training Program, positive-action measures did bring about an increase in women's share of places in training for more highly skilled and non-traditional occupations. The targeted-equity approach of the Canadian Jobs Strategy did result in high participation rates of women in many programs, although not in those leading to higher-skilled occupations. While improvements took place in women's access to training programs, however, the analysis in the chapter has shown that the equity measures had little significant impact on the nature of training women received. Throughout all the policy periods examined, the great majority of women were trained for occupations that were predominantly female, mainly in the expanding service sector. This is true even in the case of the National Training Program, where women continued to be trained mainly for sex-typed, primarily clerical, jobs in the service sector. Despite the shift to an equality paradigm, federally funded training programs continued to reflect and reinforce the existing gender division of labour in ways similar to the programs during and after the Second World War.

The explanation for this failure lies in the understanding of an active labour-market policy that informed government decision-making throughout this period. In Canada, an active labour-market policy has meant government intervention to meet more efficiently the employer-generated demand for labour. The nature of that demand has not been questioned; it has been accepted as given. This approach assumes that the demand for labour is gender neutral. The reality, however, is that it reflects an occupational and industrial structure that is highly segregated along gender lines. Increasing women's access to training programs geared to meet the gendered demand of the labour market in the period between 1972 and 1995 meant channelling women into sex-typed occupations and industries. From the perspective of women's equality, such an approach is anything but active; it is essentially passive.

An active labour-market policy with women's equality as a central concern would require measures to counteract the effects on women's training choices of the gendered demand of the labour market and, where possible, to alter the gendered nature of the demand itself. Positive-action measures to increase women's participation rates in training for more highly skilled and traditionally male jobs can help counteract the effects on women's training choices of the gendered demand from the labour market. To be effective, such measures would have to be a central feature of all training policies. However, measures besides training are required to alter the gendered nature of labour-market demand. An active labour-market policy favouring women's equality would have to include effective employment-equity legislation covering hiring and promotion, and accessible high-quality child care. Furthermore, it would require a supportive framework of macroeconomic and industrial policies that promoted employment growth as well as collective bargaining and minimum-standards legislation that ensured that the jobs available to women were well paid and predominantly full-time and full-year.

APPENDIX: FEDERALLY FUNDED TRAINING PROGRAMS, 1967–1995

Canada Manpower Training Program (CMTP), 1967–80 (under the Adult Occupational Training Act, 1967)

Institutional courses ('general purchase courses')
Delivered in provincial institutions; federal government purchases 'seats' in the institutions.
- Skills Training: pre-employment courses providing entry-level skills training in particular occupations (also called Occupational Skills Training)
- Language Training: English or French as a second language
- Basic Training for Skill Development (BTSD): courses designed to upgrade basic skills in mathematics, science, and communication for unemployed workers (originally described simply as basic educational upgrading)
- Apprentice: classroom component of apprenticeships
- Job Readiness Training (JRT): life-skills, job-orientation, or academic-upgrading courses or work-experience training targeted to chronically unemployed workers or persons out of the labour force for a prolonged period
- Work Adjustment Training (WAT): courses directed at teaching appropriate work habits and attitudes to workers with 'behavioural difficulties'

Industrial courses
These courses take place in the workplace; the federal government provides a subsidy to the employer for all direct training costs and a portion of the wage of the trainee.
– Canadian Manpower Industrial Training Program: brought together under one umbrella a variety of industrial training programs in 1972. In 1978, EIC introduced Critical Trade Skills Training (CTST).

National Training Program (NTP), 1982–5 (under the National Training Act, 1982)

Institutional courses
As under the Adult Occupational Training Act

Industrial courses (National Industrial Training Program)
– Critical Trades Skills Training (CTST): courses directed at training for occupations such as tool-and-die maker, industrial maintenance mechanic, and others where there was a shortage of skilled labour. Employers offering training for occupations recognized under CTST could receive federal funding for up to two years.
– General Industrial Training (GIT): courses directed at training workers for other occupations in demand, retraining workers affected by new technology and industrial restructuring, training the unemployed, training women in non-traditional occupations, and training adults with special needs

Canadian Jobs Strategy (CJS), 1985

Under CJS, the federal government purchased training seats from provincial institutions, commercial trainers, and non-profit organizations. The distinction between institutional and industrial programs became less relevant.
– Job Development: courses directed at the long-term unemployed, defined as those unemployed for twenty-four out of the previous thirty weeks; a combination of work experience and relevant training. Sponsoring organizations, which could be private-sector, government, or non-profit organizations, received wage subsidies and direct financial contributions to capital costs and training. The training could last up to fifty-two weeks.

- Job Entry/Re-entry: orientation-to-work courses and basic employment training aimed at helping new employees make the transition
  into the work force. The re-entry courses were directed at women
  who had been outside the paid labour force for three or more years;
  other programs, including Challenge, were directed at students entering the workforce.
- Skills Shortages: employers were reimbursed for a period of from
  three weeks to three years for the direct training costs and some of a
  trainee's wages when providing training for current or newly hired
  workers in occupations where there was an existing or anticipated
  shortage. The employer could be in a private-sector, government, or
  non-profit organization.
- Skills Investment: employers received subsidies for the wages of
  workers who were taking training and for direct training costs for up
  to three years in cases where jobs were threatened by technological
  change or market change.

Labour Force Development Strategy, 1990

Beginning in 1991/92, the CJS programs were reorganized to put more
emphasis on improving the 'employability' of people on Unemployment Insurance or social assistance and on assisting employers to train
their existing workforce. The following summary includes only those
elements of the LFDS that incorporate training.

1 Programs for unemployed workers or people on social assistance:
- Project-Based Training: training in such areas as technical skills, life
  skills, interpersonal skills, effectiveness skills; combines classroom
  and on-the job training; directed at groups that have difficulty access-
  ing the labour market
- Purchase of Training: training courses purchased from public institutions, and commercial and non-profit providers

2 Programs for private-sector employers:
- Human Resource Planning: Assistance made available to selected
  employers to assist them in becoming more self-reliant in analysing
  human-resource issues and formulating appropriate responses
- Labour Market Adjustment Assistance: (a) under the Training Trust
  Fund, the federal government assists in the creation of self-sustaining
  trust funds to pay for the training needs of employers and workers in

the private sector; (b) under Training Enhancement Assistance, financial assistance is provided for a variety of activities to promote the
development of a training culture in the private sector.
– Workplace-Based Training: federal government shares costs associated with the design and delivery of training for employer's staff.
Training is related to increased productivity and competitiveness.

3 Community Development:
– Local Projects: projects directed at communities in difficulty; they
combine training with work experience to assist participants in
improving their position in the labour market.

NOTES

1 On unemployment insurance see Porter 1993; on collective bargaining see
Fudge 1992; on minimum-standards legislation see Fudge 1991 and McCallum 1986; on training, see Pierson and Cohen 1984. For a historical treatment
that covers minimum-standards legislation, social assistance, and collective
bargaining see Ursel 1992.
2 Economic Council of Canada 1965: 170–84
3 Canada, Department of Manpower and Immigration 1970: 3.
4 Ibid. 1971: 12.
5 Ibid. 1974: 3.
6 Canada, Royal Commission on the Status of Women 1970: 196.
7 Ibid.: 196–7.
8 Ibid.: 189.
9 Ibid.: 191.
10 Canada, Department of Manpower and Immigration 1974: 3.
11 Canada, Department of Manpower and Immigration 1975: 3.
12 See the summary and description of federally funded training programs at
the end of this chapter.
13 Canada, Department of Manpower and Immigration 1975: 12.
14 Canadian Advisory Council on the Status of Women 1974: 16.
15 Canada, Employment and Immigration Canada 1978: appendix 7, 1.
16 Calculations based on Statistics Canada, 1988: table 2.
17 Statistics Canada 1990c: 78.
18 The outline of the National Training Act that follows is based on the description in the Canada, Employment and Immigration Canada 1983a: 23–4.
19 Canada, Employment and Immigration Canada 1980: 10.
20 Ibid. 1981a: 9.

21 Ibid. 1983a: 25.
22 Canada, Employment and Immigration Canada 1985: table 1. This table is the basis for all the calculations in this paragraph.
23 Ibid. 1983b: table 7.3.
24 Ibid. 1981b, 1983b: table 5.9.
25 Ibid. 1983b, 1985: tables 11.15, 3.1 and 2.7.
26 Ibid. 1983a: 23.
27 Ibid. 1985: table 11.22.
28 The 1980/81 figure was calculated from ibid. 1981b: tables 3.1 and 2.10; the 1984/85 figure, from ibid. 1985: tables 3.1 and 2.7.
29 Ibid. 1981b: table 3.1; ibid. 1985: table 3.1.
30 Ibid. 1985: table 11.15.
31 Ibid. table 11.22.
32 Canada, Royal Commission on Equality in Employment 1984: chap. 2.
33 Canada, Employment and Immigration Canada 1987: 22.
34 Ibid. 1989.
35 The $2.7 billion figure comes from ibid. 1991: 2–5.
36 Butterwick 1992.
37 Employment and Immigration Canada, Statistical Analysis Unit.
38 Canadian Labour Force Development Board, 'CJS Expenditure and Participant Data,' n.d., n.p., mimeo.
39 Canada, Human Resources Development Canada 1994: 7.

3

The Labour Market, the State, and the Reorganization of Work: Policy Impacts

M. PATRICIA CONNELLY AND
MARTHA MacDONALD

The labour market in Canada is undergoing significant restructuring. This is the dimension of overall structural change and adjustment that most directly affects people in their daily lives. Several dimensions of change have been widely observed and discussed in the popular media as well as in academic forums, including the growth of service-sector jobs and the erosion of goods-production jobs; the increase in non-standard work; the stagnation or decline of real wages; the polarization of earnings; the feminization of the labour force. These labour-market manifestations are the end result of strategies by corporations, governments, and households in a changing world economy. Households and corporations are responding to politically shaped economic forces and are themselves influencing policy and shaping economic outcomes. Government policy limits and directs the possible corporate strategies of restructuring – favouring some and discrediting others. At the same time, governments feel their hands are tied by disembodied economic realities, manifested in global corporate strategies over which they perceive they have little or no control. Households negotiate the changing terrain of livelihood provision. All of these strategic layers are gendered. Gender relations shape the government, corporate, and household strategies and the labour-market outcomes.

We are examining some of these processes and outcomes in our current research project on restructuring and gender, using case studies to better understand the processes at the level of individual workplaces and households. We are examining issues of flexibility and earnings inequality from a feminist perspective. This means going beyond a narrow focus on the paid labour market to include all kinds of work. Restructuring affects the totality of economic activities as the combined strategies of corporations, states, and households shift economic effort across the dimensions of formal/informal economy, paid/unpaid work, and productive/reproductive labour. We are interested in the direct labour-market policy adjustments being made in UI, training, and job creation that have gendered assumptions and impacts. As well, we are interested in how other policy levels, such as deficit management, affect the labour market. We are also sensitive to the regional variation in policy concerns and impacts.

This paper summarizes preliminary findings from an initial public-sector case study on home care in Nova Scotia. It is a case study of both workplace restructuring and the gendered impacts of deficit-reduction policies that target health and social services. The trend towards de-institutionalization in the health and social-services fields creates major changes in the organization of work and the nature of the jobs available in those sectors. The example of home-care workers highlights issues of the casualization of work, subcontracting, and the effects of government restraint. It is women who bear the brunt of these changes, both as workers and as primary care givers in the home. This trend in the reorganization of health and social-service delivery is occurring in many provinces of Canada and in many countries of the world, in both the North and South (Connelly 1994).

Theoretical Concerns

Both the social science and the management literature focus on the increased need for flexibility in the global market, including flexibility in the use of labour. The management literature speaks positively of the new lean production-management methods, with their emphasis on teamwork, total quality management, and a partnership between workers and managers. The term functional flexibility is sometimes used in this context to refer to flexibility in how labour is allocated across tasks. Writers such as Piore and Sabel (1984) see this as a positive step for workers, leading to multi-skilling and a more craft-based labour process. However, many political economists see it as merely another way to increase productivity, without necessarily upgrading the skills, conditions, or rewards of work.

We are critical of this literature on flexibility for its failure to recognize the gendered nature of the restructuring (MacDonald 1991; Mac-Donald and Connelly 1990). For example, in a gendered labour process functional flexibility is more typical of men's jobs, whereas women tend to be used in the more routinized, repetitive work. Our research on the fishery and that of others (MacDonald and Connelly 1990; Hadley 1994) suggests that women are more likely to be affected by strategies of numerical flexibility (flexibility in the amount of labour) through various forms of non-standard work. Strategies of wage flexibility (flexibility in compensation) are also traditionally more characteristic of women's employment. These three flexibility strategies, then, are not gender neutral. Much of women's work, whether on the line in manufacturing plants or in service jobs ranging from nursing to social work, is being made more routinized, sped up, and degraded, and made non-standard in terms of hours and the rewards of work. Flexibility strategies create marginalization for the majority of women. The changes in the delivery of health care and social services provide an excellent example of these flexibility strategies in action.

While much of the literature focuses on corporate restructuring, public-sector restructuring is particularly crucial to women, as many traditional female jobs are concentrated in that sector, including nursing, teaching, social work, and clerical work. Women are losing some of their best-paying jobs through the erosion and restructuring of the public sector. The public sector is increasingly adopting management philosophies developed in the private sector. Initially, governments responded to fiscal restraint by general belt tightening across departments, leading to staff reductions, work speed-ups, and wage concessions. This response mirrored the private-sector attack on labour costs.

Now a more fundamental restructuring of the public sector is under way in many jurisdictions in Canada and abroad. Books such as *Reinventing Government* (1993) preach the need to rethink the definition and delivery of public goods and services. A common theme is that governments should get out of the business of providing services and become purchasers of services. The implicit assumption is that the private sector is more efficient and can therefore deliver the goods and services at a lower cost. So powerful is this assumption that it often goes untested. The result is a trend for governments to re-evaluate service delivery in department after department to identify all those that could be provided privately. Even where services are not contracted out, new delivery structures are being developed, usually involving decentralization. This process is in keeping with in-vogue management philosophies of reducing bureaucracy, flatteningmanagement hierarchies, and devolving authority to smaller units.

These changes in delivery mean radical changes for workers as old jobs are lost and new ones created. In this transition jobs can be re-classified, skills redefined, and conditions of work renegotiated. Full-time jobs can reappear as part-time or casual jobs. Professionals can be replaced by lower-skilled para-professionals. Bargaining units are dissolved and union successor rights are often unclear. We are interested in the extent of the deskilling and devaluing of jobs that occur in this process and the gendered impacts of the changes.

Health and social-service delivery have been key candidates for such restructuring across Canada (Sutherland and Fulton 1994). This partly reflects their relative size in government budgets – governments under pressure to cut spending see little alternative to reducing costs in these areas. However, the need to reduce costs does not dictate the method of doing so. Public-sector workers continually reiterate alternative ways that savings can be made, without such negative labour impacts. However, they feel they are generally not consulted about how to save money. The restructuring of health and social services reflects more than the simple need to save money. It reflects a broader political shift that has accompanied the economic pressures, manifested in a rethinking of the welfare state (Yalnizyan 1993). In Canada as in other industrialized countries there is pressure for the state to play less of a role. Privatization of services is advocated. There is pressure for deinstitutionalization of patients and clients, along with a greater role for the community and family. While there are attractions to this change in focus that appeal across the political spectrum from left to right, there are serious implications for both the quality of service and the conditions of work for those providing the service. The service providers are to a large extent women – either in traditional institutions, in smaller 'community' institutions, or in the home. Often the rhetoric of community and family care is used without there being provided the necessary supports to ensure that good-quality care and needed services are available.

There is a growing literature in Canada on the restructuring of health care, showing the deterioration of both the level of care and the quality of jobs (White 1990; Armstrong et al. 1993; Armstrong and Armstrong 1995). This case-study draws on that literature and focuses on the intersection of the health and social-service systems. The growth of home-care services is one element in the deinstitutionalization strategy. It also interfaces with the unpaid care-giving work provided in the home. It is women's work in both cases, and it is women's work that replaces the higher-paid work of other women.

Case-Study[1]

The case-study that follows examines one group of workers in one department in one province. Nova Scotia, a 'have not' province to begin with, has been particularly hard hit by restructuring. The fishing industry has collapsed owing to the destructive effects of both corporate and government strategies of 'adjustment' in the 1980s (MacDonald and Connelly 1990). The province has also been particularly hard hit by federal-government cutbacks, given its dependence on transfer payments, government employment, and defence spending. The erosion of federal-provincial transfer payments has put increased pressure on the provincial government to cut spending. Despite adecade of rhetoric about fiscal restraint, Nova Scotia now finds itself with the second-highest debt/GDP ratio in the country and the highest percentage of revenue that goes to service the debt.[2]

This situation has built up slowly during the provincial Conservative governments of the 1980s, and is now being ruthlessly tackled by the new Liberal government. Hospitals are being closed, full-time hospital staff are being laid off and then rehired as part-time or casual workers, patient hospital stays are shortened, university salaries and faculty hiring are frozen, university staff are required to take several days of unpaid leave, and tuition has been significantly increased. Most recently, union contracts have been abrogated, employees receiving provincial moneys are receiving a 3 per cent wage decrease, and wages are frozen for three years. Pressure to pay mounting costs in health care and higher education has affected the province's ability to fund other areas of health, education, and welfare, such as homes for the disabled, elementary schools, and assistance to the elderly. As the federal government off-loads their costs to the provinces, the provinces have had to lay off large numbers of workers, many of whom are women, in health and education fields and have had to restructure the services they deliver in order to operate with less money.

As in many countries, a major area targeted to save money is the provision of community, social, and health services. The trend is towards privatization, de-institutionalization, and keeping people in the community. When services are reduced, women are affected, both as the majority of public-sector professionals in these fields and as the primary unpaid care givers.

The Liberal government in the province of Nova Scotia is in the process of studying its health-care delivery with the aim of creating a restructuring plan. Early reports have indicated that they intend to expand home care as a means of keeping people in their communities and of saving on the more expensive hospital care. The home-care program, previously housed in the Department of Community Services, was recently transferred to the Department of Health. Home care is delivered by agencies in three sectors: the public sector, for example the municipal government; the voluntary non-profit sector, for example the Red Cross; and the private sector, for example Comcare. We are currently interviewing samples of workers from all three sectors about changes in their workplace and in their households. We have also interviewed the provincial coordinators, the directors of the different agencies, the executive of the group that represents most of the agencies in the province, social workers, assessors, and many other people involved in the area.

A home-care worker provides personal care, meal preparation, basic housekeeping and laundry, and respite care for family care givers. The cost of this care is shared by the federal, provincial, and municipal governments and is free of charge to the elderly and physically disabled whose incomes fall below a specified level of the Canada Assistance Plan. Those who can afford to pay for the service can obtain home care from the voluntary or private sector. The goal of home care is to help people to remain living as independently as possible in their own homes. This is consistent with the province's policy of de-institutionalizing. Our preliminary analysis of home-care workers shows how the structure and quality of home-care jobs are being altered by the process of restructuring. When the case-study is completed, it will also provide an examination of household work patterns and an analysis of the impact of restructuring on the home-care workers' paid and unpaid work. It will also provide some insights into the process of de-institutionalization.

The need for home care is increasing not just as a result of the province's policy of de-institutionalization, but also because of the demographic changes currently taking place. First, Nova Scotia, like the rest of the country, has an aging population. As the baby-boom generation continues to age, the older groups will be expanded, significantly changing the age profile. Second, the population is living longer. The average life expectancy for women is projected to reach 83 years by the year 2006, and that for men, 76 years. Because women typically live longer than their spouses, they are more likely to be on their own in their advanced years of life. Third, the majority of women, who are the primary care givers, are now in the labour force and have less time to care for children, elderly parents, the sick, and the disabled. Fourth, more young families are mobile and move from home towns where elderly parents live, so daily care of the elderly becomes impossible. Fifth, there is an increase in the number of single-parent families, most of whom are poor. They struggle to care for their children and are unable to care for their elderly relatives as well.

In 1988, recognizing the increasing need, the province's existing piecemeal home-care service became part of a Coordinated Home Care Program (CHCP). The first stage of the CHCP was to provide home care to the elderly and physically disabled. It was generally felt that the program would eventually expand to include care for early hospital discharges and emergency care. It would also expand to include professional workers such as nutritionists and occupational therapists. In this way it would truly become a comprehensive and coordinated program. In 1991, however, wages and budgets were frozen at the provincial level and the program did not expand as planned. As it now stands, the program has come under considerable pressure to respond to early hospital discharges, to acute care, and to emergency situations. In extreme cases, it does respond, but it is not, in general, able to accommodate such requests. This is because its mandate has not expanded to include this kind of care and because financial and labour-power constraints do not allow it to respond.

The Workers

Home-care workers were once drawn from the ranks of middle-aged women with grown children who had never before worked outside the home. Now the majority of home-care workers are young women who are single parents and are on social assistance. This is particularly the case in the urban areas. These women are drawn to this work because they can adjust their hours to the needs of their children and to the rules regulating social assistance. With rising unemployment, some men did apply for and were given homemaker jobs, but they did not last for any length of time. Some simply did not like the work, others left the job because the clients preferred women workers. We were told that men clients did not like to see other men doing housework and women clients did not like strange men in their homes.

With regard to race and ethnicity, home-care employers do not have affirmative-action policies. There are few black workers, and we were told by one administrator that workers with English as a first language were preferred because many of the elderly had trouble with accents. A few years ago, job turnover was quite high, but given the unemployment situation today, agencies have no problem recruiting workers. In fact, they find no need to advertise; they can fill openings by word of mouth. Wages are low for home-care workers since they are considered unskilled. Also wages for these workers have been frozen for the last two years, as they have been for all provincially paid workers. With very few exceptions, these jobs are not unionized.

With regard to the structure of homework, several years ago the majority of homemakers were salaried employees. Now they are almost all part-time workers. This saves money for the province, since the government now pays only for the hours that the worker is in someone's home. Travel time is unpaid, and if a client cancels an appointment, is hospitalized, or dies, the home-care worker loses wages until the client is replaced. A replacement usually takes several days, since a client assessment must be done and paperwork must be filed. Working on a part-time basis means lower wages and, in most cases, fewer benefits for the worker. It also means that a homemaker can no longer plan on the amount of money she will bring in each week.

With regard to the labour process, isolation has increased. Administrators have been told to reduce the amount of time for in-service training and to reduce the number of meetings with homemakers. This means that workers have less contact with other workers and less face-to-face contact with assessors. Instead of being able to share problems and solutions with a group of fellow workers who are having similar experiences, they must now deal with them as individuals with direction from a social worker.

Autonomy has decreased. Homemakers once had more autonomy and flexibility to define client needs and to decide when and how to service these needs. If they saw something that needed to be done, they did it. Now they are given a list of tasks to do. These tasks are very specific and the amount of time it takes to do the task is already determined. If the worker feels that something else should be done, or if the client makes a request, the home-care worker must call the social worker for permission to do the additional work. If permission is given, then the social worker and the homemaker must carefully record the additional amount of time spent in that home in the client's file, even if it amounts to only ten minutes. One task not on the list, and not taken into account, is the affective component of care provided by the worker, that is, the emotional support and companionship or what one social worker referred to as 'tender loving care.' With the loss of this component and of the autonomy that the job once provided, it was felt that the home-care worker was being reduced to the status of a cleaning person. In an attempt to counteract this perception, the title of homemaker was changed to home-care worker. This language, however, did not change the reality of the changing labour process.

Discretion has decreased. The social workers who do the client assessments feel that the home-care worker comes to know the clients better than they do. They feel that the situation of clients changes over time and that home-care workers should be able to respond to these changes. It is unfair to expect that workers can always do a specific task in the minimum time allotted, especially if they do three or four households in one day. So they try to build in some extra time for workers to use at their own discretion. In one case, the social workers were severely reprimanded in the provincial auditor-general's program-review report. Now they are very cautious about providing leeway for the home-care workers. This increases the stress level of workers.

Skill is not counted. It is clear that the affective component of the job is not valued, is not considered a skill, and is not accounted for on the list of tasks that can legitimately be performed. At the same time, there is talk of training the home-support workers to do 'client specific tasks' such as administering eye drops or medications and other small medical tasks. These tasks would not be transferable to other clients, which would save the cost of a visit from the Victorian Order of Nurses to these particular clients. The assumption of such tasks would not, however, be recognized as increasing the skill of the home-care worker, nor would it result in an increase in wages.

Conclusion

The change from full-time to part-time work and the inclusion of 'client specific medical tasks' in the workload of home-care workers has increased the employer's flexibility and cut costs. Flexibility for the employee, however, has decreased, with lower wages, fewer benefits, more isolation, less autonomy, less discretionary use of time, and higher levels of stress. Some home-care worker skills are unacknowledged or undervalued, as the affective component of the job is ignored and the client-specific medical skills go unrecognized. At the same time, women, especially the single parents, appreciate the flexibility of arranging their work hours to suit their household and child-care needs. They also appreciate the fact that they still have some autonomy and some discretion as they make use of their caring skills.

There is, however, cause for considerable concern, first because of the negative changes taking place in the labour process and, second, because these jobs are on the increase as the economy continues to undergo restructuring. A recent study of the Nova Scotia Departments of Health and Community Services recommends that the Coordinated Home Care Program be expanded to include early hospital discharges on a short-term and acute-care basis; be operated for more than the normal business hours from Monday to Friday; be funded by diverting moneys from hospital budgets; have coordinators/assessors in all major hospitals; and be positioned as a universal-entitlement health program. This would allow more people to be de-institutionalized, to have access to home care, and to remain in their homes and communities. A worthwhile goal. But what will it mean for the women care givers? Will it mean more low-wage, part-time, routinized and downgraded paid work with irregular hours and few benefits? Will it mean an increase in women's unpaid work in the home? Will it worsen the health and well-being of women care givers? These are the questions that must now be addressed.

NOTES

1 We would like to thank Maureen Macdonald and Daphne Tucker for assisting us with this research, as well as all those who agreed to be interviewed. This research is funded by SSHRC.
2 *Mail Star*, 12 May 1994.

4

Part-Time Employment and Women:
A Range of Strategies[1]

JANE JENSON

One of the most dramatic changes in industrial societies in the postwar years has been the shattering of the representation of the 'model worker' as a man earning enough to support his dependent family by working full time, and with job security, in industry. All dimensions of this model, over the last decades of economic turbulence and restructuring, have altered. As women's participation rate in the paid labour force approaches that of men in many countries, the 'average' worker is as likely to be female as to be male.[2] As companies restructure, the full-time worker with job security guaranteed by collective bargaining and labour legislation has given way to a variety of 'non-standard' or 'atypical' employment statuses. Part-time work, temporary work, and limited-term labour contracts have become increasingly prevalent in the private and public sectors.[3] Women are disproportionately found among those workers with such non-standard contracts, especially part-time ones.[4] Furthermore, restructuring has meant that the percentage of the labour force employed in industry has declined while that in the service sector has burgeoned. The latter sector is, of course, the one that employs women disproportionately.

None of the changes in the dimensions of the model has been gender neutral, then. Indeed, it is only by understanding the extent to which a new set of gendered employment relations is at the heart of the restructured economies that we can begin to comprehend the restructuring, as well as any space available within it for generating equality. The new employment practices draw in some ways on existing discourses and practices of gender relations, depend in some ways on their having been altered, and are profoundly implicated in setting out the new limits to gender equality that are being constituted. Just as in the postwar years women's status as a 'reserve army' depended on a particular articulation of family forms, gender relations, and production practices, so too does the feminization of non-standard employment (Beechey 1988: 54).

New employment practices are central to the conditions that women now face as they struggle to achieve economic equality in an economy that is very different from the one for which, for example, the Royal Commission on the Status of Women prescribed in 1970. Not only has the crisis of the postwar Fordist model meant high rates of unemployment, loss of industrial jobs, and continued labour-force segmentation and low wages for women.[5] It has also meant the introduction of new technologies and the concomitant institutionalization of forms of employment and relations to the labour force that had little place in post-1945 economies (Hagen and Jenson 1988: 9–11; Phillips and Phillips 1993: 106). In particular, post-Fordism has brought the consolidation of a two-tier labour force, increasingly divided in many countries into 'good jobs' and 'bad jobs.' While the conditions of the former resemble those of 'standard' postwar employment, the bad jobs are characterized by low wages, precarious or contingent employment, and a stunted career ladder (Myles 1991; Economic Council of Canada, 1990).[6] Thus, post-Fordism means more non-standard or atypical employment. And, as these very labels suggest – designating what employment is *not* rather than what it is or might be – we are still struggling to make sense of these novelties. Therefore, considering strategies of response is important because the space available for generating gender equality may be narrowing. It is certainly relocating.

This paper examines part-time work, a form of employment and a time schedule that is overwhelmingly female in all 'post-industrial' countries.[7] I am using the designation 'post-industrial' in the sense that, for example, John Myles uses it, to indicate an economic structure in which industrial *production* may (or may not) remain a central source of economic growth, but the distribution of *employment* has tilted in the direction of the service sector (Myles 1991). I have selected part-time employment as the focus because it has emerged as a favourite – heavily gendered – strategy for restructuring by employers and in some countries is being actively promoted by the state as a – also gendered – 'solution' to the problem of unemployment.[8] Thus, job creation in post-Fordism means the creation of part-time jobs for women, in both the service and the goods-producing sectors.[9]

Evidence provided by the overall statistics as well as by sectoral studies shows that part-time employment is being actively created by employers as they restructure. The state plays a role too as employer, as regulator, and as program-provider. Therefore, the contribution of this form of employment to new structures of inequality merits attention, as it is one of the structures that inhibits women's equal participation in the economy (OECD 1991: 3). It is also important to recognize that the resort to part-time work does not occur by some sort of 'necessity,' whether economic, familial, or whatever. Part-time employment is a creation and not an economic necessity. The patterns of such employment reflect major cross-regime differences in the strategies of all actors involved: employers, states, unions, and women, whether organized or acting as individuals. Plenty of space remains for choosing *how* and *whether* to employ part-time, and some of these choices are more likely to promote gender equality than are others. It is for all these reasons then that the characteristics of part-time employment are worth exploring, both in Canada and in several European countries.

Why Focus on Part-Time Employment?

This paper begins from two propositions. The first is best expressed by Margaret Maruani when she says: 'On peut retourner les chiffres comme on veut, qui dit temps partiel pense femme. Aucune autre forme d'emploi – aucune autre forme de chômage – n'est a ce point sexuée' (Maruani 1992: 130). The second is that part-time work is now a strategic choice available to employers – and the state, to the extent that its policies accept, support, or promote part-time employment – in response to the economic turbulence of the last decade.[10] It does not fall from the sky, nor is it necessarily women's choice.[11] Indeed, this paper argues that part-time employment has been the *choice of employers*. Therefore, the familiar correlations of marital status, number of children, and so on are driven more by employers' offers and states' failure to provide collective services like child care than by women's real 'choices.'[12] An employer's decision to create part-time jobs is a choice that expresses an existing set of culturally shared assumptions about gender relations, about women's social roles, about men's social roles, and about the relationship between work and family. These articulate with employers' labour-force needs in ways that allow them to create different forms of non-standard employment for women and men.[13]

The advantages to employers of part-time workers in this period of restructuring are clear. First and foremost, they gain flexibility in the management of their labour forces and 'flexibility' has been the key concept in much of the restructuring of both industrial production and the service sector. Part-time workers allow employers to respond to the seasonal or other time variations in their needs for employees.[14] If new technologies encourage employers to shed workers, they also encourage them to use their machines for longer periods. In addition, in many countries, post-1945 collective-bargaining regimes and labour legislation have provided much less protection and fewer benefits to part-time workers than to those employed full time, thereby making them a cheaper source of labour. For employers seeking to save on their wage bills as pressures to keep up their productivity rates mount, this aspect is appealing. Also attractive is the fact that the wages and other forms of income of part-time employees are often at a lower hourly rate than are those of their full-time colleagues performing the same work. Finally, part-time employees are less likely to be unionized workers, which not only often provides savings on wage bills but also makes it easier to implement strategies for 'flexible' management. Thus, as the OECD says, 'le travail à temps partiel n'implique pas seulement une durée de travail inférieure à la normale; il définit aussi en général un statut inférieur de celui du temps complet. Les travailleurs à temps partiel ont dans l'ensemble des conditions de l'emploi moins favorable sous bien des aspects' (OCDE 1991: 26).

States have also seen part-time work as a solution to their troubles. Most obviously, a part-time worker is not an unemployed worker. Therefore, policy makers concerned about the political and economic consequences of unemployment have not looked askance at rising rates of part-time work. More indirect but no less important has been the contribution of states' conversion to neo-liberal economics. Moves to cut back state spending and privatize many state services have resulted in a more general shift from 'good jobs' to 'bad jobs.' Where public-sector employment has traditionally been full-time (or at least protected part-time), private employers providing services under contract to the government are subject to all the same pressures for flexibility, cost-savings, and so forth described above.

Therefore, it is not surprising that as the service economy has increased in importance and companies have sought to restructure production, in the context of an economic crisis that has generated high rates of unemployment, there has been a general enthusiasm for part-time work among employers and states and general consternation among unions and many women.

But the place of part-time employment in the restructured economies is not the only reason that this form of non-standard employment merits attention. The other major reason is that it sets limits on the political space for women to achieve economic equality with men. Indeed, part-time employment contributes to the construction of new structures of gender inequality that may not be as responsive to the traditional policy recipes for generating equality, in particular those focusing on training or even on affirmative action.

These limits are of several sorts. The independence and autonomy that are supposed to come with successful integration into the labour market are undermined by such employment practices. Having even a part-time job may mark a sea-change in woman's sense of self-worth and independence (Armstrong and Armstrong 1994: 202–3). None the less, a part-time job is not very likely to lead to a level of income, with security and job-related benefits, that is a foundation for any economic equality. In the simplest terms, it is hard to earn one's living (and support children) with only a part-time wage. Therefore, if women with a spouse are more likely to be part-time employees, this is not a recipe for equality within the family, whether considered in terms of the gender division of labour in the family or of the capacity of a woman to be self-supporting. In addition, the very notion of women's availability for part-time work and their supposed 'choice' of it simply reinforces rather than challenges traditional assumptions about and practices of the gender division of labour in the family. Moreover, such enthusiasm for part-time work means that the state and employers have another excuse for not devoting resources to public services like child care and parental leaves.[15]

Of course, such limits have been highlighted for several years. For example, they have frequently been cited in criticisms of the 'Swedish model,' in which the rates of female labour-force participation are high, but so are the rates of part-time employment and the segmentation of the labour force by industry (Canada's rates are not dissimilar) (Bakker 1988: 28). Indeed, Swedish feminists have for many years argued for a reduced working week for everyone, rather than a gender division of working time, in order to overcome this limit to achieving the 'equality contract' (Jenson and Mahon 1993a: 91). This criticism becomes even more important as the evidence mounts that the increase in part-time employment is an element of basic trends in post-Fordist restructuring. There is increasing evidence that, in the current economy, part-time employment is declining as a transitional form, responding to life-cycle needs of some types of employees. It remains, of course, a form of employment important to young people who are still within the educational system. None the less, for many workers the pattern is more likely to be movement between part-time work, other forms of non-standard employment, and unemployment rather than from part-time towards a full-time, secure job. Thus, the first years in the labour market may imprint an employment status; lack of experience and employment history may become a crucial 'sorting mechanism' within the labour market (Myles 1991: 361–2). Similarly, temporary and part-time employees are sometimes excluded from the routes upon which career and salary advancement depend – for example, seniority.[16] Therefore, if new kinds of hiring practices mean that women do not accumulate seniority, the effects will continue to haunt them throughout their working lives. Incomes are also affected because many employers differentiate among employees in their employment classification schemas or in the ways that they pay commissions.[17] In general, non-standard employees appear to operate in a distinct labour market (OCDE 1991: 27).

Even more systematic in hindering gender equality is the fact that *skill recognition follows the form of the employment contract* rather than the other way around.[18] As Maruani concludes after a study of three different kind of workplaces and the relationship between employment contract, working schedule, recognized credentials, and salaries of the employees: 'Tous convergent vers la même idée : la qualification se construit pour une bonne part autour du contrat de travail et du temps de travail. En d'autres termes, le travail à temps partiel est devenu *une variante de la sous-qualification* alors que le travail à temps complet assure à tous les niveaux un *minimum de "professionnalité"*' (1992: 133–44). Julie White's study of struggles in the Post Office confirm that employers will attempt to link part-time work and non-recognition of skill, unless unions succeed in preventing them from doing so (1993: 253ff.).

With these observations, then, the new structures of gender inequality are revealed. Such conclusions clearly undermine any strategy for generating equality that focuses exclusively on women themselves, for example by emphasizing training.[19] No matter the training that women obtain and the skill upgrading they undergo, they will not reap the full benefits *until* they have access to better employment contracts. Training is a tool for breaking down labour-force segmentation that focuses on production. None the less, restructuring does not simply involve restructuring production; it also involves restructuring employment, which may be the more important aspect (Capdevielle et al. 1990). If women are being trained, in effect, for part-time and other non-standard employment, the effects of training will not be realized as long as women's part-time employment itself is cited by employers as evidence of lack of skill.

Therefore, strategies for achieving economic equality must also focus on the story of the creation of new structures of inequality out of employers' and states' efforts to restructure and of ways to resist those that hinder gender equality.

A Range of Responses

Higher rates of part-time employment may characterize this moment in many countries. None the less, the contribution of such employment to gender inequality is not precisely the same everywhere, because of different strategies pursued by states, unions, and women to shape employers' use of it. These responses are of four types:

Response #1: Watch the rising rates of part-time employment and do nothing

This response is probably the most common, as states come late to an understanding of the effects of restructuring on forms of employment. Given a traditional understanding of part-time work as a relatively unimportant form of employment, usually a benign choice made by young women or married women with 'family responsibilities,' states have been slow to react. Moreover, in a context like Canada's, where labour relations are regulated to a large extent by collective-bargaining regimes, the question of forms of employment appears to be a matter most appropriately addressed by employers and unions.

Of course, a do-nothing stance hinders the achievement of gender equality because it leaves part-time employees (that is, one-quarter of Canadian working women and rising) not only with low incomes, but also without the standard protections and benefits that have been associated with employment in the postwar period, and for which workers and their organizations struggled precisely in order to provide some protection against the abitrariness of employers, the labour market, and their own life chances.[20] The issue, in other words, is one not simply of hours or time management, but of the relationship to the labour force, the employer, the state, and, in general, to the rights of workers. Non-standard forms of employment threaten these postwar gains as much as they threaten the workers who hold such jobs.

Therefore, this first type of stance has been increasingly difficult to sustain as workers and unions have clamoured for something to be done. Sometimes the call is to restrict the resort to non-standard work.[21] Often it is to incorporate part-time (and other contingent) employees into benefit packages, both those negotiated in collective bargaining and those provided publicly. For example, the Ontario Labour Relations Board has redefined the situation of part-time employees, recognizing that they share a 'community of interest' with full-time workers, thereby facilitating their organization in the same union locals.

Response #2: Accept the rising level of part-time work as part of employers' demands for restructuring, but institute measures to improve the benefits and protections of part-time workers

There are two different ways in which this second response has occurred. The first is best exemplified by Sweden. By the 1960s, facing a labour shortage and the rapid growth of social spending, which required more state employees, the Swedish state began to employ women in the public sector part time. These employment practices were coupled with family policies, especially with respect to parental leaves, that permitted women to move in and out of the labour force in reaction to changing family responsibilities. Progressive income taxes supported such employment practices. These jobs were not marginalized, but virtually fully incorporated into the public and union-employer programs of social protection and solidaristic wage strategies (Rosenthal 1990: 135–7). They were, in other words, not only protected but well paid.

The result of this strategy was that Sweden had, on the one hand, one of the highest rates of female labour-force participation and, on the other, one of the most highly segmented labour forces. Thus, when the women's movement appeared in the 1970s, both within the traditional institutions of representation and in autonomous organizations, it still confronted a very traditional gender division of labour in the family. Moreover, given the organization of work (often a six-hour day for state employees), women who wanted to work full time had difficulty finding jobs (ibid.: 135).

France exemplifies a second way in which part-time work has been accepted and part-time workers provided with protections similar to those associated with standard employment. France's rate of part-time employment until the 1970s was very low and then it began to rise precipitously. In the 1970s the right-wing French government was enthusiastic about part-time employment, specifically for women, seeing it as a solution to what it interpreted as the tendency of women seeking employment to drive up the unemployment rate. The Socialist party and the major unions opposed part-time work because it had the negative effects described here. They tended to sloganize that 'part-time work was part-time unemployment' and to call instead for a reduced work week for everyone.[22]

None the less, employers continued to offer more and more part-time positions. Therefore, the Socialists, who had been elected in 1981, moved quickly to try to control the situation. Legislation and decrees focused first on atypical employment, thereby recognizing its legitimacy as well as extending protections with respect to benefits and employee rights.[23] The regularization of various forms of temporary work and fixed-term contracts, as well as of part-time work, signified their legitimation and availability as a normal part of personnel management.

Nevertheless, the French experience shows that simply extending standard benefits is insufficient, much as it is helpful. Such an extension does not address the other structures of inequality embedded in part-time employment practices or supported by such practices. Such practices have become a means of redefining the very status of employees in many workplaces, creating new divisions across categories by separating women and men, young and old, skilled and unskilled, and married and single workers.[24] These structures need to be considered, even as access to benefits and protection obviously are needed too.

Response #3: Actively encourage part-time employment as a solution to the unemployment crisis

The acceptance and legitimization of part-time work has led in some cases to state efforts to encourage it. Such positive actions usually follow in those cases where the state is desperately seeking a solution to its own problems in this crisis: high levels of unemployment.

Here again France can be used as an example. The Left governments, many of whose members continued to deplore part-time work, none the less signalled their willingness to tolerate a segmented labour market, and indeed one deeply cleaved by gender, when they turned their attention to unemployment.[25] In the context of the fight against unemployment, especially long-term unemployment, further legislation was introduced to actively encourage part-time hiring. Earlier Socialist governments had instituted some inducements for hiring part-time employees but always somewhat apologetically (Jenson 1988: 166). In recent years the *mea culpas* disappeared, with the result being a sea-change not only in the structure of the labour market but also in policy goals. A 1990 *projet de la loi sur la précarité* marked 'la fin du mythe du plein emploi, de la référence symbolique au travail stable, ... le texte qui vient d'être adopté autorise en fait cette nouvelle définition du travail qui correspond à un usage moderne.'[26]

The dangers in this embrace of part-time work by policy makers are obvious. First, especially when the embrace is by a left-wing government, the criticism of labour-market segmentation and its gender biases is likely to disappear. The feminization of non-standard employment suffers a loss of attention and therefore the new structures of inequality become invisible. This has clearly happened in France, where the discourse on the problem of 'youth unemployment' completely ignores the fact that it is young women who are making a disproportionate contribution to the 'problem,' and that their career prospects will continue to be precarious, if not become more precarious, as they move into the category of part-time working woman aged twenty-five to forty-four.

A second problem is, of course, that active encouragement of part-time employment does nothing to challenge the gender division of labour in the family. Indeed, it may exacerbate the problem. If wives are earning less, husbands may have to earn more – by working overtime, and so on – thereby leaving child care and domestic labour to the partner who is bringing in less income.

Nor does the encouragement of part-time employment do anything to challenge employers' tendency to see female workers as different and to treat them differently, whether in terms of pay, rights, or working conditions. This response marks, in many ways, a return to the notion that women workers are not really like the others, being over-determined by family responsibilities and sexuality. This was the attitude that generated high levels of part-time employment in many Northern European countries in the 1950s and 1960s, and that so much of recent politics has struggled to overcome.

Response #4: Oppose the widespread imposition of part-time employment and develop alternatives

Of course, in thinking about part-time employment it is important to recognize that it does not, in and of itself, constitute a 'bad job.' If the 'choice' is truly a choice, because real options for a full-time job exist, because child care is available, because the division of labour in the family can accommodate women working full time, because a return to a full-time job is possible when the worker wishes it, and if equivalent benefits and protections are available to part-time workers, then a part-time job might be a 'good job.'[27]

Therefore, a fourth response to the increase in employers' and states' enthusiasm for part-time work involves several alternatives, including improvements in part-time work. A first step would be that suggested by the Commission of Inquiry into Part-Time Work, which made recommendations for achieving 'fair wage levels, prorating of all fringe benefits and pension plans, guarantee[s] of the same rights and benefits granted full-time employees,' and so on (Economic Council of Canada 1984: 5). In other words, an alternative would be to end part-time employment's status as a low-wage, dead-end job for women.

Given what we know about the gender assumptions embedded in wage levels – women's work is paid less because *women* do it – the gender bias in definitions of skill, and so forth, this alternative could truly be achieved only if the gender assumptions about women's 'special talents' and availability for part-time work were confronted head on. Part-time employment would have to become a form of work considered 'normal' for both women and men.

This task may not be quite as daunting as it seems. Some steps towards it can be made. One important one is to promote the unionization of part-time workers. Studies of the experience of part-time workers in unions demonstrate that when the union takes on the issue of wage rates for part-time workers as well as their fringe benefits and rights, part-time work becomes a better option.[28] The statistics dramatically demonstrate that unionization has even more benefits for part-time than full-time workers, in terms of both wages and other benefits.[29]

None the less, as this paper has claimed, the new structures of inequality associated with part-time work are deeply marked by the process of restructuring. Therefore, while efforts to improve the part-time option might be pursued, further efforts are also necessary. A second strategy is to propose a completely different way to achieve flexibility and reduce unemployment.

For many years Swedish women (and some trade-union men) have called for the six-hour day *for everyone* as a way of addressing gender inequalities. This is one version of a union demand that was popular earlier in the 1970s and 1980s on the Left, in both Western Europe and Canada. Reduction of working time (usually the thirty-five-hour week) was promoted then as a method of job creation as well as of achieving gender equality.

The idea of reduced working time has lost its allure in recent years for several reasons. First, employers were moving ahead with their own strategies, including part-time work. Organized and unorganized workers had to struggle to divert the worst effects of this restructuring of the labour process and employment (Jenson and Mahon 1993a). Second, as the idea is now re-emerging, it is most often proposed by right-wing governments (as in France) or employers.[30] Often it is simply imposed or extracted as a concession from exceedingly reluctant workers, as has been the case with several provincial governments that have forced wage cuts on their employers in the form of 'unpaid holidays.' Workers and their unions are rightly suspicious of these efforts, in which the job-creation, unemployment-fighting effects seem very limited.

There are, however, more progressive versions of the reduction of working time. A real discussion of this alternative continues to have the advantage of holding out a policy that might reduce gender inequalities in the context of current economic realities. It is a stance that refuses the dualistic labour market, thereby creating space for a parallel, articulated consideration of gender equality (Mahon 1991). It is, of course, not an easy alternative to implement, as the conflicts even in Sweden indicate (Jenson and Mahon 1993b: 96–100) and the politics of the so-called social contract in Ontario revealed. Yet, it remains an alternative to consider, one that challenges employers and the state to abandon their long-standing gendered assumptions about how the labour market does and should operate.

The last alternative, also a challenging one to implement but one that addresses the issue of restructuring at its root, is to insert the discussion of part-time employment and equality into the ongoing critique of neo-liberal strategies. A form of restructuring that emphasizes market-driven strategies and solutions will continue to interpret part-time employment as a problem of 'human capital' or of women's 'choice' for managing work and family. Yet, it is neo-liberal politics themselves that are contributing to the increase in part-time jobs. The lack of reliable and affordable child care can only contribute to the statistics in labour-force surveys in which women report 'not seeking' full-time work.[31] Moreover, cut-backs in the public sector, which used to be a primary source of 'good jobs' for women, not only put more women at risk of unemployment but push them into a labour market that is creating more part-time than full-time jobs. In addition, cut-backs in the form of privatization (Air Canada, for example) or the establishment of more independent agencies (Canada Post, for example) are liberating employers, who previously were subject to civil-service regulations, to restructure their labour forces and employment practices. In other words, part-time employment needs to be seen not only as a central component of the current moment of economic restructuring but also as a consequence of political choices of neo-liberals, both in Canada and elsewhere.

NOTES

1 Revised version of a paper prepared for the Economic Equality Workshop, sponsored by Status of Women Canada, 29–30 November 1993. For helpful suggestions I would like to thank Greg Albo, Francine Mayer, and Charlotte Yates, as well as participants in the workshop.

2 At the beginning of the 1990s, on average in the countries of the European Community, 41% of working people were female (*Bulletin* 1993: 1). In Canada the comparable statistic is 45% (Armstrong and Armstrong 1994: 16).

3 In the six years between 1983 and 1989, in the 12 countries of the European Community, part-time workers as a percentage of the labour force rose a full 2.7% (3% for women) (Commission of the EC 1991: 40).

4 In 1989 in the European Community, 82% of part-time workers were women (Commission des CE 1991: 41). In Canada in 1987, over 70% of part-time workers were women (Saint-Pierre 1993: 274).

5 For a discussion of Fordism in Canada see Jenson 1989a and Jenson and Mahon 1993a.

6 This bifurcation is the result of strategic choices, and can therefore be ameliorated by appropriate initiatives taken by unions and states, as well as as other actors. For a discussion see Mahon 1987.

7 Particularly in North America, young men (15–24) often work part time, but the category as a whole is one that is highly feminized (Duffy and Pupo 1992: 41ff.), and becoming more so (Connelly and MacDonald 1990: 27). For the Economic Council (1990: 11), non-standard employment in Canada is primarily part-time, defined as working fewer than 30 hours a week. Part-time is not the only form of employment of non-standard employment, of course. Temporary and limited-term contracts are also often increasing and these latter may have different patterns of gendering. In France, for example, limited-term contracts in industry are usually offered to men (INSEE 1991: 106–7). Moreover, in some other countries, the rise of part-time employment in the crisis may be less dramatic, because high rates already existed. This is the case of Sweden and the UK (Bakker 1988: 21).

8 Of course, part-time employment is not the only factor limiting the achievement of economic equality; low wages for full-time work obviously remain a

factor here, as does labour-force segmentation. The latter has increased over time, especially in the service sector, even as young women have entered non-traditional occupations (*Bulletin* 1993; Armstrong and Armstrong 1994: 23ff.).

9 This has certainly been the case in Canada. Although only 15% of the labour force worked part time in the mid-1980s, over 30% of job creation (and a higher percentage in some provinces) over the previous decade has been of part-time jobs (Economic Council 1990: 11–12). Moreover, since part-time employment is heavily feminized, job creation for women has clearly been at the cost of full-time jobs. In the 10 countries that were part of the European Communities between 1983 and 1989 (i.e., excluding the recent entrants, Portugal and Spain), women's labour-force participation rate rose by 12% overall, but fully 53% of that provided only part-time work, with that percentage being 87% in France and 88% in the Netherlands (Commission des CE 1991: 41).

10 Veronica Beechey's studies of several workplaces, both public and private, describe the changes in employers' strategies for using part-time employment not in response to labour shortages but in order to acquire flexibility. These findings caused her to rethink the theoretical status of part-time work (Beechey 1987: 156–7, 161–2).

11 Part-time employment is not simply a choice made by women seeking to balance work and family, as it is often represented. Indeed, many studies show that women working part time would prefer to work full time, but can find only part-time jobs (Kergoat 1984; Duffy and Pupo 1992: 65ff.; Commission des CE 1992: 42). The Economic Council calculates that 'nearly half of all part-time jobs created since 1981 have been classified as "involuntary" part-time' (1990: 11).

12 Obviously, many women do 'choose' part-time work, but the issue of whether the choice is overdetermined by other factors, such as lack of child care, needs to be explored. For a suggestive analysis of the matter see Fagnani 1992, which explores the links between public policy and decisions about fertility and labour-force participation in France and the former West Germany.

13 This is also Margaret Maruani's approach (1992), as it is that of Veronica Beechey (1987: 50–1). Both of these analysts point out that employers choose to employ women part time while offering other forms of atypical employment contracts to men. Thus, in France, for example, temporary employment (*intérim*) is dominated by men in industrial production, whereas part-time work is over 80% female in both secondary and tertiary production (INSEE 1991: 106–7).

14 It is important to note that in Canada, because of the continuing importance of work in the primary sector (especially fishing), the gender gap in part-time work over the year is smaller than that occuring when the hours per week are examined (Connelly and MacDonald 1990: 28).

15 These arguments are developed by Pitrou (1987: 26–7).

16 In France, for example, the role of seniority is extremely important for income. While women's salaries rise more slowly than men's in the younger age groups, this difference in the rate of increase disappears with age. The closing of the gap is attributed to seniority (INSEE 1987: 155).

17 In many stores, for example, full-time employees receive a substantial commission in addition to their salaries, while regular part-time employees receive only a small bonus. Seasonal part-time employees are the worst off, receiving only their salaries (Maruani and Nicole 1989).

18 This argument is a way of extending the discussion of the social construction of skill, which has demonstrated that work done by women is *perceived* as unskilled, no matter the reality of the task (Cockburn 1985; Jenson 1989b). Similarly, part-time work (a female ghetto) is likely to be seen as lacking skill, no matter what the work done. Maruani and Nicole's (1989) study is especially powerful here because they study retail work, in which the only difference among workers is their contract yet differing perceptions of skill pervade the workplace. For example, in everyday language, as well as in terms of remuneration, part-time and full-time employees doing the same job are differentially recognized. In stores the full-time employees are considered the skilled workers, with professional qualifications (a salesperson, for example), while a part-time worker is considered less professional and necessary only as a 'stop gap.'

19 Such an emphasis on training as the primary solution to gender inequalities in the labour market has characterized the experience of France, for example (Jenson and Sineau, 1995: Chap. 7). It was also an important theme in the Economic Council's analysis of non-standard work (1990).

20 In Ontario, for example, employment standards do not guarantee part-time employees the same holidays, protections from lay-offs, or other benefits. The OECD provides a similar list of the disadvantages faced by part-time employees (OCDE 1991: 26).

21 Duffy and Pupo label this reaction 'defensive resistance' and describe some instances when it has appeared (1992: 206–10).

22 This slogan was also, of course, popular in Canada (Duffy and Pupo 1992: 210–11). The validity of the charge is confirmed by Phillips and Phillips (1993: 62), who calculate that if women working part time who were seeking full-time jobs were taken into account, the unemployment (in effect, under-

employment) rate would rise by 3% and the gender gap in unemployment would be even larger.

23 In 1982, three decrees addressed part-time work, temporary workers, and fixed-term contracts. Legislation in 1986, recognizing rather than discouraging these kinds of employment contracts, was designed to extend employee rights and social protections to part-time workers and to prevent employers from using temporary workers for jobs that were normally filled by employees with regular contracts, as well as to regulate wage rates and social benefits in the direction of equality (Jenson 1990: 120).

24 The juxtaposition of family status and sex is very clear in some companies' plans for creating the 'part-time option.' This is seen as an option for *mothers*. See, for example, one program in which 'concrètement, à l'UAP, les mères de famille pourraient travailler à mi-temps en étant libre le mercredi et durant les vacances scolaires.' Francine Aizicovici, 'Le temps partiel annualisé,' *Le Monde*, 8 September 1993. Duffy and Pupo (1992: 208) describe a privatized Air Canada's strategy for employing married women as part-time workers.

25 For example, in 1992 Véronique Neiertz, the secretary of state for women's rights, was still saying that 'le travail à temps partiel, dans la crise que nous connaissons, est le premier pas, à terme, vers le licenciement.'

26 Alain Lebaube, 'L'acte de naissance d'un nouveau mode de gestion des effectifs,' *Le Monde*, 5 June 1990. A 1992 policy was even more elaborate. Martine Aubry, minister of labour, presented a law to the National Assembly in which encouragement for employers to expand part-time work was the centre-piece. Hiring a part-time worker (as long as it did not mean firing someone else) brought a reduction of 30% on the social-security payments the employer had to pay, and firms were further induced to hire young people, again for part-time jobs. While other measures in the bill were designed to constrain employers in the *ways* they handled their part-time employees, the basic thrust of the legisation was the most positive support for part-time work to date. For the details see Fréderic Bobin, 'Mme Aubry défend un temps partiel "choisi" par le salarié,' *Le Monde*, 10 December 1992, and several authors in *Libération*, 9 April 1992.

27 This list is constructed out of several discussions and practices of part-time work, including Phillips and Phillips (1993: 48).

28 Here the classic study is Julie White's work on the Canadian Union of Postal Workers. See, for example, White 1993.

29 Phillips and Phillips cite studies showing that, for example, whereas the average wage of a full-time unionized woman is 132.7% higher than that of a non-unionized woman, the comparable figure for part-time women workers is 158.6%, and the gap for fringe benefits may be even larger (1993: 116–17).

30 See, for example, *New York Times*, 22 November 1993, the ongoing debate in *Le Monde* since September 1993, and the *Globe and Mail*, 22 December 1993, where the 'temporary option' is presented as one for 'professionals and managers.'

31 As the OECD says (1991: 13), 'à en juger par l'expérience de certain pays, il existe une étroite corrélation entre l'activité féminine et les services que l'État dispense aux familles.'

PART 2: NATIONAL ECONOMIES AND SOCIAL CITIZENSHIP

5

The Nation as a Gendered Subject of Macroeconomics

SUZANNE BERGERON

Once we begin to theorize gender – to define gender as an analytic category within which humans think about and organize their social activity rather than a natural consequence of sex difference, or even merely as a social variable assigned to individual people in different ways from culture to culture – we can begin to appreciate the extent to which gender meanings have suffused our belief systems, institutions, and even such apparently gender-free phenomena as our architecture and urban planning. (Harding 1986: 17)

The current restructuring of the global economy has had a profound impact on both the developed and the developing countries. Since the 1970s the concentration of capital, the new international division of labour, and the globalization of production have led to a search for a new logic of development and national economic stability. In Europe and North America, this new logic has led to the dismantling of the Keynesian welfare state. In developing countries, it has led to a neoclassical 'development counter-revolution' (Toye 1993). In all cases, economic restructuring has shifted the boundaries between state and market, national and international, and public and private.

While the discourse of restructuring is generally cast in gender-neutral terms, feminist analyses have shown that women bear the burden of economic adjustment (Bakker 1994; Beneria and Feldman 1992). This chapter considers another entry point to constructing a feminist theory of restructuring. By exploring the metaphors through which economists make sense of the nation as an economic unit, we can begin to see that nations are gendered subjects of the economic discourse of macroeconomic restructuring.

The nation is a site that has remained somewhat resistant to our feminist gaze. This may be because one of those metaphors, the nation-as-community, appears to include all of the citizens, male and female, within its boundaries. However, the nation-as-community is defined in contrast to its others, both those outside of national boundaries and those inside the nation, in an attempt to keep its borders (both geographic and metaphoric) intact. The narrative of inclusivity impedes our awareness and examination of the oppression of those in the 'margins.' Feminist analysis can help us understand this mapping – however contradictory, slippery, and ever-changing – of the modern nation in economics. By undertaking a feminist reading, this paper hopes to begin to explore the interests that are served by naturalizing the nation in the discursive practices of mainstream economic theory.

As for my own discursive practices, the next section will offer an overview of recent scholarship on the nation and nationalism. This will be followed by a consideration of the gendered status of the nation in modern thought. The third section provides an abbreviated history of thought on the treatment of the national economy in economics. In the final section, the paper will explore some of the links between gender and nation in the narratives of macroeconomics.

Narratives of the Nation

'A Nation,' says Bloom. 'A nation is the same people living in the same place ...'
'By God, then,' says Ned, laughing, 'if that's so then I'm a nation for I'm living in the same place for the past five years.'
James Joyce, *Ulysses*

Most recent scholarship on nations and nationalism begins by deconstructing the concept of the nation as a natural and eternal entity. Eric Hobsbawm points out that the basic characteristic of the modern nation is its modernity, as it was literally invented in the eighteenth and nineteenth centuries. Before that, social groupings we think of as nations were centred around a city and had borders that were porous and overlapping (Hobsbawm 1990). Benedict Anderson's influential *Imagined Communities* (1991) emphasizes that nationality, nationalism, and nations are all culturally determined meanings, not natural groupings. The collected essays in *Nationalisms and Sexualities* (Parker et al. 1992) provocatively extend Anderson's rejection of the nation as 'natural' by stressing that the identity of a nation is based on continually shifting gender, homoerotic, and homophobic cultural meanings. Literary theorist Homi Bhabha links the emergence of the modern nation with the desire to fill the sense of loss associated with migration and colonial expansion (1990: 291). Ernest Gellner shows the variety of ways that nations link themselves to an eternal mythic past, concluding that 'nations as a natural, God-given way of classifying men, as an inherent ... political destiny, are a myth; nationalism, which sometimes takes pre-existing cultures and turns them into nations, sometimes invents them, and often obliterates pre-existing cultures: that is a reality' (1983: 48–9).

As arbitrary as national boundaries may be, they become natural, so much so that people will die for their nation. Anderson in particular argues that we can't make sense of the modern nation as a mere issue of appearance versus reality. The way that we think about the nation has a major impact on the way that nations are. He argues that the basic characteristic of modern nations is that they are *imagined* – we will never know our fellow citizens, yet we feel a sense of communion with them; *limited* – there is a space beyond which there is only the other, the outsider; and, finally, *communities* – what connects us to our unknown countrymen and women is a 'deep horizontal comradeship' (1991: 16). What is important to note here is that nations are communities that we literally create through our imaginings. They are not imaginary communities that can be contrasted to some 'real' ones out there: 'Communities are to be distinguished, not by their falsity/genuineness, but by the style in which they are imagined' (1991: 15).

While previous scholarship on the emergence of modern nation-states claimed that such imaginings were first applied to Western European nations and then eventually exported throughout the world, Anderson, among others, sees the modern nation emerging in the way that European empires, in particular the Spanish empire, dealt with their colonies (1991: 50). The colonial entities developed a self-contained nature because of the metropole's desire to maintain firm control over them. They were carved out into manageable units. The borders of colonial nations were often determined by something as arbitrary as a river or the limits of military conquest, despite our modern conceit that there really is a difference between, for example, the origins of Peruvian and those of Bolivian natives. At the same time that these units were thought of as objects of control, however, they were also thought of as subjects with their own will, not least, as it turns out, by the local Creole administrators who, in overthrowing an increasingly oppressive crown, redefined the non-Spanish-speaking natives as fellow nationals. The liberation movements of the Creoles in the eighteenth and nineteenth centuries were by and large successful in throwing off the yoke of Spanish oppression, but ironically retained the colonial boundaries as their own national boundaries, as well as retaining colonial ideas about controlling the populations within those boundaries.

Nations as Objects, Nations as Subjects

For Anderson, the representation of colonial entities in maps and censuses in large part constitutes these ways of knowing, influencing the way the colonial state imagined its dominion in terms of the nature both of its population and of its geography (1991: 164). The white colonist went out into the world and measured his 'other.' And eventually European populations came to be measured in much the same way. For example, the influential nineteenth-century statistician Quetelet was bent on discovering the nature of the nation by measuring human behaviour and production until, at last, he could define the average Frenchman, Brit, and so on (Hacking 1990: 39). His goal, and the goal of others like him, was to define the social body, filtering out the individual particularities to derive the general facts of a population. By measuring and defining the communal pathology of a people, national statistics transferred a medical notion from the individual body to the body politic, giving rise to a set of measures, assessments, and interventions aimed at the national social body as a whole (Hacking 1990: 22; Cooper 1992: 13). This creation of the social body through statistical measurement of births, deaths, populations, wealth, production, maladies, madness, and so forth transforms the way people view themselves (as normal or not) and the societies they live in – in the process transforming societies and the way we are (Foucault 1973b, 1980).

This also becomes part of the way the nation is imagined. The nation becomes an object that can be measured, assessed, known, and cured. Reflecting the conceptions of knowledge that have come to dominate Western intellectual life since the seventeenth century, this imagining is also gendered. As feminist philosophers (and others) have argued, modern science relies on a set of dualisms in which the scientist is a detached objective observer and controller of the passive natural and social world. The identification of science with masculinity, universality, detachment, and control can be contrasted with the identification of femininity with difference, connectedness, and submission (Bordo 1987, Keller 1985). The masculinism of modern science was explicit in the writings of some of its early champions, such as Henry Oldenburg, who stated that the intent of the British Royal Society of Scientists was to 'raise a masculine philosophy,' and Francis Bacon, whose book the *Masculine Birth of Time* contains the assertion, 'I am come in very truth leading to you Nature with all her children to bind her to your service and make her your slave' (quoted in Keller 1985: 52, 39). While less explicitly stated, this is still part of the Cartesian legacy of objectivism in a quest for unity, certainty, and order that dominates the natural and social sciences today.

This masculinist ontology is not universal, but is itself race and class specific. As Sandra Harding has pointed out, it reflects a distinctly European world-view (1986: 177). The objectivism and empiricism of this stand is also colonialist – it has constructed, for example, a Third World that exists out there and can be known and intervened upon. The 'imaginative geography' (Said 1979) that constructs nations as objects of control is bound with these dualisms.

The nation does not, however, exist solely as an object of discourse. Nations have subjectivities, even agency – the common will of the people. For one thing, they convey a sense of fraternity that goes well beyond simply belonging to an administrative entity. Contrast most people's attachment to their homeland with their attachment to, let's say, an object such as their trading unit: would anyone willingly die for the EC? This attachment is what is usually associated with nationalism and nation building, viewed more often than not as a vestige of our dark past, tempting us to agree with G. Lowes Dickinson that progress will be served when 'the barriers of nationality which belong to the infancy of the race will melt and dissolve in the sunshine of science and art' (quoted in Hobsbawm 1990: 38). This view is too simplistic, as most recent scholarship on this topic argues; the nation as we know it is a recent event that coincides historically and philosophically with the Enlightenment. To argue that nations can only interfere with the Enlightenment project is to forget that nations themselves, considered as communities of like-minded people, are conceived as autonomous, sovereign, and unique individuals that have rights to self-determination in the global community. In economics this is often taken for granted. Economists are nearly as comfortable discussing the endowments and preferences of a nation as those of an individual agent.

This discussion, however, raises some interesting problems, for as nations strive to define themselves as subjects, they do so by distinguishing themselves from others in asserting both their uniqueness from other nations and the solidarity of the individuals that constitute the nation. The binary logic of Western discourse again constructs difference between self and other in hierarchical dualisms (or, one could argue, 'colonizing dualisms'). Take, for example, a post-colonial perspective on this process: 'Nationalism seeks to represent itself in the image of the Enlightenment and fails to do so. For the Enlightenment itself, to assert its sovereignty as the universal ideal, needs its Other; if it could ever actualize itself in the real world as truly universal, it would in fact destroy itself' (Chatterjee 1986: 17).

Nationality, like gender, is a relational term: nations define themselves not only by what they are, but by what they are not: they are defined by what they oppose. To talk of the nation as a subject invokes its Other. This reference is not limited to distinguishing one nation from another in the world community. There is a liminality between nations as well as *within* the nation. The duality of nation/other is asymmetric: when other nations enter the narrative it is often not as equals but as unruly, childlike, passive and/or irrational. Edward Said's investigation of how the West 'invented' the 'Orient' as its undisciplined, feminized Other provides a wonderful if disturbing account of these processes at work (Said 1979).

The narrative strategies that create the limits of community within the nation are similarly constructed. The narrative of the nation-as-subject can be understood in part through its metaphor as a limited, imagined community. These imaginings allow the nation to function as a totality that exemplifies social cohesion. Not surprisingly, the representations of the nation as community have often been modelled on gender relations and norms. The metaphor of the nation as woman is a familiar one – but what kind of woman can symbolize the nation? In the West it is generally maternal, an ideal mother, an association of the nation (and womanhood) with home. But these tropes more than likely do not reflect that women have a higher status in the community than men. Women may em-body the nation, but the fraternal bonding of men in public space may be more representative of the scope of the imagined community, where woman signals 'the limits of national difference between men' (Parker et. al. 1992: 6). Gender is not itself an essence in the figuring of the nation – there is no universal set of gender relationships that will allow us to make sense of all nationalisms, but since nationalism seems to have an affinity for the male civil society of public space, gender relations will be written into the narrative of the nation as a cohesive subject.

The Nation in Economic Theory: An Abbreviated History of Thought

... and he said, 'Now this schoolroom is a Nation. And in this nation there are 50 millions of money. Isn't this a prosperous nation? Girl number 20, isn't this a prosperous nation?
'Well, what did you say?' asked Louisa.
'Miss Louisa, I said I didn't know. I thought I couldn't know whether it was a prosperous nation or not unless I know who got the money. But that had nothing at all to do with it. It was not in the figures at all.'
'That was a great mistake of yours,' observed Louisa.
    Charles Dickens, *Hard Times*

Could these broad cultural narratives of the nation also be written in economic theory and policy? Mainstream economists, with their emphasis on individual choice, individual firms, individual markets would by and large deny it. Besides, with a few exceptions, economics as a profession has clung to a narrow scientism that by definition denies the possibility of narrative, metaphor, metonymy, storytelling, or conversation in economic inquiry (McCloskey 1985). Despite the protests, however, economic theory has created a set of representations of the nation that overlap with more general social constructions. And like the broader culture, economics is ambivalent about the nation.

This ambivalence has been commonly misunderstood as a dichotomy. Marxist and Keynesian thought, for instance, has been linked to national planning and policy, while the primary focus of the neoclassical tradition is said to be the individual firm or consumer trading in a global market. This chapter takes a different approach. On the one hand, classical economists can be seen as rejecting the idea of the nation as an economic unit. Adam Smith's *The Wealth of Nations* (first published in 1776) represents a polemic against mercantilist notions that economic agents should make choices based on the well-being of the nation-state. The work of nineteenth-century classical economists Thomas Malthus, David Ricardo, Jeremy Bentham, and J.B. Say contributed to Smith's critique of economic nationalism. Say's contemporary J.E. Cairnes went so far as to insist that a theory of international trade was redundant as there was already a theory of trade between individuals (Hobsbawm 1990). In this period, the heyday of nation making, the strong emphasis on the importance of individual choice as opposed to national policy and national well-being should be noted. In fact, the cosmopolitan views of the classical economists could be seen as swimming against a dominant cultural tide.

On the other hand, the nation-state does emerge in classical economic discourse in a variety of ways. While Smith rejects the idea of the nation as a body politic with the state at its head, his uneasiness with the boundlessness of the market economy leads him to replace it with an economic collective connected by an invisible hand. Susan Buck-Morss's investigation of economic representation in mercantilist and classical economic thought shows that, in Smith's rhetoric, nations become social bodies that consist of things, and the countries with the most things are the civilized bodies (Buck-Morss 1995). 'Savage nations' are miserably poor; 'civilized nations' rich (Smith 1937: lviii).

In the nineteenth century, governments began to get involved in monetary questions, which brought up a need to define the amount of money in circulation as well as the boundaries of circulation, done in part through the development of national statistics. In addition, the work of German thinkers such as Frederich List, who considered a nation to be like a body and individuals analogous to molecules, was more influential on economic thinking than most mainstream accounts let on. Bentham's emphasis on social welfare (the greatest good for the greatest number) shifts the terrain of economic discourse from an emphasis on individual welfare to one in which the general welfare of a nation is the object of analysis. And Ricardo, individualist that he was, treated nations as individuals in his comparative-advantage theory of international trade, even as he was trying to show the benefits of thinking less about the nation as an economic unit.

Economist Richard Adelstein has documented a change in thinking about the nation as an economic entity in early-twentieth-century economic thought. Influenced by the newly emerging field of managerial science, economists such as Herbert Croly and John B. Clark were struck by the analogies between the modern corporation (legally considered an organism, a living, concrete entity) and the national economy. Wesley C. Mitchell and Simon Kuznets, in a similar vein, devoted a great deal of intellectual energy to the development of better national-income accounts that would increase our knowledge, and hence ability, to manage the national economy as well as the modern corporation was managed. These men shared a technocratic vision. If policy makers can know the nation, they can use that information to control it for the well-being of all its citizens. John Maynard Keynes turned Mitchell's aggregations into independent variables and objects of policy (Adelstein 1991:

171). The Keynesian revolution popularized the idea that intelligent control of a known and manageable object, the national economy, is not only possible but enhances our freedom, and macroeconomics was born.

The birth of macroeconomics coincides with the embrace of a 'pragmatic collectivism' that asserts the primacy of a reified community, the national economy, which we can know as a separate, concrete, and limited object of scientific inquiry (Adelstein 1991: 161). One of the most stunning examples of this thinking is Paul Samuelson's construction of national 'social indifference curves' in which the preferences of nations can be theorized in much the same way as individual preferences based on national tastes and income (Samuelson 1956). In general, the reified community can be seen in the rhetoric of representation and control that underscores macroeconomic theory and policy from the Second World War to the 1970s. More recently, the 'god's eye view' of the national economy in Keynesian theory has inspired criticism from the postmodern left and the pro-market right.

However, while the free-market neoclassical and New Classical criticisms of Keynesian-inspired macroeconomics question the role of government in stabilizing the national economy, they retain the concept of the nation as an economic unit. New Classical economists Robert Lucas and Robert Barro's analysis of macroeconomic performance, based on the well-being of a 'representative agent' who benefits when unemployment falls and when GDP rises, is underscored by the same unspoken notions about horizontality and community as Quetelet's 'average man.' In addition, the agent in neoclassical and New Classical thought is considered to be a self-interested, individualistic 'economic man,' for whom things, other people, and nature are external. While this agent is presented in economics as a simple reflection of its human nature, the gender behind this veil of objectivity is not hard to guess.

While disavowing the project of macroeconomic intervention, free-market theorists take as given the existence of a national economy that can be stabilized not by the government, but by the market. The economy, while inserted in an international market-place, is still thought of as separate, knowable, and controllable in these frameworks (Weintraub 1991). To argue that an attachment to microfoundations eliminates the nation in macroeconomic discourse ignores this key narrative foundation in their theorizing.

By bringing up some of the similarities between the market-oriented New Classical and Keynesian theories, my intention is not to deny the very real and important differences between them. Theoretically, they begin with different causal essences (individuals versus structures), proceed from different sets of methodological underpinnings, and of course come to very different policy conclusions. On many levels they are better understood as incommensurably different and conflicting discourses (Amariglio et al. 1990). However, reflecting broader discursive structures in twentieth-century thought, they are also both written in the palliative narratives of the nation that evoke social harmony and scientific control simultaneously.

Nation and Gender in the Narratives of Economics

Let us now turn our attention to the way these narratives play themselves out in economic thinking, emphasizing their gendered construction.

The construction of the nation in economic theory, predicated on the metaphor of imagined community, achieves the effect of an inclusive macroeconomic and macropolitical discourse. In this respect economic theory's view of the nation is not unlike its view of the household. Gary Becker's (1991) influential work on the economics of the household well exemplifies the gender biases of this type of analysis. His theories begin with the assumption that the family behaves as if it were an individual. Feminist criticisms of Becker point out that the assumptions of harmony and unity that pervade this work prevent mainstream economists from seeing the power or class differences by gender in the household (Folbre and Hartmann 1988; Resnick et al. 1991).

The rhetoric of inclusivity implied by the nation, however, is also based on defining the limits of the national economy, often theorized along the lines of a public/private dichotomy that privileges male/public activity. Women's activity is often marginalized. For example, little attention is given to the value of household production, traditionally done by women. Housework is not included in measures of national output such as GDP statistics even though many other types of non-market output that are difficult to measure are included in these statistics (Waring 1988). Feminists who want to simply 'add' women's work to already existing categories should, however, be wary. The current construction of national income accounts privileges the separative, masculine ideal of 'work' and may produce a garbled concept of household production.

Not taking women's work into account does have serious implications for the construction of macroeconomic theory and policy and its practice.

For example, policies that promote the production of tradeables at the expense of non-tradeables in countries with balance-of-payments difficulties are becoming popular in the less-developed countries. Diane Elson's research has shown that these purportedly gender-neutral policies put an incredible burden on women. Often, the non-tradeable goods are used by women to decrease the amount of work necessary to maintain the family. These goods include prepared foods, state-funded health clinics, and day care. As the production of these is decreased, women's work increases. Because economists assume that family maintenance is done for 'love,' they assume that the household can absorb this additional work with no problem. But it is the women in the household who become the 'shock absorbers' (Elson 1991: 186) in the wake of such policies. In addition, because the 'unlimited supplies of female labour' assumed in the conceptual framework of adjustment policies do not in fact exist, the policies have a good chance of 'failing' by their own (gender-biased) standards of failure and success.

Elson's research points out how the public/private dichotomy creates the boundaries of the national economy in which women are written in the margins. This discussion of limits could be extended to include race and class as well. If one of the key metaphors of the nation is 'horizontality' – that the well-being of the nation is shared by all of its members, floating above any conflicts – then differential effects of policy are difficult to fit into the narrative of national economic well-being. If inflation falls, doesn't everyone benefit? If GDP increases, aren't we all wealthier? Mainstream economists are often led by macroeconomic statistics to assume that the answer to these questions is 'yes,' even if those on the margins of the nation – women, minorities, the underclass – are actually worse off.

There are, however, differences between the Keynesian welfare-state approach and the more market-oriented approach in this context. While the Keynesian approach has, in fact, marginalized women primarily by granting women entitlements based on their roles as wives and mothers (in the role of a paternalistic 'husband substitute'), it did succeed in creating a space for women to ask for assistance from the public sector. Janine Brodie's analysis of economic restructuring and gender shows this process at work. The particular form of entitlement and citizenship for women created by the Canada Family Allowance Act of 1944 defined women's economic role as conditional on the nuclear family, in which the man was the primary breadwinner. It linked women's interests with family interests, and national interests with family interests as well. Yet within the market-oriented, individual-choice discourse in the current conjuncture, even these programs are under attack for being targeted at 'special interests' as opposed to the 'ordinary Canadian' (Brodie 1994: 19–23). Similar rhetoric is being employed in the current restructuring of the U.S. economy (Williams 1994). As this book goes to press, U.S. government representatives are arguing that poor women do not deserve assistance and may not even deserve to keep their children. While the paternalistic presumptions of the Keynesian welfare state are out of touch with current realities, so are the orphanage and the poorhouse of the nineteenth century.

In the current round of economic restructuring, the free-market approach is based on redrawing the boundaries between public and private and state and market. The word 'public' has itself become more pejorative in the 1980s and 1990s, associated with (decaying and underfinanced) public housing and public hospitals for the undeserving poor (Fraser 1993). Economies that once decreed that all citizens had rights to basic needs are now decrying the very idea of entitlement. While these arguments are posed in gender-neutral language, it is women and children who make up the majority of the poor in these societies. In the United States, the (incorrect) stereotype of the social-welfare recipient is a black, unmarried, urban woman with children, defined as dependent, passive, lazy, and primitive, and therefore undeserving of social rights. While welfare mothers are being told to get to work, white middle-class women are accused of abandoning their children to strangers as they selfishly pursue their careers. As the 'normal American' is defined as disciplined, controlled, part of a traditional nuclear family, and one that pays his or her own way, the struggle over rights to citizenship is coded by gender as well as race and class.

But the discussion of the boundaries of the nation goes right to the heart of the narrative of the nation as an autonomous, separate subject as well. And economics has written the national economy as an autonomous subject. National economies become entities – and in some economic theories they become rational, stable entities, dare we say masculine entities? When neoclassicals and new classicals argue that national economies are inherently stable and self-regulating, they are unwittingly writing the trope of the nation as a masculine subject. The rational economy can achieve equilibrium, the economist's version of the political 'harmony of interests.' These imaginings construct the national economy as a subject that is a unified totality with no internal conflict.

If subjects are defined by not only what they are but what they oppose, what is the 'other' that this masculine subject defines itself against? One answer might be: the less-developed economies. The LDCs are often viewed as unruly others against which we can define the developed economies. Take, for example, this quote: 'A study of less-developed economy is to economics what the study of *pathology* is to medicine: by understanding what happens when things do not work well, we gain insight into how they work when they do function as designed. The difference is that in economics, pathology is the rule: less than a quarter of mankind lives in the developed countries' (Stiglitz 1989; emphasis added).

The discursive construction of the less-developed countries is one example of the nationalistic construction of self and other in economics. Described as passive, open, dependent, and unstable, Third World nations become the Other against which the countries of the West can define themselves as controlled, independent, and stable.

Unfortunately, similarly dualistic thinking is also found in some Western feminist research. Women in less-developed nations have often been defined by feminist economists in terms of their economic dependency, passivity, and oppression, in contrast to Western women, who are independent, liberated, and in control of their own lives (Mohanty 1991b). This is not to say that Western women are in fact liberated and in control of their lives, but to say that the discursive construction of Third World difference reinforces such dichotomous thinking. In addition, it makes it difficult for feminists to see the dynamism and creativity that often accompanies Third World women's response to policy change (Beneria and Feldman 1992).

Like liberal feminists, who prescribed an integration into the market as the solution to Third World women's poverty in the 1970s, today's free-market liberals believe that the problems of the less-developed economies can be cured by getting in touch with the universal logic of the market. The free-market experiments of the 1970s and 1980s have tried to impress this lesson upon developing countries with a ruthless vengeance. According to UN and World Bank statistics, many countries in Africa, South Asia, and Latin America have more poverty today than in the 1970s. But economists argue that, like the 'irrational' peasant who is originally disoriented by market exchange, these nations can improve their lot if they just stick to the free-market path.

What complicates this story is that in their attempt to stabilize these nations and make them unified, stable, and autonomous subjects in the image of the developed economies, economists must treat them as passive feminine objects that can be controlled by the all-knowing rational economic scientist. The high-profile free-market economist flies down to a Latin American or African country, makes a quick diagnosis, and then doles out the prepackaged medicine. In the name of giving a lesson in the potential for autonomy and freedom, the experts fly in and tell people what to do.

The Keynesian approach treats nations as passive, feminine objects as well, positing as it does the all-knowing technocrat who can know and control the economy, in this case through state intervention. But the narrative construction of the nation in the Keynesian and post-Keynesian tradition differs from that of their neoclassical and New Classical counterparts in important ways. First, the nation in Keynesian thought, while seen as a totality with fixed borders, is viewed as naturally and inherently unstable. There is no necessary, universal 'logic' that every nation can follow to achieve the perfect unity/social harmony of equilibrium. The nation as a subject is characterized by instability, multiplicity, and contingency. There is no universal, ahistorical, essential national economy in Keynes's framework (Crotty 1990). By identifying the nation with these concepts – instability, multiplicity, the body – Keynesian discourse constructs a feminine subject whose unstable and irrational nature can be controlled by the scientist to ensure freedom and progress. It can recognize that different countries take different paths to growth, stability, and development.

The Keynesian approach is also slightly more at ease with the notion of internal difference. James Tobin's critique of the New Classical representative-agent model is a good example. Tobin is insistent that there are aggregates or groups out there in the economy with distinct characteristics and goals, and worries that Lucas's replacement of this reality with a representative agent misguides theory and practice (Tobin 1980). Yet Keynesianism's reliance on the horizontality of agents within a nation, its goal of achieving 'common good for the common people,' generally neutralizes any sense of conflict that its own theorizing brings up. Once again, the nation becomes a site of social harmony, this time with a little help from technocratic government intervention.

Conclusion

Feminist economists often critique mainstream economics for 'leaving gender out.' This chapter argues that gender is already 'in' macroeconomic theories. It has been argued that the purportedly universal individual agent of economics – a unified, knowing separative self – is a masculine subject (Nelson 1992). This chapter demonstrates some of the ways in which the other subject of macroeconomics, the nation, is gendered. The gendered construction of the nation in macroeconomic theory is visible in the boundaries that determine the space of the imagined community of the economy. It is also visible in the differential treatment of less-developed countries as passive and unstable. Finally, the very project of macroeconomic science relies on ideas of detachment and control that reflect masculinist ideas about power over nature and society.

While the nation is presented in macroeconomic discourse as a stable, unified subject, it is a subject that is fraught with contradictions and instabilities. Feminists concerned with the impact of macroeconomic restructuring need to be aware of the political spaces that are opened up by these contradictions (Brodie 1994). An understanding of the gendered metaphors that undergird macroeconomic theory can contribute to this project.

6
Restructuring and the New Citizenship

JANINE BRODIE

Canada, like all Western democracies, is currently experiencing a profound shift in state form and governing practices. It is now widely acknowledged that the foundations of the Keynesian Welfare State (KWS) have not survived the combined forces of prolonged recession, jobless growth, the so-called globalization of production, and neo-liberal governing practices. The broad consensus that grounded the KWS and structured the pattern of federal politics for almost a half-century has gradually, but certainly, given way to a very different set of assumptions about the role of government and the rights of citizens. These new assumptions and understandings – the emerging neo-liberal consensus – inform different forms of domination while, at the same time, reshaping more familiar ones rooted in gender, race, and class.

There is a growing body of gender-sensitive research, as the chapters in this volume demonstrate, that provides compelling evidence to show that the gendered impacts of restructuring are pronounced and multiple. To date, most of the empirical data on the gendered dimensions of restructuring have come from developing countries where the effects of structural adjustment policies (SAP) were first felt and most severe. These policies, which usually entail reducing the public sector and re-orienting national economies to external trade, have tended to affect women in five fundamental ways. First, poverty everywhere is increasingly gendered. The so-called feminization of poverty is particularly acute among female-headed households and among elderly women. Second, women have acted as 'shock-absorbers' during adjustment both by curtailing their own consumption and by increasing their workload to compensate for household-income loss. Third, women tend to be more directly affected by reductions in social-welfare spending and public programs. Privatization and welfare cuts often simply mean that social services are shifted from the paid work of women in the public sphere to the unpaid work of women in the domestic sphere. Fourth, gains made towards the goal of gender equality during the 1970s are being rapidly eroded owing to shifts in the labour market that are producing few good jobs for women (or men for that matter) and because of reductions in child care, education, and retraining programs. Finally, public-expenditure constraints have a direct impact on women's employment and working conditions within the public sector itself, since many women find employment there (U.S. Agency for International Development 1992; xiv; Bakker 1994a). Progress towards employment and pay equity, for example, has come to a virtual standstill.

In this chapter, I intend to examine the cultural and discursive transformations that have accompanied this round of restructuring and explore how the new ways of thinking about citizenship and welfare provision affect women. The passing of the welfare state represents much more than a series of state responses to the changing international economy or to the so-called debt crisis. It signals a paradigm shift (a new way of thinking) in governing practices – a historic alteration in state form that enacts simultaneous changes in cultural assumptions, political identities, and the very terrain of political struggle. Restructuring is a key word that represents a prolonged and conflict-ridden political process during which old assumptions and shared understandings are put under stress and are eventually either rejected or transformed, while social forces struggle to achieve a new consensus – a new vision of the future to fill the vacuum created by the erosion of the old.

Feminists have long argued that state discourses and practices around social welfare are critical to understanding both the character of gender relations during any period and the way in which women both identify with and mobilize in politics (Orloff 1993). The new discourse around social welfare, especially as it is expressed within the federal government's social-policy review, is no exception. The cultural understandings rendered by the restructuring process are multiple, complex, and often quite contradictory. This chapter will explore only two dimensions that relate to changes in popular conceptions of citizenship. First, I will examine the implications for Canadian women of the notions of citizenship that inform the new thinking about social-welfare provision, that is, changes in our shared understanding of social citizenship. Second, I will explore the gendered implications of targeting – the current buzzword for social-service delivery in the emerging new order.

Unlike the postwar welfare state, the emerging neo-liberal order seeks to limit women's political citizenship rights by attempting to deny the importance of gender and gender representation in the politics of the late twentieth century. Redefining citizenship is a critical task for the emerging neo-liberal state. In many ways, it is foundational, because the way we define citizenship is intimately linked to the kind of society and political community we have and want (Mouffe 1993: 60). It is also precisely neo-liberalism's limited conception of citizenship that provides the first and necessary point of opposition for Canadian feminists.

The Postwar Consensus

Canada is not the only country to be submerged into a politics of disruption, uncertainty, and change in the late twentieth century. In Britain, for example, this period of profound transformation is called the 'New Times.' Elsewhere the terms 'post-industrial' and 'postmodern' are used to suggest that we are in the process of fundamental transition – at a point of no return to the 'good old days' of Keynesianism and postwar prosperity. Since the early 1980s, Western liberal democracies have been forced to re-examine many of their governing assumptions and practices, moving from what some political economists have called a 'Fordist' past to an unknown 'post-Fordist' future.

According to the regulation theorists, the economies and politics of Western democracies were organized around what is termed a Fordist 'mode of regulation.' By this they mean that for much of the post–Second World War years, there was a widespread consensus that national governments should take an active role in managing the economy through Keynesian demand-management techniques; that the labour process was organized around the assembly-line and mass-consumption industries; and that redistribution was accomplished through social-welfare spending and collective bargaining (Lipietz 1987).

In contrast to the previous doctrine of the laissez-faire 'negative' state that governed the Western world until the Great Depression of the 1930s, the postwar years brought new shared understandings about state intervention in the economy, an elaboration of bureaucratic institutions and governing instruments, and an expansion of the very meaning of citizenship itself. The Keynesian state asserted the primacy of the state over the 'invisible hand' of the market and engendered widespread public expectations that governments were responsible for meeting the basic needs of its citizens. The postwar consensus changed our common-sense notions of the government–market relation and, indeed, of what it meant to be a Canadian. Contrary to contemporary political discourse, it was widely believed that there was no such thing as a self-regulating market. Political control of the economy was 'almost a moral imperative' and Canadian citizenship came to mean more than simply having formal rights such as the right to vote, speak one's mind, or join a union. Instead, the menu of citizen rights came to include social welfare – social citizenship rights – which all could claim simply because they were Canadians (McBride and Shields 1993: 10, 15). In summary, then, the postwar consensus was a whole package of relations, institutions, and arrangements that linked a logic of economic development during a particular historical period with an equally particular and complementary set of norms, habits, laws, regulations, and representations of reality about, among many other things, the welfare state and popular notions of the rights of citizenship (Harvey 1989: 121–3).

Although the regulation theorists are decidedly silent about gender, the postwar order also rested on a very particular model of the workplace, the home, and the gendered division of labour. It presumed a stable working/middle-class nuclear family supported by a male breadwinner, containing a dependent wife and children, and resting on women's unpaid domestic labour. The state guaranteed through collective bargaining and welfare measures that there would be a 'family wage' – that an individual male worker could earn enough to care for his family. Women's paid labour, thereby, was deemed unnecessary or, failing that, secondary to that of her husband. Each of these cultural forms, in turn, was supported and reinforced by the welfare state (McDowell 1991: 400–2).

If the KWS reinforced a particular family form and gender order, it also created new political spaces and identities for women. Unlike the laissez-faire period, which cast women as the moral force in politics, the welfare state largely spoke to mothers framed within the context of a nuclear family headed by a male wage earner (Brodie 1995a). After the Second World War, women were actively encouraged, if not forced, to leave the workforce and return to the home, with all the unpaid domestic labour that it entailed. The new welfare ideology shifted the emphasis of state discourse on welfare from the protection of women and children through regulation of working hours and the like to the administration of income and social services for the male-headed nuclear family.

The Family Allowance Act (1944, a.k.a. 'mothers' allowance') was one of Canada's first universal social-welfare programs. It was also somewhat unique among social-security measures because it was unanimously endorsed by all parties in the House of Commons and because its beneficiaries never lobbied for it (Ursel 1992: 190, 205). Designed to shore up the family wage, this welfare provision recognized women primarily as mothers and homemakers. The welfare state readily transferred money from working women who did not fit the dominant cultural model to women who did – mothers (Pringle and Watson 1990: 236). In a very real sense, then, postwar welfare policy was directed less at women as a social category worthy of assistance than through mothers in order to reinforce a particular family form, gender order, and the postwar organization of the labour force.

Redefining Citizenship

It has become increasingly apparent that the new neo-liberal state marks a distinct shift in shared understandings of what it means to be a citizen and what the citizen can legitimately ask of the state. Although varying considerably among themselves, postwar welfare states rested on a broad but ultimately fragile consensus about the rights of citizenship. The postwar notion of social citizenship conveyed the idea that poverty was not always an individual's fault and that all citizens had the right to a basic standard of living. The general consensus underlying the creation and maintenance of the welfare state was that Canadians should not have to repeat the harsh lessons in public administration dealt out by the Great Depression of the 1930s. The postwar consensus held that the public could enforce limits on the market, that people were not forced to engage in market activities that denied their safety or dignity, and that the national community was responsible for the basic well-being of its individual members.

It is precisely these postwar ideals of social citizenship that are currently under attack in the new order. A defining mark of the emerging neo-liberal state is the 'subordination of social policy to the demands of labour market flexibility and structural competitiveness' through the progressive 'hollowing out' of the welfare state (Jessop 1993: 9). Neo-liberalism is less concerned with the actual size of the welfare state than its underlying values, especially the idea that everyone is entitled, as a right of Canadian citizenship, to state protection from unpredictable market forces. Even though the debt has been cited by both the Mulroney and the Chrétien administrations, the issue is less about budgets than about cultural forms and public expectations (Yeatman

1990: 118, 123). Changing public expectations about citizenship entitlements, the collective provision of social needs, and the efficacy of the welfare state has been a critical victory for neo-liberalism.

During the past decade, the postwar social safety net has been stressed and redesigned almost beyond the recognition of its creators. This assault began in full force after the re-election of the Mulroney Conservatives in 1988, when they effectively put an end to the principle of universality in welfare provision. Since then, the list of social programs that have been reduced or altered by federal and provincial governments has grown daily. These changes in the postwar conception of social citizenship, moreover, have usually been implemented 'stealth style.' This style of politics, which was perfected by the Mulroney government and subsequently embraced by the federal Liberals and many provincial governments, enables governments to enact immediate and significant changes in social policy by means of complex changes in regulations and repeated budget cuts without prior warning, consultation, or media scrutiny (Gray 1990: 382). The politics of stealth was used to put an end to the principle of universality in Canada's Old Age Security and Family Allowance programs and has severely restricted the capacity of the provinces to implement fundamental components of the postwar consensus, particularly in the areas of welfare, health care, and post-secondary education.

During the past decade, then, there has been a decided shift away from the postwar ideals of universal, publicly provided services and social citizenship. Moreover, the social safety net is poised for a major transformation to make it fit with the market-based, self-reliant, and privatizing ideals of the new order. The rights and securities guaranteed to all citizens of the Keynesian welfare state are no longer rights, universal, or secure. The new ideal of the common good rests on market-oriented values such as self-reliance, efficiency, and competition. The new good citizen is one who recognizes the limits and liabilities of state provision and embraces her obligation to work longer and harder in order to become more self-reliant (Drache 1992: 221).

Many of the changes to the social-welfare system have occurred incrementally and almost invisibly, usually implemented by cash-strapped provincial governments desperately seeking any way to reduce expenditures by 'reforming' social-welfare policy. Some governments, in fact, have tried to make the poor disappear both literally and conceptually. Alberta, for example, will give welfare recipients a free *one-way* ticket to British Columbia and keeps payments for so-called single employables so low that it encourages them to seek social assistance elsewhere (*Toronto Star*, 24 December 1993, B1). Similarly, the Mulroney government established a parliamentary subcommittee, which the opposition parties boycotted, to redefine what it meant to be poor in Canada. According to this committee's analysis, Canada's poverty numbers were 'grossly exaggerated' and were 'hurting Canada's international reputation.' It recommended that a new poverty measure be designed – one that would establish the income necessary only to ensure that the poor could meet their most basic needs (*Toronto Star*, 9 June 1993, A1).

Other provinces, with the encouragement of the federal government, have begun to 'target' welfare populations that have been identified as drains on the system. Single mothers have been targeted as an especially immediate problem throughout the country. Although the child-caring activities of single mothers previously were considered to be of overriding importance, effectively making them unemployable until their children were of school age, this is no longer the current thinking. Public policy is reshaping the social identities of single mothers and their capacity to make claims on the state by redefining them as a welfare problem – as undeserving, employable, and dependent (Evans 1995).

New Brunswick, the province that federal Human Resources Minister Lloyd Axworthy calls an 'incubator of reform,' has launched two programs targeted at single mothers. Axworthy has praised this province for its initiatives in social-welfare reform: 'rather than using [social assistance] in a passive way for people to get some limited income security, it gives them a launching pad into the job market' (York 1993). These initiatives, NB Works and the Self-Sufficiency Project, attempt to nudge single parents (read women) from the welfare rolls onto the job market. More recently, the federal and Manitoba governments have launched a $26.2-million program to help that province's four thousand single parents currently on welfare to find work (*Globe and Mail*, 10 September 1993, A4). In each case, single mothers are being targeted as 'a problem' within the existing welfare system. Their identities in legislation and practice are rapidly being transformed from women who were previously seen primarily as mothers, and thus temporarily unemployable, to women who are seen as burdens on the state and potential workers who are responsible for the maintenance of themselves and their children. As discussed below, single mothers are also targeted in the federal government's thinking about social-welfare reform.

All of these provincial initiatives pale in comparison with Ottawa's current 'rethinking' of the social-welfare system. There has been a great deal of build-up and promotion about the redesigning of the social safety net – a process that essentially puts an end to the postwar social compact. The Chrétien government has announced a total redrawing of Canada's social-welfare system by 1996 – an undertaking that Finance Minister Martin has called 'the most comprehensive reform of government policy in decades' (Canada 1994a: 2). On the release of the federal government's discussion paper *Improving Social Security in Canada* (Canada 1994b, hereafter ISSC) in October 1994, the prime minister said that 'reforming social security' was on top of the government's legislative agenda. All Canadian women will be affected by these changes in so far as they are aimed at reviewing unemployment and welfare benefits. The forthcoming reforms in Canada's postwar social-welfare regime represent nothing less than a 'constitu-(tive)-tional' change in cultural understandings.

Improving Social Security in Canada (ISSC)

The new welfare thinking is premised on a human-resources model that sees joblessness as an individual rather than structural problem. It assumes a radical individualism that 'locates the causes of social problems in individual failure or misbehaviour and identifies social change as being effected by individuals trying to maximize their personal self-interest' (J. Williams 1991: 22). This is, at best, an optimistic assumption, especially during what some have termed Canada's 'jobless recovery.' New Brunswick's Premier McKenna suggests that this should not be a concern because 'if you have the training, the jobs will take care of themselves' (*Globe and Mail*, 15 January 1993). For the federal government, Canada's mounting social-welfare rolls reflect a 'skills deficit' that can be reversed by creating a better-trained workforce. Critics of the new thinking about 'active' social policy are less convinced (McFarland 1993). For many, especially for a generation of young Canadians who have virtually been shut out of the labour force in recent years, the greatest disincentive to employment is not the absence of skills but, quite simply, the absence of jobs!

The ISSC attempts to degender women and obscure the gendered division of labour by defining them as employable individuals instead of as mothers, and then regenders them as welfare 'dependents' in need of therapeutic intervention. In fact, it is hard to find women in this discussion paper, even though we know that the provision of social welfare is highly gendered. Some 60 per cent of single mothers, for example, live below the poverty line, and this group finds strong representation among the ranks of welfare recipients. Under the previous welfare regime, these women were primarily seen as mothers, but ISSC shifts this identity to that of potential employables. The problem of single-parent poverty is no longer a problem. Instead, single mothers are cast as employables – potential workers – who are a burden on the state, their children are the 'vulnerable' poor, and 'deadbeat dads' become the cause of their poverty.

As the discussion document explains, 'one key reason why there is such a close link between poor children and lone-parent families is inadequate, unreliable or unpaid child support payments.' ISSC sees the lone-parent family as a degendered one when, in fact, we know that the vast majority of these families are female-headed. Putting gender back into the equation might have identified other 'key reasons' for child poverty within lone-parent families – among these the poverty of single mothers, the large and persistent wage gap between men and women, the gendered segregation of the labour force, the increased number of women who can find only part-time jobs, and, most obviously, the declining availability of affordable quality child care in this country.

According to the federal government's new analysis, poverty is very much a problem of skills deficits among individual Canadians who, in turn, become dependent on the social-welfare system for survival. The discussion paper is full of reference to dependency; in fact, the category 'welfare recipient,' which carries a small measure of dignity, is largely replaced with the term 'dependent.' Moreover, the discussion paper argues that dependency is a trap that is 'both costly and cruel' (ISSC 1994: 8). The function of social-welfare policy, then, is not to provide the poor with a minimum standard of living but, instead, to break the dependency by putting recipients back into the labour force.

The idea that welfare recipients are dependent on welfare carries with it a barrage of negative images that stigmatize the poor and make them appear to be personally to blame for their condition. This discursive gesture is not unique to Canada but is, instead, integral to the neo-liberal state. Fraser and Gordon have traced the meaning of dependency across history. They argue that in pre-industrial societies, colonies and servants were deemed to be dependent but this did not carry a negative connotation. With industrialization, dependency was assigned to those who were not in the paid labour force. For paupers the term 'dependent' did impute a weak moral character, but for women dependence on the male breadwinner was judged to be natural and proper. Fraser and

Gordon argue that in the current period the idea of welfare dependency, similar to drug addiction, is seen to be an individual shortcoming – one that is both blameworthy and avoidable. All adult 'dependency' on the state is now suspect and avoidable. Only children are now able to claim a benign dependence (Fraser and Gordon 1994).

The dependency metaphor also suggests certain policy responses and not others. It raises the spectre of the pathological and dysfunctional and thus invites surgical or technical intervention (Beilharz 1987). In the case of the federal government's proposals, this outlook involves identifying the diseased, 'the dependents,' the otherwise employable, and subjecting them to treatments such as retraining and counselling or creating disincentives to break their habit in the form of workfare, or more restrictive and declining benefits. The latter is the rationale underlying the ISSC's proposed two-tier UI system, which would pay the 'frequent user' (the addict) less than the 'occasional user' (the recreational user).

The links between social assistance, dependency, personal culpability, and gender are implicit in this analysis, but the discussion paper goes further. At one point, it suggests that the problem of Unemployment Insurance dependency is more pronounced among particular groups, among them, women, members of visible minorities, persons with disabilities, and aboriginal people (ISSC 1994: 48). And, at another point, it suggests that a single mother should be helped to 'leap successfully from social assistance to the independence of a job – even a low paying one' so that she does not transmit her pathological behaviour to her children. As the discussion paper puts it, 'the price of staying on welfare is high ... Children who grow up on society's sidelines risk the continuation of a cycle of low achievement and joblessness' (ISSC 1994: 70).

The ISSC fits comfortably into the newspeak of neo-liberal governments, which attempts to make structural inequalities invisible and, in the process, silence groups that protest these inequalities. This rhetorical strategy conveys the clear message that is up to every 'good individual' to become more flexible and self-reliant and to make fewer demands on the state. But a deeply entrenched and unequal gender order, by definition, means that women can only be gendered individuals. As much as this rhetoric tries to cast women as individuals detached from a deeply gendered social order, then, it must necessarily recast them as 'bad individuals' – the ones who are different, dependent, and blameworthy for not successfully leaping into independence. This is the gendered message that shines through the optimistic lines of the ISSC.

In *Improving Social Security in Canada*, the federal government sets out its three principal objectives for reforming the social welfare system:

1 jobs – helping Canadians to get and keep work by ensuring that we have the knowledge and skills to compete with the best labour forces in the world
2 support of those most vulnerable – providing income support for those in need, while fostering independence, self-confidence and initiative, and starting to tackle child poverty.
3 affordability – making sure the social-security system is within our means and more efficiently managed, with a real commitment to end waste and abuse (ISSC 1994: 10).

While these objectives seem worthy enough, the suggested mechanisms for their implementation are not. Among other things, the government has put on the table workfare and other penalties for 'frequent users' of social welfare and unemployment insurance. Moreover, any increases in welfare spending, the ISSC suggests, should be directed towards counselling rather than income maintenance. The discussion paper states its new understanding of citizenship quite unambiguously. 'Improved government support,' it suggests, 'must be targeted at those who demonstrate a willingness and commitment to self-help.' It is the primary task of the reform 'to gear them more effectively towards helping individuals achieve the satisfaction and dignity of work' (ISSC 1994: 25, 82).

Targeting

A central theme in the work of Michel Foucault is the idea that the manner in which cultures define the normal or ordinary as opposed to the deviant or special both gives people their social and personal identity and acts as an instrument of political domination and bureaucratic administration (Foucault 1973b). The current thinking about citizenship and welfare provision has increasingly employed these 'dividing practices' to minimize the relevance of gender itself in the new cultural order – an impositional claim that attempts to delegitimize the women's movement. Increasingly, the social category 'woman,' which found some unity, however misleading, in the welfare state and in second-wave feminist discourse, is actively being deconstructed. Women, it is argued, do not have similar political interests. Individual women are being redefined as members of specially disadvantaged groups that require 'targeted' social programs to address their special needs/short-comings so that they too can become ordinary 'degendered' citizens (Yeatman 1990: 134).

The idea of targeting is entirely consistent with the hollowing out of the welfare state. Its overt rationale is that, in an era of fiscal restraint, scarce resources are best targeted at those who need them the most. Thus, universal entitlements such as the family allowance are transformed into a child tax credit available only to those whom the government defines as truly needy. Similarly, initiatives designed to combat violence against women are structured to target what are deemed to be high-risk groups – aboriginal women, women of colour, immigrant women, lesbians, and women with disabilities.

Women's different experiences of oppression cannot be denied or ignored. But responsiveness to difference is not the primary outcome of targeting. Instead of exposing the structural links among race, gender, poverty, and violence, targeting serves to pathologize and individualize difference as well as place the designated groups under increased state surveillance and administrative control. It disassembles and diffuses the collective claims of the women's movement, recasting it as a 'ghetto of disadvantaged groups' (Yeatman 1990). The idea of targeting, as Esping-Anderson suggests, is the mirror reflection of universalism and is made possible by the rejection of the universal delivery of social programs. 'Universalism in social policy,' he writes, 'manufactures its own universal political constituency, which in turn helps maintain a basic sense of social solidarity and shared responsibility.' Universalism, in other words, 'undermines both the stigmatizing nature of poor relief and ... the self-reliance mechanism of private insurance' (Esping-Anderson 1983: 30). To be 'targeted' is to be effectively stigmatized as being outside the norms of the new citizenship – someone who has to be subjected to some kind of rehabilitation to make her normal. Since the gender order puts women in a structurally subordinate position, then, the new welfare thinking effectively casts them outside of the ranks of 'normal' the citizenship and outside of the political community.

Conclusion

Yeatman has argued that the abandonment of the discourse of citizenship by dominant groups at this time is a (the neo-liberal's) response to

the increasing effectiveness of claims on citizenship by groups historically identified as 'other' or, in contemporary parlance, 'minorities'
(Yeatman 1994: 83). Although restructuring discourse attempts to hail
women into the public either as non-citizens with special needs or as
genderless citizens, the restructuring process is, needless to say, neither
gender nor race neutral.

The disappearance of universal social programs and the erosion of the
social safety net obviously gives less substance to the postwar construction of citizenship. The federal government's proposed reform represents a number of foundational shifts. It has reintroduced into political
discourse concepts such as the 'deserving and undeserving' poor and
'genuine' versus 'non-genuine' poverty (Yeatman 1990: 122). There is
also a shift in what the reformers refer to as an active welfare model as
opposed to the passive postwar one. It is difficult to ignore the obvious
valorization of the new order encoded in these terms. They signal a
change in the philosophy of welfare provision away from the protection
of people who are either temporarily or permanently displaced by the
wage economy to a new regime where retraining or participation in the
job market is a condition for social assistance. The idea here is that all
able-bodied people, very broadly defined, are effectively 'undeserving'
of social assistance if they do not either endeavour to retrain to better
compete in the job market or take some form of work to 'top-up' their
social assistance incomes, and thus reduce the burden they impose on
the state.

Canada's social-welfare system is being redesigned to make it more
restrictive, especially for those deemed to be 'employable,' and to force
them back into the job market even if the only jobs available are 'non-
standard' – that is, insecure, part-time, and poorly paid (Yeatman 1990:
130). It is no coincidence that these are precisely the kinds of jobs that
are being created in Canada's restructured economy. Second, 'active'
social-welfare programs serve to rediscipline the workforce both by
making the poor dependent on some form of employment to qualify for
social assistance and by constructing an image of the 'undeserving' poor
as those who do not participate in some form in the job market. Third,
all of these factors serve to negate systemic thinking about poverty and
unemployment. We are encouraged to think of poverty in terms of
undeserving, deficient, and wrongly skilled individuals instead of Canada's 'restructured' political economy and its seeming incapacity to provide employment, much less good jobs, for an unacceptable and ever-
growing number of Canadians. The gaze of policy makers is directed

away from structural factors (which go unchallenged) to the micro-individual self-help solutions. And, it would seem that Canadian women are among those most in need of this kind of therapy. A highly unequal gender order, in fact, ensures this outcome.

Postscript

In February 1995, the federal Liberal party dealt the death blow to the social-security consultation process and to Canada's postwar welfare state. Instead of redesigning the national system, Finance Minister Paul Martin used the so-called debt crisis and the budget process to shift federal responsibility for social welfare, health care, and post-secondary education onto the provinces. The budget set a two-year limit to phase out the Canada Assistance Plan (CAP) and Established Program Financing (EPF) and to introduce a new block-funding program called the Canada Health and Social Transfer. Under the proposed new regime, the federal government will give a block of funds to individual provinces that they can use as they wish in the social-welfare field subject to vague and increasingly unenforcable national standards. At the same time, the federal government indicated that its contribution to these programs would decrease in future years – indeed, by an estimated $7 billion in the 1995–7 period alone.

Although the federal government has passed the responsibility for social programs to the provinces, there is little reason to believe that the program changes implemented at this level will reflect different governing assumptions than those telegraphed in the social-security consultation process. Some provinces such as Alberta and New Brunswick have already embraced a neo-liberal conception of citizenship while Ontario, Canada's most populous province, is now poised to adopt workfare and other neo-liberal governing instruments. In other words, the Canada Social Transfer simply marks a change in the site of the implementation of the new citizenship and not a change in its intent or content. In fact, decreasing federal revenue for social welfare virtually ensures that the provinces will redesign and contract their social welfare budgets. In the meantime, the federal government has set its sights on the two remaining programs that remain in its policy arsenal – unemployment insurance and old-age security – again with the intent of reducing its commitment to the social-welfare of Canadians.

More broadly, however, the social security consultation provides yet another example of the curtailment of democratic citizenship rights under the flag of the neo-liberal state. Public consultations have become a familiar legitimizing instrument of the neo-liberal state. They give the appearance of democratic input and enable governments to implement policy agendas that were, at best, only alluded to during an election campaign. In fact, during the first year of the federal Liberal government's mandate, it deployed public consultations in relation to the budget, immigration policy, and social security.

The functions of the public consultation, as a governing instrument of the neo-liberal state, are threefold. First, it serves to silence informed voices in a specific policy field by labelling them as 'special interests' with positions and motivations that are unrepresentative of and potentially antagonistic to those of 'ordinary Canadians.' Second, the public consultation acts as an effective device for limiting the parameters of the debate. So-called 'ordinary Canadians' are provided with information kits that structure the debate and, ultimately, its outcome. Finally, the public consultation provides the illusion of democratic policy-making even though, as in the case of the budget, immigration policy, and social policy, the eventual policy change was imposed through what has been termed 'the politics of stealth.' This politics enables governments to enact immediate and significant policy shifts through the budget and spending cuts under the guise of fiscal imperatives. The Canada Health and Social Transfer has been imposed by the politics of stealth much to the detriment of national standards, the life-chances of Canada's growing number of poor (who are disproportionately women and children), and the postwar consensus about social citizenship.

7

Tax Policy and the Gendered Distribution of Wealth

LISA PHILIPPS

This paper examines a dimension of women's economic position that is relatively invisible in policy debates; that is, the unequal distribution of wealth between women and men. Discussions of economic inequality in Canada focus primarily on income disparities. Our empirical and symbolic markers of poverty and class tend to be income-based: the poverty line, the gender wage gap, the increasing polarization of incomes, the number of affluent people who pay no income tax, the poorly paid or unpaid status of much work done by women. Since most of us rely on wages or other income payments to survive, this does seem like an obvious place to concentrate our intellectual and political energies. However, talking about inequality and redistribution solely in terms of income also has the ironic effect of keeping *wealth* disparities safely outside the boundaries of debate.

This habit of overlooking wealth distribution means that economic policies are formulated and assessed by reference to an incomplete picture of the nature and degree of inequality in our society. The reality is that wealth is distributed even more unequally than income in Canada, and that wealth disparities are gendered and probably raced. Moreover, lack of access to wealth poses special problems for women that go beyond those of income-poverty. This aspect is of particular concern in the current context of economic 'restructuring.' The ability to survive and 'adjust' to a shifting, contracting labour market may depend heavily on the availability of savings or other forms of capital. At the same time, many aspects of state policy are being 'restructured' under intense pressures both to respond to increasing poverty and to reduce government expenditure. I argue here that taxation and other economic-policy reforms must take wealth disparities into account, if we are serious about including women in all aspects of economic life, and if we wish to create a more equal society.

Part 1 will explain how a lack of access to or control over wealth contributes to women's economic disadvantage both qualitatively, in the ways it affects personal security and autonomy, and quantitatively, in terms of the empirical evidence on wealth distribution. Part 2 will look at the historical failure of Canadian tax policy to address itself to wealth disparities, and will link this failure to the economic subordination of women within the family-household system. I argue that the privatization of support obligations within the family not only obscures the unequal distribution of wealth between women and men, but also places significant constraints on the state's ability or willingness to redistribute wealth through the tax system. Part 3 will consider the way forward. The challenge is to enact tax and other policies that will equalize wealth holdings and in particular enhance women's economic power, without jeopardizing the security of those women who at present depend on assets accumulated by husbands or fathers.

Let me be clear about the point of all this. I am *not* suggesting that we should strive to ensure there are as many wealthy women as wealthy men in Canada. Instead, I would hope for a society in which people's autonomy and security, and their role in political processes, rest far less on private-property ownership. This chapter attempts to expose the forms of deprivation and disempowerment currently entailed by wealth-poverty, as well as the ways that taxation policy evades and reinforces them, and to show how both of these phenomena are deeply gendered.

1. Wealth Ownership in Canada: Not Just a Question of Class

Before going any further I should clarify what I mean by 'wealth.' Economists have defined wealth in various ways, for a variety of purposes.[1] For my purposes here, 'wealth' means the money value of the stock of assets owned by an individual at a particular point in time (excluding lifetime earning capacity or 'human capital'), minus her total debts and liabilities at that time. It is important to see that this definition is itself loaded with ideological assumptions. Concepts like 'wealth' and 'property' are of course socially constructed and culturally contingent. They beg fundamental questions, such as who has the power to distinguish property from non-property, and to define what has economic value.[2]

I am particularly struck by the individualistic focus of my definition of wealth. It is rooted in a world-view in which resources are parcelled up among private owners who have the right to exclude others from their property. As Leroy Little Bear has said, it reflects a Western European philosophical tradition of linear reasoning, with its tendency to fragmentation and singularity.[3] He illustrates this cultural specificity by contrasting European understandings with the fundamentally different notions of property and community present in many First Nations societies.[4]

These epistemological questions require a much deeper treatment than I am ready to give them here. I mention them in part because I think they are connected to an issue that surfaces repeatedly in this chapter: the power of empirical data to shape knowledge. It is no coincidence that my definition of wealth matches up neatly with those most often used by economists and statisticians to measure wealth distribution. This similarity enables me to provide some quantitative analysis of relative wealth ownership between various social groups. By bringing in scientific measurements I reinforce the authority of my arguments, but also subtly adopt the ideological framework embedded within the statistics. One response to this problem is to demand that statistics be gathered in a way that better reflects women's lives, for example, by showing how unpaid domestic work contributes to the production of wealth. More radically, this analysis suggests that we should be suspicious of the assumption that our claims about the world are not credible unless they can be measured and quantified by social scientists.[5]

Wealth and the Quality of Women's Lives

Property ownership is a major determinant of power and status in our society. Many of the barriers faced by women in economic, political, and family life are closely related to their lack of access to wealth. In a period of economic recession or 'restructuring,' these barriers take on added significance. Although the same might be said about lack of *incomes*, wealth inequalities deserve special consideration for several reasons.

Perhaps the most basic is that reserves of wealth provide greater long-term economic security and independence than a stream of income alone. Wealth forms the basis for a secure retirement from the paid labour force necessitated by old age, illness, or disability – the times when many women experience poverty.[6] It also provides greater freedom to withdraw from the labour market to care for children, the elderly, and others, to leave a violent partner, or simply to live as a single person without being poor. These are areas in which women too often lack acceptable choices. People with saved or inherited wealth live more stable, less stressful economic lives, because they are not as vulnerable to financial crisis. The possibility of losing one's job, or being faced with emergency expenses, is even more threatening if there are no resources to fall back on.

Lack of access to wealth may also seriously diminish an individual's opportunities in the market-place and her ability to survive in a changing labour market. Without any capital base, it is difficult to obtain significant credit or other financing for a business enterprise, a house, or other major investments. It may also constrain educational options, by placing limits on where, what, and how long one can afford to study. For instance, in the absence of state or family support, a worker with no financial reserves may not even consider leaving paid employment temporarily to get education or training aimed at enhancing her labour-market potential. Similarly, lack of wealth may limit mobility – the capacity to relocate in search of new work. Thus, it not only detracts from current living standards, but may also reduce the possibility of improving or changing one's economic position over time. The blockage of opportunities that results from having little or no access to wealth may be one reason why women get stuck in poorly paid or otherwise undesirable jobs, or in the unpaid sector. It may also place women at a disadvantage in 'adjusting' to a new economic order.

There are a myriad of other benefits that flow to wealth holders in the form of political clout and social standing. To give some of the more obvious examples, those who own or control wealth can influence political decision-making through their power to determine when, where, and how capital will be invested, by financing election campaigns and lobbying activities, and through the ownership of (or tax-deductible access to) mass media. The power of property owners was demonstrated succinctly in British Columbia during the spring of 1993 when the NDP government hastily retracted a proposed education surtax on homes valued over $500,000, following loud complaints by the tiny percentage of taxpayers who were affected.[7]

This influence and status also have a private side. Within families, a great deal of power is wielded by the persons who own and/or control decisions with respect to major assets. Few would dispute that gender is implicated here. Savings, investments, and other forms of juridical property tend to accrue to male family members, in part because women's labour is paid more poorly than men's, if it is paid at all. Contrary to ideological notions of the heterosexual nuclear family as a realm governed by altruism, there is a good deal of evidence that many men do not share their higher incomes or wealth with women to the extent that is generally assumed. Thus, many women are at least to some extent dependent upon assets owned by a husband or common-law partner for security in old age, despite having worked all their lives.[8]

A husband or father who controls access to capital in the family has power to affect the opportunities, lifestyle, and security of other family members. The wealth owner can also determine how, when, and subject to what conditions his property will be distributed following death.[9] Women living without men are also affected by the maldistribution of wealth, of course. Though they may not be directly dependent on a man's assets, we will see in the next section that woman-only households have dramatically lower wealth holdings.

To the extent that wealth inequality is recognized as a distinct phenomenon, it is generally framed as a problem of class or socio-economic justice. I am suggesting that wealth distribution is also a function of gender, and most likely of race and other social characteristics as well. The following section revisits the empirical evidence on wealth and income distribution with this thesis in mind.

The Gendered Distribution of Wealth

Our knowledge about wealth distribution in Canada is quite limited. Detailed statistics on *income* distribution are collected and published regularly by the government, but there is a dearth of equivalent material on household wealth.[10] Moreover, the published data generally look at wealth distribution across the whole population, and give little information about the sex, race, ethnicity, or other characteristics of wealth holders. This statistical deficit speaks volumes all by itself about our insensitivity to the gendered and raced contours of inequality. Despite these limitations, it is possible to sketch out a rough picture of how wealth is distributed from various bits of direct and indirect data.

The most important general observation is that wealth disparities are more extreme than income disparities across the population as a whole. In 1984 the wealthiest 20% of (government-defined) 'family units' held about 69% of the country's total net household wealth.[11] By contrast, the top quintile of income earners received a comparatively low 43% of all income in the same year.[12] One problem with these figures is that they do not fully convey the extreme concentration of wealth at the very top.

One economist has estimated that the wealthiest 1% of the population holds a full 25% of household wealth.[13] At the opposite end of the scale, the least wealthy 20% of Canadians actually had negative net wealth in 1984. That is, their aggregate liabilities exceeded the value of their assets. Indeed, the bottom 40% held only 2.1% of national wealth. Again, a comparison with income figures shows that wealth is distributed more unequally. The lowest-earning 20% of family units received about 4.5% of total income, and the lowest-earning 40% received a 14.8% share.[14]

It should be remembered that these data include many non-income producing assets, such as vehicles and homes. If we look only at financial assets, the degree of inequality is even more severe. The wealthiest 20% of Canadians owned about 94% of private business equity in 1984 (interests in sole proprietorships, partnerships, and private corporations), and 74.7% of all other financial assets (including cash, deposits, savings bonds, publicly traded stocks, and RRSPs).[15]

The second general observation is that, while wealth inequalities are more extreme than income inequalities, there is a positive correlation between the two. That is, people with low incomes tend to have little or no wealth, and people with high incomes are likely to have significant wealth.[16] Many individual exceptions exist, of course, but income data can nevertheless be considered as a proxy for estimating wealth inequalities among different social groups.

This type of indirect evidence is important when we come to look at gender. It is difficult to determine with any degree of precision how wealth is distributed between women and men. The main problem is that wealth surveys have used the 'family' as their unit of measurement, rather than looking at individual asset holdings. This distorts our picture of wealth distribution in several ways. For one thing, there are many individuals who live in households that do not conform to any of the models of 'family' used in the surveys. For example, lesbian couples with children may simply be lumped into the category of 'single parent households headed by women.' Nor is there any category that can accommodate aboriginal households where aunts, sisters, and other extended-family members may play a very significant role. Moreover, as Marjorie Cohen and others have pointed out, using the white heterosexual nuclear family as the unit of analysis assumes that resources are shared equally between women and men within households, and that women's welfare is indistinguishable from that of their families.[17] Women are thus made invisible vis-à-vis wealth by being subsumed into narrowly defined family households.

Despite the shortcomings of the wealth data, there are several statistical indicators that tend to confirm that women are at a serious disadvantage relative to men in terms of property ownership. First of all, we can assume that the well-documented income gap between women and men also translates into a wealth gap, given the positive correlation between wealth holdings and income levels. In terms of direct evidence, the government data do identify wealth holders by gender in one case – for lone-parent families. When such households are headed by women, they have a median wealth of $4800, compared with $33,612 for male-headed lone-parent families. Moreover, 50.5% of families headed by female single parents had net worths under $5000, compared with 24% of those headed by male single parents. In addition, census results suggest that men are far more likely than women to own, rather than rent, their residences.[18] Home ownership is a key indicator of wealth. The 58% of family units who owned their own homes in 1984 together held 91% of national wealth. The median wealth of home owners was $79,947, compared with $3283 for those who rented their living space.[19]

Divorce is also a major factor in women's economic lives. Studies indicate that women's average incomes drop sharply relative to men's after separation or divorce, and that such women are much more likely than their former male partners to have incomes below the poverty line.[20] Given the high correlation between wealth and income levels, this disparity suggests that women probably also have less wealth than their male ex-partners. Although there is not yet any Canadian wealth data to back this conclusion up, it is supported by abundant literature on the qualitative failings of the property-division laws enacted in the 1970s and 1980s. The statutes do not even purport to assist women in common-law or lesbian relationships, or the large proportion of women in low- or no-wealth households.[21] Moreover, family-law regimes only provide for deferred sharing of property. That is, wives obtain no legal rights to wealth accumulated by their husbands so long as the marriage subsists, but only upon obtaining a legal divorce.[22] Even in traditional marriage situations where there is property to divide, women's legal claims are undermined by illegal evasion and legal avoidance planning, by the exclusion of business assets from divisible property in many provinces, by the unfavourable exercise of judicial discretion, and by extreme pressures to agree to unfair settlements through threats of a custody battle, a costly litigation process, or physical violence.[23] Nor do family-law statutes apply to matrimonial homes on Indian reserves, according to the Supreme Court of Canada.[24]

At least one American study has measured post-divorce wealth distribution directly. It found that separated men had a median wealth of $5547, compared with $1200 for their female counterparts. The figures for divorced men and women were $12,850 and $9375 respectively.[25]

How do women fare with respect to ownership of business assets? We know that this form of wealth is very highly concentrated in the wealthiest sector of the Canadian population. There are undoubtedly some women in this privileged group, but the data do not reveal how many or the relative value of men's and women's business holdings. Knight's interesting study shows a strong bias in favour of sons over daughters as inheritors of family businesses, suggesting that women have limited access to established business wealth through this route. Only 15 per cent of business owners had identified a daughter to succeed them, and the rate was even lower in families with both male and female children.[26] Knight found that 'most CEO fathers felt that their daughters were not interested in [the] family firm, although they had never discussed the issue with them, much to the frustration of the daughters.'[27]

Many women are starting their own businesses, either in response to labour-market upheavals or in frustration with the glass ceilings they experience in their jobs. How promising is entrepreneurship as a means for women to gain access to wealth? There are many successful women-owned businesses, of course. But the evidence suggests there are also many gender-related barriers to the establishment and growth of business concerns. Financing especially has been identified as a principal area of complaint. Since women have lower incomes, they probably have less personal savings to offer as collateral for business loans, and this in itself is a major stumbling block. But even when their financial characteristics are the same as men's, women report discriminatory attitudes and practices on the part of lenders and creditors. These include being rejected outright, getting asked for more collateral, and being required to have a spouse co-sign – all suggesting a perception that women are not legitimate business persons in their own right, or are greater business risks. Other factors that women have identified as inhibiting their success include the need for more management training, a lack of support networks, and the failure of male partners to share child care and household labour.[28]

There is even less empirical data to go on when we try to factor race into the picture, not to mention sexual orientation, physical ability, or other factors that may be related to socio-economic status. There are no

Canadian studies that focus directly on ethnic or racial-group wealth holdings. However, income statistics and other forms of indirect evidence suggest that wealth disparities in this country are probably raced, as well as gendered.

First of all, it is clear that aboriginal people, particularly aboriginal women, receive incomes that are markedly lower than the Canadian average, a fact that hints at even greater inequalities of wealth.[29] As discussed earlier, I suspect that my definition of 'wealth' may be quite inappropriate for many First Nations communities, resting as it does upon culturally specific notions of property that centre around individual private ownership and the right to exclude others. Still, I think it is worth considering how aboriginal people stand in relation to wealth as understood by the dominant culture. For example, aboriginal people living on reserves have only a limited legal interest in reserve lands, which cannot be sold or mortgaged to anyone who is not a status Indian. Similar restrictions apply to prevent personal property situated on a reserve from being mortgaged or otherwise used to secure a debt.[30] While it may be argued these legal restrictions are advantageous in some respects, they also make it difficult to finance economic enterprise through mainstream commercial channels. Financing problems are consistently identified as one of the most significant barriers to the establishment and growth of First Nations businesses. In addition to the inability to pledge collateral, other problems include the lack of personal savings owing to low incomes, conservative lending policies, and negative stereotyping of First Nations borrowers.[31] Furthermore, income and wealth generated on reserves often does not remain within the First Nations economy precisely because of the lack of a self-sustaining economic base (Le Dressay 1993: 215).

It seems fair to infer from these and other factors that aboriginal people probably have significantly less wealth than other sectors of the population. It is possible that settlement of the many large land claims that remain outstanding in Canada will to some extent redress this inequality.

There is some evidence that other ethnic and racialized groups are also disadvantaged in terms of income and wealth. Peter Li's analysis of 1981 census data on seventeen ethnic groups found that the lowest average incomes were received by non-white persons, and people of South European origin. After adjusting for variables such as age, gender, and education levels, non-whites still received the lowest average incomes.[32] It is also notable that researchers in the United States have consistently found severe inequalities in the wealth holdings of blacks and whites. One recent study noted that while black families receive 50 to 60 per cent of the income of white families, their median wealth was found to be only 8.5 per cent of that for whites. Black female-headed households were the least wealthy of all groups studied, with a median wealth of 2.4 per cent of that in white households. Moreover, when non-income-producing property such as homes and vehicles was removed from the calculation, the average black household had zero net wealth.[33]

People with disabilities, and especially women with disabilities, are also disproportionately represented among those who are poor according to *income* standards.[34] The same can be said of elderly women not living with husbands.[35] Again, I suggest that these data most likely understate the deprivation these groups experience, because their wealth holdings are probably also very low.

As Oliver and Shapiro (1990) have remarked, the condition of poor households and individuals appears 'far more precarious, marginalized and unequal' when wealth is factored into the picture (p. 139). One of the things this means is that women and other wealth-poor groups face barriers to economic and political life more severe than we commonly recognize. It also means that anti-poverty strategies designed to meet minimum income needs are inadequate by definition, because they address only one aspect of the problem. Likewise, state policies designed to redistribute income are necessary but far from sufficient, because they do not deal with the causes or consequences of women's unequal access to wealth.[36] The next section considers how Canadian tax policy has treated the wealth question.

2. Towards a Wealth-Sensitive Feminist Analysis of Tax Policy

We know that the Canadian tax system fails women in a variety of ways. The most pervasive problem is simply the lack of progressivity in the overall incidence of taxation.[37] This is especially unfair to women, given their over-representation at low income levels, and their lower average incomes. This general inequity is aggravated by a variety of specific provisions that tend to disadvantage women, such as the taxation of spousal and child support payments, and the inadequate and poorly structured deduction for child-care expenses.[38]

Feminist critiques of the tax system may still be understated, however, because we typically focus on the distribution of *income*. As I have tried to show in the last section, this approach may overlook how *wealth* inequalities affect women's lives in qualitatively and quantitatively distinct ways. This to my mind is an important gap. In this section I will sketch out the beginnings of a wealth-sensitive feminist analysis of Canadian tax policy. There are three main insights to be gained from such an analysis.

The first point is that the incidence of taxation is in fact less progressive, and more biased against women, than even its harshest critics have generally argued. This is because income levels are almost always used as the sole indicator of ability to pay, ignoring the additional social and economic benefits enjoyed by wealth holders, as well as the disadvantages faced by those with little or no wealth. For example, income levels are used to set marginal rate brackets, to determine entitlement to the GST Credit, the Child Tax Benefit, and other concessions, and to establish thresholds for 'clawing back' Old Age Security.[39] Given that wealth is distributed much more unequally than income, all these components of the tax system may be seriously underestimating the taxable capacity of the wealthy and overestimating that of the poor. Similarly, by measuring the distribution of the tax burden according to income levels only, we minimize the degree of inequality among taxpayers, and therefore exaggerate the progressivity of the tax system. This has particular implications for women, who are disadvantaged relative to men in terms of wealth, as well as income. Using income as a proxy for ability to pay therefore obscures the full nature and extent of gender bias in the tax system.

Interestingly, the need for a more realistic measure of ability to pay is one of the arguments often advanced in favour of personal-wealth taxes.[40] This takes me to my second point. If we applied a wealth-sensitive feminist analysis to the tax system, we would probably notice more often that, unlike the United States and almost all other OECD countries, Canada has no personal-wealth tax. This was not always so. From 1941 to 1971, the federal government imposed an estate tax that applied to the very wealthiest testators and their heirs.[41] Soon after this tax was abolished, the provinces began repealing their succession duties in a race to the bottom. The last succession duty was repealed in 1985, when Quebec finally left the field.[42] The fact that no Canadian government currently imposes a personal-wealth tax is in one sense remarkable, considering the amount of hand-wringing by politicians about budget deficits and growing economic inequalities. Certainly the recent NDP government in Ontario back-pedalled on the subject, after being elected on a platform that promised a new wealth tax.

The policy arguments usually advanced in favour of personal-wealth taxation include the need for greater progressivity or vertical equity in the tax system, and the need to equalize the distribution of wealth for moral, economic, and political reasons.[43] My point here is that we should revisit these traditional arguments to take account of gender. The exclusion of personal wealth from the tax base is not a gender-neutral policy. Lack of access to wealth causes particular difficulties for women, and probably the more so for racialized women, elderly women, and disabled women. The ability to inherit and hold wealth free of tax primarily benefits men, and helps to preserve the economic ine-qualities that are a hallmark of women's subordination.

My final point, which is more complex, is that our failure to redress wealth inequalities through the tax system is linked in important ways to the privatization of women's economic lives within families. By this I mean that our tax policy has for the most part reacted to women's lack of economic power simply by facilitating or leaving space for the provi-sion of support for women in private, within families, presumably by men. In order to do this, the tax system must assume a social universe populated by heterosexual couples composed of (male) breadwinners and (female) dependents. It is true, of course, that many women are at least to some extent materially dependent on the income or wealth of men. However, these assumptions are informed as much by ideology as by the concrete practices of taxpayers.[44]

Familial ideology constructs inequality between women and men within the nuclear-family household as natural and private. Indeed, the family is seen as an inner sanctum of privacy, set apart not just from the state but also from the world of commerce. The self-interested, arm's-length transactions of the market-place are ideologically alien to the family sphere, where 'economic' needs are expected to be met by altru-istic (male) breadwinners, and 'care' is to be provided by selfless wives and mothers.[45] In taxation and other state policies, this normative view of the family translates into various assumptions about behaviour, one of which is that women's economic needs should (and typically will) be addressed privately, as a family matter.

One of the most powerful illustrations of this assumption is the long-standing use of spousal exemptions in the tax system. Under the current system, for example, property can be transferred to a 'spouse' free of capital-gains tax, either during their joint lives or upon death.[46] Federal and provincial inheritance taxes, when they were in force, also tended to provide generous relief for spousal bequests. In fact, shortly before it was repealed, the federal estate tax was amended to exempt from tax entirely any property passing to a spouse.[47] Although marital exemptions often use gender-neutral language, it is clear that the main recipients of such transfers are expected to be wives. This is nicely illustrated by the comments of one MP on the introduction of the first federal succession duty, who protested that 'if a man during his lifetime has accumulated an estate for the support of his widow and family, he should not have part of it confiscated by any government.'[48] In Ontario the spousal exemption was at one time expressly limited to wives, and was not made completely gender neutral until 1970.[49]

The policy of relieving spousal bequests or transfers from tax reflects a decision that the state should defer to private support arrangements within heterosexual family households. It assumes and accepts a relation of support and dependency between husbands and wives, of which property transfers are a part. This relation is treated as natural, in the sense that it precedes the state and should not be disrupted by it. At the same time as it offers immediate financial relief for some women, the spousal exemption declares the state's unwillingness to take responsibility for the distribution of resources within the private world of the heterosexual family. As in so many other areas of the law, it simply gives women the right to keep whatever they manage to obtain from men privately.[50] The presence of spousal exemptions in the *Income Tax Act* also tends to normalize the economic inequalities that exist between male and female members of households. The tax system thus reinforces dominant familial ideologies and helps to reproduce the conditions of inequality that they describe.

Other state policies go further than spousal exemptions by attempting to give women a positive claim to their husband's assets at the end of the marriage or to protect them from total disinheritance.[51] But these programs also ultimately deny public responsibility for women's welfare. Rather than offering a public support system external to the family, they aim to ensure that testators and ex-husbands provide for the security of dependent family members out of any private wealth they have accumulated. As Fran Olsen has pointed out, such reforms have been successful in limiting the husband's power to abuse the control he exercises, but are unsatisfactory insofar as they leave the husband in control.[52]

Not surprisingly, these same familial ideologies have helped to fuel political resistance to wealth taxation in Canada. The political rhetoric around inheritance taxes has often evoked images of the state intercepting family businesses and other legacies meant for widows and children.[53] The gender politics of wealth taxation, however, have not received a great deal of attention. Tax-policy analysis has generally revolved around a more traditional left-right axis on this issue, where the relevant conflicts are between private-property owners and the state, or between property owners and the unpropertied.[54] Such analysis overlooks the fears raised by policies that seem to interfere with the privacy of the family, or to threaten its perceived economic-support functions. I worry that these family fears severely constrain the radical possibilities of wealth taxes because they cut across class and political affiliations, offering a common ground of opposition to wealth taxes among people with otherwise quite divergent opinions about economic inequalities. Even those who strongly advocate wealth taxation tend to qualify their support when it comes to family bequests or property associated with the family.

One of the best examples of this hesitancy can be found in New Democratic Party policies. The federal NDP has consistently made strong statements about the need to redistribute income and wealth through the tax system, but has been careful to develop a position on wealth taxation that does not impinge on family privacy. Beginning in 1969, party resolutions calling for higher succession duties or the reintroduction of estate taxes have supported the concept of spousal exemptions and relief for family farms and family businesses.[55] In the most recent federal election campaign, the NDP platform included a promise to introduce an annual net wealth tax, but again subject to protections for homes, farms, and small businesses.[56] Although these concessions may seem like minor exceptions to a policy that is basically egalitarian, in fact they could seriously reduce the redistributive potential of a new wealth tax.[57] Moreover, they imply a profound acceptance that any attempt to tax wealth must respect the boundaries of family.

I do not mean to suggest that we should call for the immediate abolition of spousal exemptions from taxation. As the next section will discuss, this would ignore the real conditions of dependency in which many women live today. Rather, my intention here has been to show how gender politics and familial ideologies have shaped the way our tax system deals with wealth. The conclusion that follows will consider what changes might improve women's situation vis-à-vis the distribution of wealth.

3. Making Women's Access to Wealth a Public Policy Issue

A long-term strategy for addressing the issues raised in this paper should in my view be informed by a vision of the world in which the distribution of resources is radically more equal and public policy is directed first and foremost to ensuring the adequate provisioning of needs. The question I want to address here is what changes we might look for in the shorter term, within the current political-economic context of Canadian society, that might move us closer to such a world.

I do believe that Canada should impose personal-wealth taxes on those with significant assets. The tax system is one of the most powerful tools governments have right now to effect distributive changes. A wealth tax could play a meaningful role in making the overall tax system more progressive, and in equalizing the distribution of wealth. This effect could counteract some of the 'harmonizing down' that is occurring at present in the Canadian labour market, as discussed by Pat Armstrong in this volume, and could help to offset the trend to increasingly polarized incomes. Moreover, a wealth tax could provide new revenue to support existing social safety nets and to fund some additional affirmative measures that I will outline shortly.

I am not convinced, however, that a wealth tax on its own would do very much to remedy the harms caused by wealth inequality, in particular the harms to women. A significant wealth tax that did not exempt spousal and other intra-family transfers could conceivably worsen the position of some women whose security currently rests upon accumulated male wealth.[58] As I have discussed, however, the political constraints imposed by the family are such that any wealth tax imposed by a Canadian government would likely be heavily qualified to protect intra-family wealth arrangements. Even under these conditions a wealth tax would still be worth the effort, because of its potential to erode the gross disparities of wealth among households. However, it is also a recipe for the continued invisibility of women's lack of access to wealth *within* households.

A strategy for dealing with the gendered and raced dimensions of wealth inequality must directly tackle the familial ideologies that privatize women's economic interests and subsume them into the family. It must also aim at making the lack of access to wealth experienced by women and other subordinated groups a matter of public responsibility and positive state action. Certainly, statistics should be collected in a way that does not mask but rather exposes how women, racialized groups, disabled persons, and others are excluded from wealth in our society. In addition, public policy on matters such as income support, housing, training, education, pensions, and small-business assistance should be developed with a greater sensitivity to the particular barriers and deprivations facing those without any savings or assets. Social policies must be more attentive to the causes and effects of wealth-poverty, if we hope to do better at enhancing women's autonomy and security in an era of 'restructuring.' The state can help by establishing much more adequate support structures external to the family, so that women are not faced with impossible choices when they wish to leave a relationship, raise children on their own, invest in their future earning capacity through education, relocate to a more active job market, or run their own businesses.

It must be kept in mind, of course, that the roots of this problem are much deeper. What women are really entitled to is full recognition of the value of their labour. The fact is that women do produce wealth, even if the legal rights and social power to control it at present accrue largely to men. The policy suggestions I have made here could help some individual women. They will not, however, substitute for more basic changes in how power is distributed and contributions are valued in both the family and the market.

NOTES

1 See, for example, Aaron and Munnell 1992: 121; Mintz 1991: 250; and Wolff 1987: 3–5.
2 See Hirschon 1984, and Cassin 1993. Two examples spring to mind to illustrate the ways in which definitions of wealth are politically configured, in this case by a masculinist bias. First, they obscure the extent of men's economic dominance by failing to recognize certain forms of economic power as 'wealth.' For instance, Canadian courts have on the whole rejected the argument that professional degrees and other 'career assets' are a form of 'property' that is divisible on marriage breakdown. In cases where the husband's professional credentials are the major source of economic security for the couple, the effect of this doctrine is to substantially diminish the wife's potential claim against the husband: see Caratun v. Caratun (1992), 42 R.F.L. (3d) 113 (O.C.A.) (leave to appeal to the Supreme Court of Canada dismissed without reasons 27 May (1993); and Hatch 1993. Second, the notion of wealth used by law fails to recognize that wealth formally accruing to individual men is in fact in large part constituted by unpaid labour performed by women: see Cassels and Philipps 1994; and Finch 1983.

3 Little Bear 1976.

4 See also McLuhan 1971 and Turpel 1990: esp. at 14–17 and 29–34.

5 See Postman 1992.

6 See Gee and Kimball 1987: 53; National Council of Welfare 1990: 99–115; Oja and Love 1988: 48, table 6; Statistics Canada 1990a: x–xv and 5.15–5.16; and Statistics Canada 1990b: 16, 17 and 27.

7 The government estimated the surtax would apply to 2.5% of residential properties: 1993 Budget, Province of British Columbia, pp. 16, 17 and 55–7. Minister of Finance Glen Clark announced the retraction of the surtax less than a week later, on 5 April. See Gillian Shaw, 'It's a taxpayers' revolt, and the New Democrats don't get it,' *Vancouver Sun*, 3 April 1993; Stewart Bell, 'Vancouver homeowners hit hardest,' ibid.; Barbara Yaffe, 'Fair taxes? That's rich,' *Vancouver Sun*, 6 April 1993; and Neil Hall and Keith Baldrey, 'Homeowners' protest kills school surtax,' *Vancouver Sun*, 8 April 1993.

8 See, for example, Edwards 1980, Wilson 1987, Pahl 1989, and Blumberg 1991a and 1991b.

9 For analyses of the relationship between economic resources and marital power, see England and Kilbourne 1990, and Blumstein and Schwartz 1991: 261.

10 Canadian wealth-distribution figures are generally derived from the periodic surveys of household wealth conducted by Statistics Canada. The most recent survey was done in 1984. In countries that impose some form of personal-wealth tax, more detailed and up-to-date information can be obtained from tax returns. For a more comprehensive analysis of wealth-distribution statistics, see Ontario Fair Tax Commission 1993, app. A.

11 Oja 1987: stables 1 and 4.

12 Statistics Canada 1986a: table 74.

13 Davies 1991: 283.

14 Oja 1987: tables 1 and 4; Statistics Canada 1986a: table 74, n. 9; and the Ontario FTC 1993: A17. International comparisons show that Canada's experience is far from unique. Large wealth inequalities are common in other industrialized countries: see Kessler and Pestieau 1991: 316; and Wolff 1987: 2. In particular, patterns of wealth distribution in the United States are broadly similar to that in Canada, although even more extreme: see Chawla 1990.

15 Oja 1987: 27, table 4. In fact, the government figures should be seen as conservative estimates of wealth inequality for several reasons. The surveys do not take into account households on Indian reserves, many of which may have low wealth holdings. Nor do they include inmates of institutions. Moreover, there is a serious problem of non-reporting or under-reporting by

the wealthiest households. These factors may be offset to some degree by the fact that pensions and insurance are not counted, which are probably among the more widely held forms of wealth: see Statistics Canada 1986b: 81–3; Oja 1987: 18–20; and Davies 1991: 281.

16 Statistics Canada 1986b: table 4; and Rashid 1980: 45, 46.

17 Cohen 1982. See also Edwards 1980; England 1993: 47–9; and Folbre and Hartmann 1988: 186–93.

18 The 1991 census determined that about 70% of households maintained primarily by men were privately owned, compared with about 45% of those maintained primarily by women. A household 'maintainer' is defined as the 'person or persons in the household who pay the rent, or the mortgage, or the taxes, or the electricity, etc. for the dwelling.' A 'primary household maintainer' is generally 'the person who contributes the greatest amount toward the payments for shelter expenses': Statistics Canada 1992b: 176, table 13, and definitions at 181, 182 . The data show clearly that female single parents are less likely to own their residences than male single parents or husband-wife families: see Statistics Canada 1993: table 1; and Lindsay 1992: 41.

19 Chawla 1990: 4.5 and table 2. See also Statistics Canada 1986b: 44, table 14.

20 Perhaps the most famous study is Weitzman 1985, which compared the economic consequences of divorce for men and women in the U.S. For Canadian data see Finnie 1993: 205, Pask and McCall 1989, Stewart and McFadgen 1992.

21 In recent years the courts have fashioned common-law remedies that allow common-law spouses to make property claims in some circumstances. See *Pettkus v. Becker*, [1980] 2 S.C.R. 834; *Sarochan v. Sarochan*, [1986] 2 S.C.R. 38; and *Peter v. Beblow*, [1993] 101 D.L.R. (4th) 621 (S.C.C.). These cases are discussed in Cassels and Philipps 1994, and by the Ontario Law Reform Commission 1993b, which has recommended the extension of property-division rules to all heterosexual common-law couples, and to same-sex couples who elect to file a document constituting them a 'Registered Domestic Partnership.'

22 For a general overview of the law in each province, see Holland and Bissett-Johnson, eds, 1980, and supplements; see also Hovius and Youdan 1991.

23 These and other problems are discussed variously in Cassels and Philipps 1994, Eichler 1990–1, Morton 1988, Kerr 1992, Mossman and MacLean 1986, and Rogerson 1990. See also Ontario Law Reform Commission 1993a, Wolfson 1989, and Zier 1994: 12.

24 See *Derrickson v. Derrickson*, [1986] 1 S.C.R. 306, and *Paul v. Paul*, [1986] 1 S.C.R. 306, and the analysis of these cases in Turpel 1991.

25 Oliver and Shapiro 1990.

26 Knight 1989.

27 Knight 1988: 9, 10.

28 See *Survey of Women Business Owners in B.C.* (British Columbia 1986), Knight 1989, *Women in Business* (British Columbia 1991), and Belcourt, Burke, and Lee-Gosselin 1991. I found one study that disputes these conclusions: Wynant and Hatch 1990. According to their data, women-owned businesses are smaller than men's in terms of both assets and sales, and women's average success rate in obtaining loans is indeed lower (exhibits 11.2 and 11.3). However, they conclude that the differences in financial institutions' treatment of male and female business owners is not statistically significant. The authors note that in follow-up interviews some women did attribute problems in dealing with banks to gender bias, but discount this experience by pointing out that men experience similar financing problems. They caution that women's concerns in this regard 'can be heightened by individual incidents and anecdotes that are widely repeated and popularized in the press,' suggesting that women are simply imagining sexism in the commercial world (p. 343).

29 According to Statistics Canada's *1986 Census: Profile of Ethnic Groups*, the average income for 'North American Indians' and 'Aboriginal Peoples' of single origins was approximately 68% of the Canadian average. The income of women from these groups was about 47% of the Canadian average: tables 2–39 and 1–64. The 1991 Aboriginal Peoples Survey indicates that 77% of aboriginal adults had incomes below $20,000, compared with 57% for the total adult population: Statistics Canada 1993a: xiv, xv. See also Canada, Secretary of State 1991: 20.

30 See the *Indian Act*, R.S.C. 1985, c. I–5, as am., ss.20, 24, 28, 29, 89, 90; and Woodward 1989: 220–33, and 288–94.

31 See Bherer, Gagnon, and Roberge 1990; Lemmon and Kirkpatrick 1990; and Tunnicliffe 1993.

32 Li 1988: 85–98 and 114–22.

33 Oliver and Shapiro 1990: 139. See also Wolff 1992: 555. Another study focusing on younger families found somewhat less extreme, though still very serious, racial wealth inequalities: Blau and Graham 1990.

34 See National Council of Welfare 1990: 115, and Statistics Canada 1990b, 1990a, and 1992a: 21. It is notable that the disability rate among aboriginal people is more than double that for the Canadian population as a whole (31% vs. 15%): Statistics Canada 1994: vii. This illustrates very clearly the intersecting nature of social categories such as gender, race, class, and disability.

35 See National Council of Welfare 1990: 99–103, and Gee and Kimball 1987: 53.
36 Blau and Graham (1990) have raised a similar alarm in the context of racial inequalities: 'Most studies of economic well-being focus solely on income, but if wealth differences are even greater, then these studies will underestimate racial inequality and policies that seek to narrow income differences will not be sufficient to close the wealth gap' 321–2.
37 A tax is generally termed 'progressive' when the rate of tax increases with the taxpayer's ability to pay. Conversely, 'regressive' taxes are those that impose relatively greater burdens on those with lesser ability to pay. Despite the progressive marginal rate structure of the federal income tax, the effective rate of all taxes on high-income people is not much greater than that on low- and middle-income earners. This is because progressivity is undermined by deductions and credits that tend to benefit high-income people and by the regressive impact of property taxes, sales taxes, and payroll taxes: See the Ontario FTC 1992a: 20–5; and Gillespie 1966.
38 See the *Income Tax Act*, R.S.C. 1985, c. 1 (5th Supp.) as am., s.56(1)(b),(c) and 60(b),(c), (alimony and maintenance), and s. 63 (child-care expenses). In May 1995, the Supreme Court of Canada rejected an equality-rights challenge to the taxation of child-support payments, holding that the tax system does not violate the equality guarantee in s. 15 of the *Charter of Rights and Freedoms*: see *Thibaudeau v. Canada* (court file no. 24154). The two women justices, McLachlin and L'Heureux-Dubé JJ., dissented. See Lisa Philipps and Margot Young, 'Sex, Tax and the *Charter*: A Review of *Thibaudeau v. Canada*,' 2 *Review of Constitutional Studies* 1995: 221, on the decision at the Federal Court of Appeal level, and Lisa Philipps, '*Thibaudeau v. Canada*: Tax Law versus Equality Rights?' *Canadian Bar Review* (forthcoming, 1995), for an analysis of the Supreme Court reasons. In the earlier case of *Symes v. The Queen*, [1993] 4 Supreme Court Reports 695 (December 16, 1993), the Supreme Court of Canada held that Revenue Canada's refusal to allow a self-employed woman to deduct child-care costs as a business expense did not contravene s.15 of the *Charter*. See Young 1994a. For an analysis of how women are unfavourably affected by these and other provisions of the Income Tax Act see Ontario FTC 1992b. Other studies examining the impact of the tax system on women include National Association of Women and the Law 1991, Lahey 1985, Maloney 1989 and 1993, and Woodman 1990, and Young 1994b and 1994c.
39 See the *Income Tax Act*, s.117(2), 122.5, 122.6, and 180.2.
40 See, for example, Bale 1989: 12; Bird 1972: 7–11; Brooks 1990: 18, 19; Hartle 1988: 420, 421; Maloney 1988; and Michalos 1988. Personal-wealth taxes are those based on some comprehensive measure of an individual's total wealth in all forms. They can take a variety of forms, including capital transfer taxes

(such as estate or inheritance taxes) and annual-net-worth taxes. Although they may exempt specific assets (for example, homes) or specific transfers (such as spousal bequests), they can be clearly distinguished from taxes imposed on only one type of asset, such as municial property taxes. For a description of different personal-wealth tax models see Ontario FTC 1993.

41 It has been estimated that less than 5% of Canadian taxpayers were affected by death taxes, and that these few held at least one-third of the country's total wealth at the time the federal estate tax was repealed: Bird 1970: 458, and Bird 1972: 11. According to then finance minister Edgar Benson, more than half of the revenue from the tax was collected from estates valued over $500,000: House of Commons Debates, 5 February 1969, 5179. One economist calculated that the repeal effectively relieved these individuals of about $12.5 billion in future taxes (Bossons 1972: 54, 55).

42 S.Q. 1986, c.15. Ontario repealed its *Succession Duty Act* as of 11 April 1979: S.O. 1979, c.20. For a more detailed analysis of this period of fiscal history, see Bird 1978.

43 See authors cited at note 40. There are of course opposing views: see, for example, Ward 1980, Wagner 1980, and Crawford 1993.

44 See Cassin 1993: 110–12.

45 See Olsen 1983, Pateman 1983, Barrett 1988, Gavigan 1988 and 1993, Fudge 1989, Williams 1991, Kline (1994), and Philipps and Young (1995).

46 *Income Tax Act*, s.73(1), s.70(6). These provisions generally applied only to legally married persons before 1 January 1993, when the definition of 'spouse' was broadened to include heterosexual common-law partners who have cohabited for at least a year or who have parented a child together: s.252(4).

47 *Estate Tax Act*, S.C. 1958, c.29, s.7(1), as am. by S.C. 1968–69, c.33m, s.3(1).

48 Hon. G.S. White, Debates, House of Commons, 7 May 1941, 2635.

49 See Cullity 1972: 47; and *Succession Duty Amendment Act*, S.O. 1970, c.51.

50 See MacKinnon 1987: 99–102.

51 In British Columbia, see the *Family Relations Act*, R.S.B.C. 1979, c.121, as am., Part 3, and the *Wills Variation Act*, R.S.B.C. 1979, c.435. The latter gives a discretionary power to the courts to make an award against a testator's estate, where a will does not 'make adequate provision for the proper maintenance and support of the testator's wife, husband or children': s.2. The Ontario counterparts are the *Family Law Act*, R.S.O. 1990, c.F.3, as am., and the *Succession Law Reform Act*, R.S.O. 1990, c.S.26, as am., Part V.

52 Olsen 1983: 1541. See also MacKinnon 1987: 38.

53 See Philipps 1992.

54 See, for example, Gardner 1981, MacDonald 1985, and Banting 1991.

55 New Democratic Party (Canada) 1976: 32–4.
56 *Strategy for a Full-Employment Economy* 1993: 56.
57 The Ontario Fair Tax Commission's Wealth Tax Working Group recently estimated that a full spousal exemption would reduce the revenue-raising capacity of a provincial estate tax by around 60% (OFTC 1993: B27).
58 See Bennett, Heys, and Coward 1980 for a discussion of this dilemma.

PART 3: GLOBALIZATION(S):
CHALLENGES AND ALTERNATIVE STRATEGIES

8

NAFTA and Economic Restructuring: Some Gender and Race Implications

CHRISTINA GABRIEL AND
LAURA MACDONALD

Recent changes in the global economy have prompted nation-states to adopt a variety of restructuring initiatives. Trade liberalization, as epitomized by the North American Free Trade Agreement (NAFTA) is one such strategy. NAFTA will facilitate the continental integration of the national economies of Canada, the United States, and Mexico. This process of restructuring is mediated by relations of gender, race, and culture and will likely produce contradictory and multiple outcomes for women within nation-states and between women in Canada and Mexico. These dimensions have largely been neglected in the debate around NAFTA.

Women in Canada, the United States, and Mexico are struggling to bring these issues to the fore. Gathering at Valle de Bravo for the First Trinational Working Women's Conference on Free Trade and Continental Integration, participants stated: 'Because economic integration is based explicitly on women's exploitation in the paid and unpaid labour force, we – Women in Mexico, Canada and the United States – demand that our respective governments guarantee basic rights to adequate education, health care, food, nutrition, housing, stability of employment, living salaries and training, voluntary maternity and peace (that is the ability to live free from violence) within any tri-lateral agreement.'[1] This chapter offers an assessment of some consequences of trade liberalization for women in the North and South. Women of colour,[2] regardless of their geographic location, occupy a particular position in the global economy. For this reason we have chosen to focus on the case of Third World women in Canada. In doing so we hope to highlight the complex political interconnections that exist between women in Canada and Mexico by considering the differing and multiple impacts of NAFTA on women, both within and between countries, and women's organizing responses.

NAFTA makes visible the common links that exist between Third World women in Mexico and their counterparts in Canada, within a post-colonial, global economy. These links, however, need to be contextualized. A singular focus on gender as an analytical category will ultimately lead to a flawed analysis. The effects of the current restructuring on women in Canada and Mexico must be understood relationally in terms of gender, race, and class. As Vasuki Nesiah states, 'Feminists cannot invoke "women" without speaking to the specific politics and conditions of struggle through which women are socially constructed and against which women are socially situated' (1993: 203). Thus, NAFTA also challenges feminists to confront the contradictions that exist between women. While the claim 'Sisterhood Is Global' has been challenged by Third World women for its universalizing and homogenizing direction, the subsequent recognition of 'difference' can often be reinscribed with neo-colonialist overtones. In these cases, as Mohanty (1991) has argued, the failure to develop a socially located analysis and acknowledge the particular struggles and agency of women casts Third World women in the role of 'victim' and Western feminists as the bearers of a transformatory and liberatory politics. In contrast, Nesiah calls for a 'feminist internationality' that confronts the notion of universality embodied in global sisterhood and speaks to a transnational political alliance of women whose differences are 'acknowledged ... and are confronted rather than ignored' (1993: 190).

Thus, feminist organizing must confront the differences and tensions that exist between women arising from race, class, and imperialism, particularly as these cleavages are implicated in the process of hemispheric restructuring. Organizing by women in Canada and Mexico may hold the prospect for a feminist internationality insofar as it creates the potential for cross-cultural and cross-national feminist solidarity and organizing (Gabriel and Macdonald, 1994: 536).

Canada – From the Local to the Global: Free Trade Round Two

Trade liberalization, in concert with the privatization of, or cuts to, many of the functions of the welfare state, is responsible, in part, for the ongoing and dramatic restructuring of the Canadian economy. Women in Canada, as women's groups predicted during the 1987 free-trade debate,[3] have borne the brunt of this restructuring. In general, women's position in the labour market has worsened. More women are working part time. One in five Canadian women today is either unemployed or underemployed and the '49% of women who work on less than a full time, full year basis suffered an 8.2% fall in real earnings between 1989 and 1991' (Canadian Labour Congress, 1993: 1). And, increasingly, women's employment has been characterized by a shift from direct to indirect forms of work. It is expected that NAFTA will intensify and accelerate this ongoing process of restructuring, because it incorporates elements of the existing U.S.-Canada FTA and expands it by adding sectors.

The Gender and Racial Implications of Economic Restructuring

In assessing the consequences of trade liberalization we would argue, however, that the overall impact of economic restructuring on women cannot be considered in terms of gender relations alone. A singular focus on gender not only supports the dominant construction of Canada as white, but also ignores the fact that relations of class, gender, and race are mutually constituted and both shape and structure the subordination of differing groups of women. Consequently, the current social and economic changes resulting from trade liberalization are inadequately theorized and understood when gender is given priority. In an effort to move beyond an account of patriarchy and 'women,' and consider the articulation between racism, class relations, and gender, we briefly examine the effects of trade liberalization on women of colour in Canada.

As Swasti Mitter has demonstrated in *Common Fate, Common Bond* (1986), the mobility of international capital is predicated on the politics of race and gender. The process of uneven capitalist development on a global scale has been a major factor in the large-scale migration of peoples from the Third World to the industrialized economies of the North. It is this experience that informs the active opposition of many Third World women in Canada to NAFTA. As the Coalition for Visible Minority Women told the recent Ontario Cabinet Committee on NAFTA:

Free trade and free trade zones are all too familiar to us. They conjure up memories of low wages, horrific working and living conditions, sexual harassment, and the suppression of union organizing. We remember governments all too willing to suppress the democratic rights of their citizens in order to compete for the 'prizes' offered by transnationals.

We are familiar with all this because the free trade zone experiment was piloted and refined in third world countries, like Korea, Hong Kong, Taiwan, Indonesia and Malaysia, Philippines, India and Sri Lanka. Many women were casualties of free trade in their home countries – that's why they left. Filipino domestic workers have told us, 'We've been squeezed dry once and now it is happening again.'[4]

These women arrived in Canada as part of the global division of labour that is underpinned by colonial exploitation (Mitter 1986a). In Canada, as Roxanna Ng has argued, they constituted a labour-market category – 'immigrant women.'[5] Ng observes that 'non-English speaking women, particularly those from visible minority groups tend to be concentrated in the bottom rungs of most service and manufacturing sectors in the so-called "non-skilled" and dead-end positions' (Ng 1990: 107).

Many women of colour, as they are all too aware, are particularly vulnerable to the ongoing processes of restructuring because of their social location in Canadian society. This location itself is rooted in the narratives of 'colonialism and imperialism in which white settler colonies, like Canada, played a subordinate but favoured role. The economy still continues along the same imperialist path and its long worked up ideology of racism still continues to be the important ideological force' (Bannerji 1993: 146). Not surprisingly, systemic racism as well as sexism mediates the entry of women of colour into the labour market.

Women of colour were constructed as 'immigrant women' and as 'dependent.'[6] Any skills or training they received in their countries of origin was often devalued upon their entry to Canada. Moreover, the failure of the federal government to provide adequate job and language training to those it designated as not destined for the labour market – read dependant on a male breadwinner – and systemic racism forced many of these women into occupational job ghettos. As a result, many Third World women are heavily over-represented in 'declining' industries including clothing, textile, and leather products.[7] Not surprisingly, these sectors are projected to be highly affected by NAFTA. What kind of adjustment support can these women expect?

In an effort to confront changes in the economic environment and address the structural weaknesses in the economy that trade liberalization deepens and intensifies, the Province of Ontario's 1992 Industrial Policy supports a sectoral development approach. Through a tripartite arrangement the government's Sector Partnership Fund 'will provide $150 million over three years to approved cooperative sector projects that strengthen the competitive fundamentals and promote sector development.'[8] However, despite the policy's familiar espousal of 'equity' and 'fairness' and the recognition of 'traditionally disadvantaged groups,' it is questionable whether this strategy will be targeted at the sectors in which women work, and if it is, whether women workers will benefit. As the International Ladies' Garment Workers Union and INTERCEDE recently wrote: 'The impact of the industrial policy on women in the labour market has not been analyzed. How will immigrant women benefit from this policy? To date, there is no sectoral adjustment or partnership for industries or sectors dominated by immigrant women and workers within the most vulnerable sections of the labour market' (ILGWU and INTERCEDE, 1993: 6). Similarly, the Coalition of Visible Minority Women, commenting on the negative effect of the FTA on the garment industry and its workers, questioned, 'We often wonder whether the fate of the industry would have been the same if these industries were staffed with white, able-bodied men whose first language was English. Maybe there would have been stronger public outcry and earlier government intervention.'[9]

The experience of the 1988 FTA demonstrates that there will be few if any adequate industrial or labour adjustment programs to address changes in women's economic roles because of trade-liberalization strategies. Under NAFTA there is no commitment on the part of the federal government to provide any new labour adjustment measures. This fact has significant consequences for women, and most particularly women of colour.

Labour adjustment is generally difficult for all groups of displaced women workers. Women's family responsibilities may limit their flexibility to relocate or retrain. Existing programs are often characterized by lack of child-care provisions, as well as inadequate and unsuitable curricula for women. A 1993 Ontario Ministry of Labour study of displaced workers concluded that women take a greater cut in pay compared with men when displaced: 'Women fare worse than men. This statement is true even if all other factors – such as displacement, income, tenure, education, success in finding a new job, occupation at displacement and the industry of the old job and of the new job are taken into account and held constant. In other words, after controlling for all other factors that explain post displacement earning differential – *the fact of being a woman costs the displaced worker $2,283*' (Ontario Ministry of Labour, 1993: 10). The same study indicates that the negative consequences of displacement are greatest for those with longer tenure in the displaced job, those who worked as semi-skilled production operatives, those with less education, and women. These results are particularly significant for women of colour working in NAFTA-sensitive industries such as textiles, electrical products, and clothing. A majority of these workers (Jones and Huff 1989: 22) fall into one or more of the risk categories identified by the Ministry of Labour study. As other data indicate:

Immigrant women are not responding as effectively to changing labour markets as non-immigrant women. There are many possible explanations for this, including language problems, difficulties with recognition of credentials and discrimination in the labour market.

The experience of more recently arrived immigrant women from traditional sources (i.e. Europe and North America) supports the structural change model [i.e., immigrants respond to the need for labour in expanding parts of the economy, thereby facilitating structural change] whereas evidence for recent immigrants from non-traditional sources (i.e. Asia, Africa, Caribbean and Bermuda, Central and South America, and Oceania and other) does not support the model. (Seward and Tremblay, 1989: ix)

These findings underscore that women of colour who are displaced in the current context of restructuring will likely experience a difficult adjustment process.

As we have attempted to illustrate, the current costs of restructuring and the resulting economic insecurity have not been spread evenly within Canada. The labour market is increasingly polarized.[10] The terms 'core' and 'periphery' are often used to describe this stratification. The former refers to secure, stable, unionized, full-time jobs with benefits (white, male jobs), while the latter refers to non-unionized, non-standard forms of work. The description, however problematic, is not without irony given the fact that many of the workers in the 'periphery' of the internal labour market originate from the Third World. Changes in the labour market replicate and strengthen existing gender and racial divisions.

Economic insecurity has been a common experience of many people of colour in Canada. As Dionne Brand argues, the reality of black women's lives dictated that they could not subscribe to a notion of white femininity, in which females play the role of a passive dependent wife reliant on a male breadwinner, because black men have never had access to the intrinsically racist power structures developed during slavery, colonialism, or the current phase of capitalism. Consequently, she argues, 'Black women have always had to work as a condition of their race. It is not, then, a question of the right to work outside the home, but a matter of economic imperative of wage work and a question of the kind of work available to them' (1993: 231). Any assessment of the impact of restructuring on women of colour has to consider how their male counterparts fare. If these men are structurally positioned in declining sectors and/or those that are NAFTA-sensitive, the process of restructuring will deepen already existing inequalities. Women of colour will necessarily have to take whatever work is available.

Similarly, the same processes have to some extent sharpened the divisions that exist between groups of women. Recent 1991 Canadian census data indicate that seven out of ten women work in just five occupational groups: teaching, nursing or other health-related occupations, clerical, sales, or services. Job ghettoization and occupational segregation are particular problems for Third World women.[11] The same data also highlighted the fact that female economists, lawyers, accountants, and auditors all increased in number. These women, a small group of affluent workers in the core, are increasingly held up as the example other women should emulate. It has been argued, however, that one possible outcome of earnings, skill, and job polarization is that economic and political differences among women will increase (Bakker 1991: 272).

Where most women cope with domestic responsibilities by working part time, doing shift work, and relying on family networks, more affluent women can purchase domestic labour. Indeed, INTERCEDE, an advocacy organization for domestic workers, reports that the 'demand for domestic workers has exceeded supply especially for live-in domestic workers who are available to their employers 24 hours a day' (ILGWU/INTERCEDE 1993: 6). The commodification of domestic labour itself has created a source of employment for migrant Third World women workers. However, this employment is characterized by lack of status, low pay, few benefits, and little legislative protection. These factors render domestic workers, as well as industrial home-workers, the archetypal flexible worker.

Indeed, employers have responded to changes in the economic environment by adopting a 'flexible low cost labour strategy.'[12] In such an environment, plants downsize, relocate, or close down. Wherever possible, capital attempts to lower direct labour costs. Under the provisions of NAFTA, these trends will continue. The garment industry in Ontario offers a case in point. As the International Ladies' Garment Workers Union told the Ontario Cabinet Committee on NAFTA: 'Our main fight today, thanks to free trade, is on two fronts: first, against plant closures and secondly, with the rise of homework as a low wage strategy here in Canada. We are seeing sweatshops emerge in Toronto similar to sweatshops at the turn of the century' (1993: 1). Homeworkers often earn below the minimum wage and receive few or no benefits (Cameron and Mak 1991). The ILGWU reports that garment manufacturing is often the first and only source of employment for women, particularly immigrant women. In Metro Toronto, in 1986, 94 per cent of all sewing-machine operators were born outside Canada (ILGWU 1993: 2). Increasingly, as women's available employment options are severely curtailed, they are often forced to turn to homework. Thus, the ILGWU has so eloquently argued: 'When we examine the impact of free trade on the garment industry we are not looking at a neutral labour market, we are attacking an industry made up mainly of women and most often immigrant women' (1993: 2). Homework is but one expression of the fragmentation of women's work and the growing inequality many women are experiencing because of trade-liberalization policies such as the FTA and NAFTA.

Challenging the Outcomes of Trade Liberalization: Women's Organizing Efforts[13]

The negative experience of the FTA has prompted many women to organize a concerted opposition to NAFTA. Women have organized against NAFTA – in feminist groups, in their communities, through their unions – and have worked in broad-based coalitions such as the Action Canada Network (ACN). However, what distinguishes women's organizing around NAFTA from the earlier mobilization against the FTA is the explicit recognition of global restructuring and the espousal of international solidarity by more mainstream groups such as the National Action Committee on the Status of Women (NAC).

In October 1991 NAC set up a Global Strategies committee. Linda Yanz,[14] a member of the committee, stated that it had a mandate to monitor the impact of free trade and economic restructuring on women, to foster a network of women activists across Canada, and to strengthen NAC's commitment to international solidarity. She reported that its efforts bore fruit by NAC's next annual meeting in June 1992, when members not only endorsed a campaign against NAFTA, but also called for new ties to be forged with international women's groups. This meeting also included guests from Nicaragua, the Philippines, South Africa,

Chile, Mexico, the United States, and South Africa – a marked contrast to NAC's previous AGM, when two international guests did not play a significant role in the proceedings except for one workshop on free trade. Yanz observed: 'The change represents a shift in NAC ... and a growing consciousness within the women's movement – including NAC's leadership – that international solidarity must somehow become a more integral component to women's struggles in Canada' (Yanz 1992: 3). NAC has also initiated a cross-country participatory research and popular-education project called the Future of Women's Work Campaign. It will highlight the experiences of older women, displaced fishery workers, women with disabilities, domestic workers, visible-minority women, and aboriginal women in the home, in the workplace, and in their communities. It aims 'to document and make visible the changing trends in women's work and to examine/consider these trends within the context of restructuring of the Canadian and global economies' (NAC 1993: 1). The Domestic Worth Project in Ontario focuses on domestic workers; its coordinators are already reporting that the experience domestic workers from the Philippines left behind is similar to the current experience of Canadian women.

There are other independently based Woman to Woman and Global strategies groups working in NAC's national network, based in Toronto and Vancouver. In 1991, Women to Women Global Strategies and the British Columbia Federation of Labour Women's Committee sponsored a joint tour on free trade. They invited two Mexican women activists to participate. Of their visit Denise Nadeau, a member of Women to Women Global Strategies, wrote: 'We got much inspiration from these women who, with fewer resources to work with, were working to build a new solidarity both nationally and internationally. We also learned that Mexican women, as well as American women along the U.S./Mexican border, were looking at strategies that move beyond the workplace into the neighbourhood and were using methods of organizing that have a strong cultural dimension' (Nadeau 1992: 162). BC women adopted several strategies to confront NAFTA.[15]

In Toronto, a broad-based coalition of community groups, unions, and women's organizations have joined together in The Coalition for Fair Wages and Working Conditions for Homeworkers to address the issue of flexible labour.[16] Drawing on the organizing experiences of the Leicester Outworkers Campaign and the West Yorkshire Homeworkers' Unit, the coalition adopted a strategy to raise consumer awareness. The Clean Clothes Campaign asks consumers to buy garments from manufacturers who pay fair wages and provide decent and safe working conditions. It has significantly raised consumers' awareness of homeworking. Similarly, its postcard campaign exerted pressure on retailers such as Eaton's and The Bay, forcing them to confront, if not actually acknowledge, their role in the rise of homeworking. The efforts of the coalition also brought the issue of homework to the forefront of the women's movement. The theme figured prominently in the 1993 International Women's Day (IWD) event in Toronto, when IWD marchers stormed the Eaton Centre and targeted retail stores that were not carrying clean clothes. The coalition's efforts forced the Ontario government to consider ways and means of providing employment protection for homeworkers. By November 1993 the government introduced limited protection. These fell short of the coalition's demand, however, that retailers be held jointly responsible for the failure of their suppliers to observe employment standards.

In conjunction with the Clean Clothes Campaign, the ILGWU is attempting to organize homeworkers into a Homeworkers' Association – the first union-initiated association of its kind. To this end, the ILGWU has had to adopt strategies developed and pioneered by community and women's groups outside of Canada. Many of the organizing initiatives developed by Third World women, such as those pioneered in India by the Self Employed Women's Association (SEWA), demonstrate that homeworkers can be organized. In February 1992, the ILGWU hired a community organizer to recruit members. 'The most successful tool of the homework drive involved extending the traditional notion of organizing to include social activities, especially for families' (Borowy 1993: 310).

Building on this organizing initiative, the coalition and the Public Service Alliance of Canada (PSAC) sponsored a conference on organizing around homework. It brought together workers, community activists, and researchers from England, Mexico, Nicaragua, and the United States. More than one hundred homeworkers, unionists, and researchers attended. This meeting highlighted the extent to which homework, both telework and industrial homework, was a low-wage strategy and the global dimensions of its scope.

Increasingly, women in Canada are recognizing the need to build links globally and to find strength in the collective experience of women if we are to confront the consequences of economic restructuring. As one Canadian participant told women at the First Trinational Working Women's Conference on Free Trade and Continental Integration (February 1992):

We didn't come here to tell our Mexican and U.S. sisters what to do. But we did feel a responsibility to come and share what three years living with the FTA has meant for women.

We're excited about what we accomplished together. We go home feeling stronger knowing that we will be working in coalition with our sisters in the U.S. and Mexico to ensure a just and equal place for women in our economies.[17]

Mexican Women and NAFTA

Canadian women tend to anticipate the effects of NAFTA through their experiences with the FTA. In contrast, in Mexico, the twin processes of expansion of the *maquiladora* sector on the U.S.-Mexican border and of earlier economic liberalization initiatives provide a basis to assess the impact of NAFTA on women. Some analysts believe that the most important aspect of the NAFTA agreement for Mexico is its entrenchment of earlier economic reforms, making it difficult for subsequent governments to adopt more egalitarian or nationalistic economic development programs (Grinspun and Kreklewich 1994). Women, already suffering the brunt of structural adjustment, will be affected by the consolidation and extension of that process in the form of NAFTA.

Consolidating a Neo-Liberal Program: Gender Outcomes

The experience of the *maquila* sector is significant for evaluating the gendered effects of NAFTA. Women's availability as low-wage workers is the major attraction for foreign companies to the existing *maquilas*, mostly located on the U.S.-Mexican border. Some analysts believe NAFTA will turn Mexico into a 'giant *maquiladora*,' based on the expansion of female-dominated, labour-intensive, low-wage, transnational-owned industry with a largely female force throughout the territory of Mexico (Kopinak 1993: 157). The *maquila* industry is a particularly important sector for gauging the future impact of NAFTA on women. Organizing by Mexican women in response to NAFTA has concentrated to a large extent on the problems faced by women workers in the *maquiladoras*.

Both NAFTA and the Border Industrialization Program (BIP), which created the *maquiladora* sector, result from Mexico's subordinate position in the international division of labour in general and its specific relationship with the United States. The Mexican government's transition from a highly nationalist position to an espousal of free trade cannot be explained without taking into account Mexico's dependency on the United States, the failure of import-substituting industrialization, and the crisis of the peasant economy. The debt crisis gave international actors greater leverage over domestic policies and encouraged 'modernizing' élites to adopt neo-liberal economic policies.

Assessments of Mexico's political economy have tended to neglect changing forms of gender subordination and their articulation with multinational corporation strategies. Women working in the *maquilas* in many ways 'embody and personify the intersection of sexual, class, and racial ideologies' (Mohanty 1991: 28).

Ironically, the *maquiladora* or Border Industrialization Program (BIP), which resulted in the large-scale integration of women into the Mexican industrial labour force, was originally initiated as an attempt to respond to the problem of *male* unemployment in the border region (Bustamante 1983: 233).[18] The BIP encouraged the establishment of assembly plants or *maquiladoras* by U.S. firms to take advantage of low labour costs in Mexico. The U.S. government hoped (as with the NAFTA initiative) that Mexican industrialization, in addition to increasing U.S. firms' profitability, would deter the entry of Mexican 'wetbacks' into the United States (ibid.: 236).

The 'success' of the BIP cannot be understood without an analysis of the changing sociological patterns in the Mexican border region. According to Jorge Bustamante, in 1975, approximately 90 per cent of the 56,253 workers in the *maquiladoras* were women (1983: 252). Female employment has declined to current levels of 68 per cent for reasons we will explore below. One study (Tiano 1990) showed that more than a third of the women workers in the *maquiladoras* lived in households with no adult male members. In other households, women's salaries made a vital contribution to the family economy. Moreover, it should be noted that the economic crisis of the 1980s has reduced real wages, so that families require two or three minimum wages just to survive (Kopinak 1993: 156).

As in other world-market factories, the reasons for the employment of women centre on their gender-ascribed characteristics: they are viewed as possessing greater manual dexterity, as bearing tedium better than men, and as being less likely to cause trouble by affiliating with unions. Employers view women's 'docility' and 'nimble fingers' as inherent, natural qualities, ignoring the role of gender socialization and the training that women receive in skills such as sewing from an early age (Elson and Pierson 1981). The preferred employees are young, single women.

William Mitchell, an expert on the *maquila* industry in Juárez, describes the policy: 'Put yourself in place of the guy who has a plant. Experience shows that they have trouble with married vs. single women. The old man gets sick and she has to take off. She is more subject to have children, and if she has children, they get sick and she drops off. He is down there taking the money away. You could go on and on' (ibid.: 34). As new sectors, such as the automobile industry, are converted into *maquiladoras*, the rate of female employment tends to rise (Kopinak 1993: 147). However, the rapid expansion of the industry since 1982 has resulted in reduced availability of the desired young, single, educated female employees. Instead of raising wages, management has increasingly hired men (ibid.: 148).

Many conventional analyses of the macroeconomic impact of the *maquiladora* program and the likely impact of NAFTA ignore the gender dimension of economic restructuring in Mexico. Among those who do examine the high levels of integration of women into the workforces in export-assembly industries, there are several different perspectives. Supporters of the *maquilas* argue, from a modernization perspective, that they offer positive opportunities for gainful employment that will contribute to the erosion of traditional norms that lead to the subordination of women. Ellwyn Stoddard argues, for example: 'Compared to other wages and working conditions available in the same community or region, maquiladora wages are consistently higher and working conditions mostly better' (1987: 63). As well, 'Comparisons of multinational maquiladoras and those which are Mexican-owned show that the female worker in the former has a much better ambient, more benefits, less harassment, and can avoid supervisor pressures more readily than in the Mexican-owned plants. Yet feminist critics have almost exclusively focused on the multinationals in their search for better treatment for women' (ibid.: 66). Male incomes are higher than female incomes in the *maquiladoras* as a result of the type of jobs they perform, with more men in 'professional' positions, to which Mexican labour law assigns higher minimum wage scales: 'Thus, gender-wage differentials are a function of government policy, not arbitrary managerial antifemale actions as some have claimed' (ibid.: 66). From this perspective, NAFTA would represent a clear benefit to women, since it would expand the availability of these higher-wage jobs. It is true that gender wage differentials are encouraged by state policy that undervalues women's skills, but multinational corporations are attracted to Mexico precisely because of this gender subordination.

Analysts on the left frequently share the modernization perspective that women's traditional subordination can be addressed through the integration of women into the labour force (Elson and Pierson 1981: 144). However, in the context of debate around NAFTA, opponents of the deal in the United States and Canada often focus on the high rates of female employment in the *maquilas* as a sign of the dangers to Northern (white male) workers. Employment of women is portrayed almost as an unfair labour practice, in the same category as child labour.

Critics focus on the low wages paid to women workers in contrast to Canadian and American industrial wages, the long working hours, the abysmal living conditions, the endemic sexual harassment of workers, and the health risks to workers in the *maquilas* and those living nearby as a result of toxic dumping. While these analysts correctly identify the abusive and exploitative conditions often associated with employment in the *maquilas*, there is a tendency to portray women workers as passive victims of the multinational corporations, ignoring their status as subjects – 'as agents who make choices, have a critical perspective on their own situations, and think and organize collectively against their oppressors' (Mohanty 1991: 29). The *Wall Street Journal*, for example, described Mexican *maquiladora* workers as 'joining the ranks of the most crudely exploited humans on the planet. The result has been conditions along the Mexican side of the border that rival any of the well-publicized disasters of the worst Stalinist regimes' (quoted in Sinclair 1992: 57). NAFTA critics also frequently ignore the heterogeneity of women working in the *maquilas*.

More sensitive accounts of the lives of women Mexican workers describe the ambiguities and contradictions of their situation. Although *maquila* salaries are abysmally low compared with those paid to workers in the North, they still are relatively high compared with those of other available jobs. Carrillo's study shows workers in the *maquilas* in Monterrey, Juárez and Tijuana to be earning almost three times the legal minimum wage (Kopinak 1993: 156). As well, as Swasti Mitter states, it is not surprising that 'in a trade-off between the oppression of family life and the drudgery of ill-paid work, most women prefer the latter.' Susan Tiano's survey (1990) of *maquiladora* workers suggests that women in Mexico, like women in the North, express a complex mixture of motives and opinions about their work. They are not, as the 'agentless' approach would suggest, driven purely out of desperation, but work both out of economic necessity and for personal satisfaction.

Also, in contrast to the *Wall Street Journal* version, there are important elements of economic stratification among women workers. According to María Patricia Fernández-Kelly, the women working in the most 'modern' electric/electronics branch of the *maquiladora* sector tend to be young (with a median age of twenty-one years), single, and relatively well educated.[19] Most of them left their homes as young women to find jobs in the *maquilas*, and therefore can be considered urban rather than rural. The textile and garment factories, by contrast, employ older women with less than six years of schooling. Moreover, women's employment opportunities are considerably more diversified. The border cities are highly tertiarized, with large informal sectors. Jobs are also available for women in the service sector, homeworking, and as domestic servants. As these positions tend to be unstable, and associated with lower pay and few benefits, the *maquila* jobs are seen as the most desirable, and are occupied by women who are relatively privileged compared with the Mexican population as a whole.

However, the same woman may occupy diverse occupational locations throughout her lifetime, depending on her age, marital status, and socially constrained choices. The high turnover rate in the *maquila* sector has been frequently commented upon. Job tenure in the sector averages only three years. According to Fernández-Kelly (1983: 220), there are multiple reasons for the transitory nature of the work experience. In part, employers discourage permanent employment by either laying women off or persuading them to leave voluntarily. The highly repetitive, monotonous, and accelerated nature of the work process means most women cannot tolerate the working conditions indefinitely and many choose to leave to enter other forms of employment.

As well, women leave in order to marry, to have a child, or to care for their children. Women who marry or have children are expected to return to the home to perform their 'normal role.' At this point they may perform homework or work in the informal sector while caring for children. Homework is paid considerably less than *maquiladora* work, but does not conflict as much with patriarchal norms and also permits women to perform the household labour that their male partners are unlikely to assume. However, because of economic exigencies, women usually have to return to the formal labour market, where their labour is undervalued because of the fact they are married or have children, so they are unlikely to be hired in the electronics *maquiladoras*. They are then forced either to seek work in the textile and apparel industries or to travel to the United States as undocumented workers.

As is clear from this account, the *maquiladoras* may provide increased autonomy, income, and status within the household for some women, but the women who are seen as desirable workers represent only a small fraction of the total Mexican female population. As indicated above, the rapid expansion of the *maquiladora* sector in the 1980s did not erode these corporate preferences for young, educated women, but rather led to increased masculinization of the workforce. According to Gary Gereffi, 'the stereotype of Mexico's *maquiladora* plants as being unsophisticated, female-dominated, labour-intensive operations is no longer accurate. The last decade has witnessed the emergence of new technology- and capital-intensive *maquiladora* plants, especially in automobile-related manufacturing and advanced electronics assembly, that employ much higher percentages of skilled male workers' (1992: 36). This trend is likely to continue with the implementation of NAFTA, although it is unlikely that the 'old' *maquiladoras* will disappear. NAFTA may lead to the increased segmentation of the workforce, with the 'old' *maquiladoras* continuing to exercise a downward pressure on wages. The implications of NAFTA for women's participation in the industrial labour force are thus unclear. The existing *maquiladora* model, however, has clear limits on its contribution to women's empowerment and economic status.

The provisions on services in NAFTA will also probably lead to the expansion of transborder service industries in Mexico, including software programming and data processing. According to Gereffi, these changes 'move us beyond the "global factory to the global office," where white collar as well as blue collar jobs will be networked from disparate sites around the world' (ibid.: 150). While Gereffi says nothing of 'pink collar' jobs, it is likely that women will be heavily integrated into the labour force in these service industries. At the same time, 10,000 to 13,000 women's jobs are threatened by the privatization of Telmex, the government phone company, and the introduction of digital technology (Nadeau 1992: 158).

The impact of NAFTA and economic restructuring may be even greater on rural women. The Mexican agrarian sector has been undergoing a sustained economic crisis for several decades, resulting from the commercialization of agriculture, monetization of the peasant economy, and a stagnant market for agricultural labour. Women, who provide much of the household and agricultural labour in rural communities, and who have had to sustain their families despite declining rural incomes, have been the hardest hit. Young women were the first to migrate from rural areas, because discrimination against women in agriculture, commerce, and services meant there were more local opportunities for employment for young men (Arizpe and Botey 1987: 78).

Currently, the combined effects of Mexico's entry into the GATT, IMF-induced structural adjustment, and NAFTA have already led to rapid privatization in the agricultural sector, eroding the traditional *ejido* (collective farm) system and subsistence production. Previous Mexican policy, including high producer prices and consumer food-price subsidies, has been dismantled. Agricultural tariff reduction that would occur under the Uruguay Round agreement and NAFTA would undermine peasant basic-grains producers and increase the commercialization of agriculture (Josling 1992). The already significant proletarianization and semi-proletarianization of peasant women is therefore likely to increase under NAFTA, 'freeing' women to migrate to the border region, Mexico City, or the United States, or to serve as a seasonal labour force on the agribusiness estates (Arizpe and Botey 1987: 79–80). Homeworking is also an option for rural women, although increased competition from cheap imports has restricted employment in national industry. Arizpe and Botey warn that, while proletarianization is likely to continue, this trend remains 'invisible' to both the state and social institutions (ibid.: 80).

Gender Responses to Trade Liberalization[20]

Mexican women have not remained passive in the face of these challenges. However, the heterogeneity of Mexican women has meant that they have organized in diverse ways. Some have attempted to work within labour unions to organize women and push traditional unions to take account of women's needs and demands. However, the very nature of the *maquiladora* industry makes union organizing difficult. As well, official Mexican unions are closely tied to the governing party and supportive of government policy, including NAFTA. Ana Maria Flores from the Centro de Integración y Desarrollo Humano en América Latina summarized the frustrations involved in the struggle to democratize unions at the trinational meeting of women workers in 1992: 'The issue isn't whether or not we want unions, but rather what kind of new unionism do we want. What alternative can we develop to patriarchal, paternalistic unionism? What are we going to do about demands for productivity? We've been talking about a democratization campaign – but we've been in that very struggle for decades now, and the independent unions are full of the same practices as the authoritarian ones.'

Mexican unions, whether official or independent, have historically failed to recognize the specific problems of women workers, even if a majority of their members were women (Red Mexicana 1992: 231).

Because of the specific nature of gender issues, union strategies focused solely on the workplace fail to address the intersections of the public and private spheres, of production and reproduction, which lead to women's subordination. Like Third World women in Canada, Mexican women are seeking new ways of organizing that bring together these domains. Gloria Tello, a Mexican woman with an NGO that organizes in the border areas, states:

The tremendous mobility among *maquiladora* workers and the exhaustion caused by the double day make it very difficult to organize among these women. That's why we feel we can work better in the neighbourhoods. Women feel strongly connected to their communities, and they are supported by being able to be close to their families ... Women don't compartmentalize the world – they integrate the work lives with their home lives.

The city itself and the transformation of the cultural of these women who have immigrated in from other parts of the country are elements we have to take very seriously as we develop new forms of organizing. ('Memoria Testimonial' 1992: 13)

Mexican women have also been active in the struggle for political democratization at the national and regional levels. Ana Alicia Cepeda from *Mujeres en Lucha por la Democracia* (Women Struggling for Democracy) states that 'the combination of women and democracy produces a dangerous mixture for perfect dictatorships' (Red Mexicana 1992: 141). The opposition in Mexico has demanded that any North American accord target the authoritarian nature of the Mexican political system.

Mexican women are just beginning to develop a gender analysis of NAFTA (*Correspondencia* 1992: 26). According to Ximena Bedregal and Norma Mogrovejo, the Mexican feminist movement has until recently focused largely on concrete, short-term demands related to women's different forms of reproduction: biological, cultural, and social. So far, feminists have failed to develop alternatives at the global level. Bedregal and Mogrovejo argue, however, that feminism's epistemological position, which denies 'the possibility of a single truth' as an answer to social problems, means feminists can present a broader perspective on NAFTA.[21] In this respect, feminism supports the democratic project that is such a crucial element of oppositional politics in Mexico: 'As a civilizing project [democracy] has sought to recuperate the diverse knowledges of women which the patriarchal system has made invisible. The alternative to NAFTA thus must emerge by drawing out each specific aspect of the deal: the urban, the environmental, the cultural, the productive, the symbolic, the economic ... to counterpose them in a creative ... fashion to the unitary logic imposed by the new order. It is necessary to understand that NAFTA is not just an economic project, but a specific route to a new totalizing social project which signals one single path toward a supposed development' (Red Mexicana 1992: 238). Women's groups have participated in the opposition to the NAFTA initiative in Mexico. However, unlike the Action Canada Network, which has focused on demands for abrogation of the FTA and NAFTA, the Red Mexicana de Acción frente al Libre Comercio (RMALC) has focused on long-term analysis and alternative strategies for regional trade that respect human rights and the environment. Mexican women are also establishing linkages with women in Canada and the United States aimed at challenging the underlying logic of current processes of trade liberalization that ignore the effects on women.

Conclusions: Towards a Feminist Internationality

Women are recognizing that an analysis of the global economy based on a centre-periphery division provides an insufficient guide to action. Multinational strategies are articulated with divisions in the labour force based on gender, ethnicity, age, and class in all parts of the world (Nash 1983: 3). Feminist strategies in response to NAFTA must reflect the differences not just between women in the North and in the South, but between women *within* both the North and the South. Unlike the Free Trade Agreement between Canada and the United States or that of the European Economic Community, NAFTA brings together two advanced industrialized countries with a developing country with high levels of poverty and social and economic inequalities. It thus raises difficult issues of race, class, development, and imperialism. Nevertheless, NAFTA also provides a common context of struggle, and as such it is a valuable point of encounter between women from the North and from the South. Initial organizing links do demonstrate the potential for the creation of a new form of internationality based on respect for difference.

NOTES

We would like to thank Teresa Healy for the use of her files and William Walters for his helpful comments. Some of the themes and ideas introduced in this paper regarding women's organizing and trinational responses to NAFTA are further developed in our paper 'NAFTA, Women and Organizing in Canada and Mexico: Forging a "Feminist Internationality," in *Millennium*, 23 (3) (Winter 1994).

1 From *Women's Plan of Action*, resulting from discussions that took place at the First Trinational Working Women's Conference on Economic Integration and Free Trade, Valle de Bravo, Toluca, Mexico, February 1992.

2 For the purposes of this paper, 'Third World women' and 'women of colour' are used interchangeably in an effort to, as Chandra Mohanty writes, designate a 'political constituency, not a biological or even a sociological one. It is a sociopolitical designation for people of African, Caribbean, Asian and Latin American descent ... What seems to constitute 'women of colour' or 'third world women' as a viable oppositional alliance is a *common context of struggle* rather than colour or racial identifications.' Mohanty 1991: 7.

3 The National Action Committee on the Status of Women (NAC) waged a hard-fought battle around the FTA. For an account of this struggle see Bashevkin 1991.

4 Ng 1993. The Coalition is an umbrella group representing members from 12 different communities.

5 Ng (1990) points out, 'Not all women who are landed immigrants, however are considered to be 'immigrant women'. In everyday life, when we think of immigrant women, we have an image of a woman who does not speak English properly, who is a member of a minority group, notably from the Third World and who has a certain location in the labour market (i.e. sewing machine operator or a cleaning lady). In other words, the term 'immigrant women' is a legal, social and labour market category.'

6 As Dionne Brand points out, 'with the exception of ... [the] early immigration of Chinese men and of Black women, immigration policy has always certified men's control of women by ruling that women with spouses come as dependents' (1984: 33). Similarly, Tania Das Gupta notes, 'Immigrant women have traditionally entered Canada as "family class" or sponsored relatives of their husbands, fathers or sons. As such, we were seen as "dependents" and not recognized as equal members of society. As dependents, our skills and education are not taken seriously and our contributions represented by waged work and rearing of families is not given much recognition. In fact, our potential as labourers is hidden in official labour statistics categories.

Our employment is part-time seasonal and piece work is not reflected in the yearly records of national work activity' (1986: 16).

7 Non-traditional female immigrants – that is, those from Asia, Africa, the Caribbean and Bermuda, Central and South America, and Oceania – account for 23.5% of employment in the clothing industries, 12.3% of employment in textiles, and 10.8% of employment in leather products. They account for 6.3% of the total female labour force. (Note: these figures do not include women of colour who were born in Canada.) Tremblay 1989.

8 From 'An Industrial Policy Framework for Ontario' (Ontario 1992). Competitive fundamentals include continuous innovation, raising skill levels, increasing technological capabilities, establishing domestic activities, building linkages and networks, and building international capabilities.

9 Ng 1993.

10 The Economic Council of Canada characterizes the segmentation of the labour market in terms of 'good' jobs and 'bad' jobs. The latter are characterized by non-standard work forms – part-time, short-term, own-account self-employment, temporary-help agency work. Its findings indicate that non-standard workers generally earn less than others in full-time, more permanent jobs in the same occupations and the same industries, and that, in the majority of cases, they have fewer benefits. 1990: 12–14.

11 1986 Statistics Canada data indicate that racial-minority women are underrepresented in middle- and upper-level management positions, over-represented in the manual field, and, like women as a group, are heavily concentrated in the clerical field. And, in addition, many of these women appear to be underemployed. For example, over 14% of racial-minority women who are clerical workers have university degrees compared with 4% of women in the rest of Ontario's population. Ontario Women's Directorate 1993.

12 This strategy is characterized by a reduction of a firm's permanent labour force, flexible payment systems, 'the use of contract workers, temporary labour and out-sourcing through the use of homeworking, or subcontracting to small informal enterprises that are not covered by labour or other regulations that bear the risks and uncertainties of fluctuating business.' Standing 1989: 1079

13 See also Gabriel and Macdonald 1994 for a discussion of how Canadian women's mobilization around NAFTA was influenced by the changing character of the domestic women's movement and the dynamics of broader coalition politics.

14 Yanz's account of NAC's Global Strategies committee is documented in her memo to NAC's AGM participants, August 1992.

15 The to-do list for women who wanted to join in the struggle to defeat

NAFTA also included ringing bells to warn people of the dangers of NAFTA; vigils, marches, and occupations; making signs; reading more about NAFTA and phoning friends to discuss it; watching ACN videos; and writing letters to MPs and newspapers. From *Kinesis*, February 1993.

16 The campaign is outlined in Borowy et al. 1993.

17 From unpublished personal notes – Teresa Healy.

18 In 1964, when the U.S. government suddenly terminated the *bracero* program, which had permitted Mexican workers to travel to the United States on short-term work permits, some 200,000 *braceros* were left without work, leading to unemployment rates of 40 to 50% in towns on the U.S.-Mexican border (Bustamante 1983: 233).

19 Most *maquiladora* operators have completed at least six years of schooling, while the average educational level for Mexican workers in general is 3.8 years (Fernández-Kelly in Nash and Fernández-Kelly 1983: 215).

20 See also Gabriel and Macdonald 1994 for a further discussion of Mexican women's responses to trade liberalization.

21 Red Mexicana de Acción Frente al Libre Comercio (RMALC) 1992: 230.

9

New International Trade Agreements: Their Reactionary Role in Creating Markets and Retarding Social Welfare[1]

MARJORIE GRIFFIN COHEN

Throughout the world there is a sense of enormous changes occurring that are associated with the way economies are shaped. The very terms used to describe these events convey the vastness, inclusiveness, and apparent inevitability of what is happening: globalization, restructuring, new international economic order, post-welfare state, age of global capital, new world economy. A political message, which has moral overtones, is associated with the changes: the timid (or 'economically challenged') fear the dislocations restructuring brings, but those with courage understand that whatever pain occurs is a necessary process.[2] The old order may be falling apart, but this destruction has a silver lining because along with the tearing down of old institutions there is a simultaneous building up of new and better forms of organization. Destruction becomes part of a growth process and the old familiar 'pain but gain' bromide reasserts the belief in the positive and progressive features of change.

My main point in this paper will be to show that these changes are not progressive and are not in the interests of democracy or equality. Peoples' rights, particularly the rights of women and disadvantaged minorities, are subverted through the destruction or increasing irrelevance of the very institutions that supported the ideas of equality and democracy in industrialized societies. The trajectory of the global marketization process is reactionary, and whatever is created, as existing social institutions are torn down, further undermines democratic traditions that have developed over the past two hundred years. It is the institutions associated with collective security and community that are being destroyed. The most visible targets are the social programs; less obvious is the undermining of the political institutions that support whatever democratic tendencies exist in industrialized countries. The institutions being destroyed are replaced by market-creating institutions that, at a global level, assume a supranational legitimacy replacing the power of nation-states.

The primary agencies of the global-marketization process are the new international trade agreements, which generate a whole new order of international governance. For some time feminists have recognized the dangers of the internationalization of capital and have pointed to the facilitating mechanisms of the IMF and the World Bank to impose reactionary kinds of economic policy in poor countries.[3] These organizations have been important in shaping the ideology and economic climate for global economic integration. The new dangers for equality-seeking groups are trade agreements like the Canada-U.S. Free Trade Agreement (FTA), the North American Free Trade Agreement (NAFTA), and the General Agreement on Tariffs and Trade (GATT).[4] These agreements are dangerous because they contain features that go far beyond the regulation of trade in that they codify social, economic, and political behaviour in ways that used to be left to nation-states. Through trade agreements, nation-states' power is subsumed under the market-creating activities of international regulations. The minimalist role of the state is, in a very determined way, made secure through the institutionalization of the 'unfettered' market mechanism as the ideal form of economic behaviour.

In this chapter I argue that equality-seeking groups' successes have been inextricably linked to market-correcting activities of social and economic policy. These successes are being undermined through the process of creating, globally, a single market without mechanisms for even minimal controls over international finance and investment activities. I will show, through the experience that women of Canada have had with free trade, some examples of how democracy is threatened and, finally, will suggest some possibilities for the political action that will be necessary if the future is to turn out differently from the destiny that free trade would bring.

Market Correction and Equality Rights

The rise of democracy is often associated with the development of capitalist markets and industrial society. For women and disadvantaged minorities, the path was not a linear one, and every inch of the route towards equality defied the normal working of the market system. The market itself does not foster equality and may actually require fairly large amounts of inequality to function according to economic notions of efficiency. There certainly is no inherent logic in the system to insist that women and men, black and white, poor and rich, and young and old be treated as equals.

Over time institutions have been developed, as a result of pressure from people, to modify or supersede the market in order to humanize its most brutal aspects. The point of economic and social policy is either to counter market failure or bring about social goals that cannot be ful-filled through the normal workings of the market. If the market were self-correcting and the ultimate outcomes were the kinds of societies people found tolerable, there would be no need for economic or social policy. But if anything about the market mechanism has become known over the centuries during which it has controlled economic life, it is that the process of buying and selling alone cannot meet all needs and is not invariably the most efficient way to organize production, distribution, and general human welfare.

The relationship between women and the welfare state is complex. Feminists are fully aware of the state's patriarchal aspects, yet they rec-ognize the necessity to use state power to bring about a social order that would not occur without this kind of intervention in a purely market-oriented society. The goal of feminists has been to refashion the state to reflect women's needs, and to some extent, through the market-controlling institutions of the state, women and minority groups have been able to pursue equality and redistributive goals. While their suc-cess in achieving these goals has been limited, nevertheless, for all of our impatience at the pace of progressive change, more power has been accorded to traditionally disadvantaged groups. Even though these groups still do not have parity with white males in the formal manifes-tations of power, they are recognized as political actors with consider-able influence whose views cannot be ignored. At the very least, the public discourse about rights recognizes the legitimacy of minority views and acknowledges that these groups should not be excluded from democratic organization, planning, and participation.

Under the new free-trade agreements these disadvantaged groups will experience a dramatic constriction in the various ways in which social policy can be influenced. Even the limited redistributive features of the welfare state that now exist will contract as the power of the state, at the national level, dwindles. The critical issue will be the failure of nations to control international capital because of the inability to build supranational institutions capable of fulfilling the traditional function of nation-states. Most specifically, the state's ability to enact market-controlling and redistributive policies will be affected.

Two main assertions, then, underlie my following arguments. The first is that collective public control of the market is positive for women and minorities (all people for that matter), and measures that undermine market-controlling institutions will negatively affect the goals of disadvantaged groups. The second is that national and sub-national governments, and the politics at this level, have been significant vehicles through which disadvantaged groups locate their struggles. When the trade agreements, as legal documents, limit the effectiveness of these state entities to respond to redistributive demands, the possibilities for democratic participation by disadvantaged groups are severely constrained.

Restructuring with a Single Market

In a system of more or less closed national economies, even governments and business élites have understood the wisdom of the stabilizing effects of well-developed social systems. The logic of full employment and high wages was clear: unemployment meant that without incomes, people would not be able to buy what the corporations sold. As Henry Ford understood, people needed to earn enough to buy the goods and services they produced for wages, for if this didn't occur there would be no point to production. Mass production required mass consumption. The shift in this logic began with the proliferation of export-led growth strategies in wealthy, industrialized countries.[5] When corporations, in general, did not have to rely mainly on a population within a nation to buy what they produced, the uncoupling of the relationship between production and distribution systems began. Foreign markets were ideal because products could be sold when domestic markets were saturated or when unemployment was high. The best feature of this system (from the perspective of corporations) was that wages could be driven down and held low indefinitely. The internationalization of capital has significantly changed the nature of export-led growth from the type of policies that were pursued when corporations were associated with specific nation-states. Now corporate success does not involve simply the physical trading of goods and services between nations. The ability to invest and locate within nations at will has become an integral part of the international economic system. This increased capital mobility threatens the logic of national economic and social policies as nations are held hostage to the possibility of capital flight if favourable conditions for capital are not created. As a result, economic and social policies designed precisely to counter market forces are abandoned in favour of the marketization process. The role of social and economic policy has changed and increasingly consists mostly of providing supports for market-creating activities.

Several critical changes in the relationship between the state and economic activity have occurred with the new trade agreements, and they severely limit the ability of social policy to temper or modify the actions of international capital. The most significant has been the attempts to form a single world-wide market. The recent round of the GATT will go a long way towards making this goal a reality. In the meanwhile, regional free-trade zones have accomplished prototypical examples of how the single market can be organized. Agreements such as the FTA and NAFTA are not regional trading blocs in opposition to the objectives of a single market, as is sometimes claimed, but share the GATT's philosophy and complement the GATT's objectives. Their job is to create a single market, develop institutions to enhance capital mobility, and ensure the rights of corporations within the region. In some regional trade agreements these market-creating features have gone much further than the GATT and have been the testing grounds for trade-liberalization features that have met with opposition from some countries.[6] These agreements are harbingers of what is to come.

In North America, through the FTA and NAFTA, a single market has been created that places corporate behaviour in the advantageous position of being beyond the regulatory control of a single state. The international institutions created are primarily devoted to market-supporting activities to ensure capital mobility,[7] and have no mechanisms through which measures to control corporate behaviour can develop. The result is the creation of a single market without a single state to discipline it.

Another change concerns the reduced role of the individual state in controlling economic activity. The institutions to balance or control market power remain at the national level, but ultimately with much less power than they had when the market and the state occupied one space, that is, within a nation. The limits of nation-state power over market activity in these circumstances are in some senses obvious. As nations compete for the favours of capital, the ability to exert any type of discipline over corporate behaviour comes into direct conflict with capital's increased mobility. Unless all nations that are party to an agreement behave in the same way with regard to corporate discipline, the corporations will not be disciplined at all. Any one nation, by acting on its own, will be disadvantaged by behaving in a stricter way. Since there is no mechanism for the nations to act collectively, individual state action is critically weakened. But this new advantage for capital is not only generated through the market mechanism itself. Equally important are the explicit measures in the trade agreements that place strict limits on the future development of social policy within nations. These measures, which will be discussed in the next section, specifically circumscribe state action while at the same time create greater freedom for the private sector.

Ensuring Uniformity

The need for harmonizing conditions between trading nations has been the rallying cry for those supporting free trade. During the very heated political debates about free trade in Canada, the argument used repeatedly by the business sector supporting it was that a 'level playing field' was essential for access to markets. This means something a great deal more than removing tariffs or quotas: what it requires is a uniformity of economic and social systems. If economies, either in part or wholly, do not operate by the dictates of the market, they are deemed to be unfairly subsidizing their national industries. In Canada the move towards economic uniformity has resulted in massive economic and social restructuring that occurs, not through a democratic process, but through the invisible conditioning of the trade agreements.[8]

Since the trade agreements are essentially massive economic constitutions, it would not be possible in this chapter to show the encompassing ways in which nations' economic and social policy is affected.[9] What is most distinct about them is that they prohibit substantial differentiation in economic policy between nations. In a country like Canada, which has unique features and problems, following economic policies that were designed to deal with the conditions of another country (the United States) simply does not make sense. Canada is gigantic in size and most of it is very cold for much of the year. There aren't many people in the country relative to the land mass and they are spread out. It is a country with special problems in communicating, keeping warm, and feeding its population, and it has gone about meeting these challenges by establishing institutions that make sense for the conditions here.

Canada has, for example, set up supply-management schemes for the agricultural sector and exerts a strong public presence in the transportation and communication systems. Also, special kinds of economic and social programs were developed to deal with the inequalities between regions and people within the country. Many Canadians are critical of the country's provision of social services, which are rather underdeveloped compared with those of most of the industrialized world. Still, they are significantly superior to those provided by our neighbour to the south, the U.S.A., and certainly to Mexico's.

Canada's social and economic programs are rapidly changing under the harmonization requirements of the FTA, NAFTA, and the GATT. The following are just a few examples of the ways in which the agreements specifically have changed these programs and have removed public policy from the domain of democratic institutions.

Resources

Canada is highly dependent on natural resources. The unusually high degree of foreign ownership and exportation of these resources resulted in the underdevelopment of secondary processing industries within the country. In order to combat this problem of a poor integration of resources and manufacturing, export restrictions were placed on some resources to ensure that a certain portion of the wealth of the nation remain within the country. The bizarre reality now, as a result of the trading agreements, is that public planning for resource use is simply not permitted. The attempt to foster a rational, integrated economy based on the intrinsic wealth of the nation is considered restraint of trade and is illegal under new international trade laws. Canada can no longer restrict the export of unprocessed materials, nor can it require that a certain proportion of the resources be used within the country in order to create secondary industries, provide items at relatively low costs, and give people work.

For example, until very recently Canada was in a position to insist that all the salmon caught in its waters be processed in Canada before any was exported. This was rational, not only from a short-term economic view, but also from a conservation view. Because the economics of the industry made secondary fishing industries viable (which was particularly important for women, who are the main workers in the fish-processing industries), salmon-spawning rivers were not directed for alternative uses. But now that fish may be processed elsewhere (mainly in low-wage U.S. states by non-unionized migrant labourers making about one-third what Canadian unionized fish-processing workers make) the rationale for maintaining the fish habitat is disappearing as the value of the fish-processing industry in Canada rapidly declines. Fish-stock preservation holds less interest for governments who want to encourage revenue-producing industries. As a result, there is tremendous pressure to use the salmon-spawning rivers for hydro-electric projects.[10] Fish conservation does not make sense, economically, when rivers can be dammed, the hydro-generated electricity exported, and revenues can flow to the governments.[11] The inability to plan for resource use, because of the rigidities of trade policy, results in the destruction of a healthy industry and threatens the viability of a whole species.

The Public Sector

NAFTA specifically constrains the public sector in ways that are totally new in international trade agreements.[12] The language of the whole document indicates the extent to which the public sector is considered an anomaly to the principles of free trade: everything referred to in the public sector is labelled a 'non-conforming measure.'[13] Both NAFTA and the FTA greatly facilitate the privatization of public-sector entities, either wholly or in part, and virtually prohibit putting something in the public sector that is now privately held. The main way in which new programs are prohibited is through a series of clauses that would require not only the permission of trading partners for initiating a new public program, but compensation for any losses the private sector might incur.[14] Considering the extent of U.S. corporate involvement in the Canadian economy, this restriction would make the cost of any new program prohibitive. Any government, should it be so inclined in the future, that decided it wanted to establish a national day-care program or provide a national dental or disabilities insurance scheme would certainly be discouraged by the trade agreement's enforcement of prohibitively expensive compensation to U.S. providers of these services in Canada.

Even more alarming is the *requirement* that the public sector be reshaped to reflect a commercial approach to providing goods or services. The agreement specifically says that any government entity must 'act solely in accordance with commercial considerations.'[15] Commercial considerations are defined as those 'consistent with the normal business practices of privately-held enterprises in the relevant business or industry.' Yet the whole point of public-sector activity is to provide goods and services in ways in which the private sector cannot or will not.

Using Trade Legislation to Challenge National Autonomy

The new trade agreements have fostered fairly extraordinary challenges to what were considered normal ways of managing economic and social life in Canada. As I write this piece, a great many issues are being contested by the United States through NAFTA: a few examples will give a flavour of the extent of their reach.

Intellectual Property

One important challenge deals with the investment and intellectual property rights of cigarette companies. Canada is discussing the elimination of all differentiation in cigarette packaging by replacing advertising with black-and-white packaging and strong language about smoking's lethal nature. U.S. cigarette manufacturers claim this is a violation of the trade agreement and have argued before the House of Commons Standing Committee on Health that, while Canada has the ability to prohibit the use of harmful products, it cannot 'attempt to discourage the consumption of products through measures that violate its obligations under international agreements.'[16] The companies argue that the plain-packaging requirement constitutes the expropriation of trademarks and would make the tobacco companies eligible for compensation of hundreds of millions of dollars.

The use of trade law to uphold the right of cigarette companies to protect their 'intellectual property' comes into direct conflict with the responsibility of government to protect its citizens. If the cigarette companies are able to argue successfully this way, the ability of governments to regulate industries will evaporate.

Compensation

Another NAFTA challenge involves the federal government's ability to maintain a national airport as a public entity. Just preceding the last federal election (fall 1993), the Conservative government decided to privatize the nation's largest airport, located in Toronto, and made the sale to a consortium of private firms. The whole move was a terrific political scandal because the people who would gain considerably from the sale were a group of businessmen closely aligned with the Conservative party. The Liberal party opposed the deal and promised, when elected, to reverse the decision. In an untypical move, the Liberals did keep their campaign promise to cancel this privatization move once elected. Now the U.S. firm Lougheed, which was part of the original consortium, threatens to claim compensation under NAFTA provisions that provide for such action when something is transferred from the private to the public sector.

New Social Programs

A third example of the ways in which NAFTA provisions constrain normal prerogatives of government involves the attempt of a provincial government to institute a new social program. This was the case of a political party that had campaigned on the promise of instituting public auto insurance.[17] Upon winning the election the new government moved quickly ahead on this issue, but was immediately challenged by U.S. auto-insurance companies. The proposal never did get far enough to be adjudicated by a trade panel, but the arguments of the insurance industry regarding compensation were so compelling that the premier of the province withdrew the proposed program and said it would never be tried again.

The point of recounting these examples is to show the ways in which the deliberate wishes of people through the actions of elected democratic governments are being superseded by the international trade rules. At the supranational level, panels have been established that interpret and decide rulings: these panels are not elected and do not have to respond to people's wishes, since people have no access to them. It is becoming increasingly irrelevant politically what economic and social issues parties decide to pursue and what they promise to people. Once they are elected, even if their intentions to carry out promises are good, they soon understand the tremendous effort that would be involved in defying the trade agreements in order to do so.

The examples I have given do not begin to cover the extraordinary range of intervention in national sovereignty. These are merely the most recent direct challenges that have occurred and have come to the attention of the public. Typically, self-censorship on the part of governments will be the way in which the trade agreements will be enforced. As the conditioning factors of the trade agreements become more familiar, there will be fewer and fewer dramatic examples of the ways in which these agreements impinge on the ability of the public sector to meet its obligations to people. Programs will simply be presented as 'too costly,' without proper explanation of why they would cost so much. Few governments will have the political courage to take the kind of bold action necessary to counter the power that the trade agreements give international corporations. I fully expect, for example, that the Canadian federal government will shortly find (as a result of expert testimony) that plain packaging of cigarettes does not really deter people from smoking cigarettes, and the whole issue will be dropped.

Action for Feminists

Over the long history of feminist struggle, women have managed to gain a voice in our societies through generally unpopular assertive behaviour. The campaigns to be part of the public realm, beginning with the struggle for suffrage, were pursued because women recognized that society, as it had been constructed and governed by men, did not reflect women's interests and did not treat women fairly. Having the vote was an important tool for women everywhere; not, obviously, because we all voted en masse and quickly advanced feminist and progressive objectives throughout the world – if only our projects had been that easy. The vote was important because it established our right to be part of ideas about equality and to participate (however removed initially) in the decision making of our society. It took a long time for the reality of women's participation to take shape, but slowly women have managed to begin to change the world through the use of tools associated with democracy and the welfare state.

Now the world is changing quickly and the political institutions with which women have struggled no longer have the kind of power to shape the structures of our societies that they once did. Women, minorities, and the disadvantaged are confronting a deterioration in their ability to be effective in having their interests met in the public sphere, primarily because these groups are confronting the problem of having even less democratic participation than in the past. It is not that we will have less formal participation in government bodies; this form of representation is likely to increase. But real decision-making power will elude us as the site of power itself shifts.

Because the changes in democratic institutions are not keeping pace with or corresponding to changes in economic ones, women will need to expand the focus of political pressure beyond that of our nation-states. The first task will be to understand the new economic environment: its reactionary nature is not simply the result of a neoconservative revival (even social-democratic governments are participating in the surge), nor does it involve restructuring in the abstract sense of an apolitical process that is under way because of normal market forces. The trade agreements being put into place are not natural outgrowths of normal processes, but are deliberate governance strategies to give shape to a world economy that benefits large international corporations.

At the international level, women need to find political ways in which we can be effective in arguing for economic pluralism as a necessary precondition for the multiple avenues people may pursue to exercise their autonomy and control. There is not much point to differentiation in political systems through nations if these nations can have only minimal scope for action on social and economic policy. Economic problems are not standard, and economic methods and institutions cannot be either. Feminists are accustomed to arguing for political diversity, and just as we understand that politically there is no one set of answers to all anticipated and unforeseen problems, we need to make this connection also to economic systems.[18] Women and disadvantaged minorities in wealthy industrialized countries need to join others in this world, primarily in poor countries, who recognize the dangers of the economic uniformity imposed by the trade deals.

We in wealthy, industrialized countries seldom hear of the protests against the international trading order occurring in poorer parts of the world. The demonstrations against the GATT's provisions on intellectual property rights in India, for example, have been dramatic. The Lok Sabha had to recess for four days because of protests by opposition members when the Indian government agreed to the latest GATT proposals.[19] Earlier, more than half a million farmers in Bangalore demonstrated against the agreement, providing the largest protest yet against the GATT, and in April 1994, 300,000 people in New Delhi protested against it.[20]

On NAFTA's inauguration date, 1 January 1994, peasants in the state of Chiapas, Mexico, seized a city and three towns through armed conflict that has resulted in the deaths of over one hundred people. They were protesting NAFTA, which they characterized as 'the death certificate for the indigenous people of Mexico.'[21]

The strongest protests against the new trade agreements are about food, for very good reasons: the poorest people on this earth lose everything when they lose their ability to feed themselves. The new trade agreements have designed rules to benefit the highly capital- and energy-intensive agricultural industries in countries where food production at most involves only single-digit percentages of the labour force. These rules are devastating for countries where huge segments of the population rely on farming for their subsistence. For the people of countries like India and Mexico, the principles of the trade agreements affect more than a way of life, a standard of living, sovereignty, and democracy, as they do in industrialized countries: a report on the GATT prepared by a panel of judges in India described India's acquiescence to the new trade rules as 'an abdication by the State in respect of its obligations to protect the people's right to life.'[22] The protests of these people in poor countries may be a political avenue for change and a rallying point for nations that can afford neither to withdraw from the international trade agreements nor to abide by their rules.

Any political initiatives at the international level will need to make the common links between peoples around the world. So far the actions of people in wealthy industrialized countries have not been as dramatic as those in poorer ones. Nevertheless, substantial anti-free-trade campaigns have occurred. In Canada women's groups were instrumental in the founding and activities of anti-free-trade organizations.[23] While the protests against the deals were not able to either stop the agreements or change their most damaging aspects, these protests did succeed in making the population recognize the harmful effects of free trade.[24] In recent years women in Canada, Mexico, and the United States have come together in their understanding of the problems they commonly face in the wake of the free-trade agreements. These kinds of organizational links may be a beginning for ways to advance some international institutions to bring about market control. This is a huge task and requires, as a preliminary step, the true democratization of our own nation-states. Only through intense pressure from the people within individual nations will there be any hope for the development of social policy that can exert some discipline on the market at the international level.

The true task for people within nations is to continue to work for ways to democratize their own countries so that the main function of nations is not to discipline their populations for international trading regimes, as it appears to be now. It becomes very difficult to argue for national sovereignty at the international level when nations themselves are not responding to popular sovereignty. The major political task is to find ways to ensure that domestic governments respond to the will of the people, so that these governments can then insist on international trade agreements that meet the needs of people and not just those of corporations. Meeting people's needs will entail designing rules of trade that can accommodate variations in social and economic policy internationally.

Conclusions

The new power given to the corporate sector through international trade agreements places nations in about the same stage of control over capital as they had at the dawn of the industrial revolution. For women and other minorities who have long struggled to have a voice in the ways in which our societies are run, this 'restructuring' that limits the power of democracy is extremely threatening. The process is presented to us as a natural outgrowth of the market mechanism. Women can fatalistically accept a framework which says that nothing can be done and we can continue to limit our economic goals to obtaining equality under the framework decided on by the market.

There is, however, an alternative to submission and the reduction of state functions to minimalist activities. Neither people nor nations are prevented from acting in response to the increased power of the corporate private sector. But it is important that this action occur soon, before all the institutions have changed to accommodate the new international order. We need to work simultaneously for two changes in the direction of the world economy. One involves the creation of international institutions to exert control over the global market. The other requires a change in the philosophy of trading agreements to permit a differentiation in economic policy between nations to meet different conditions and promote different objectives. Through women's collective actions we have been able to change our world to begin to reflect our needs. We cannot now surrender this objective because of the imperatives of international capital.

NOTES

1 This chapter is adapted from a paper delivered in Adelaide, Australia, in October 1994 at a conference 'Women, Power, and Politics,' celebrating one hundred years of women's suffrage in South Australia.

2 While Joseph Schumpeter's words are not used, the notion of 'creative destruction' is the justification given by business élites and most govern-

ments for moving in unpalatable directions. See *Capitalism, Socialism and Democracy*, 3rd ed. (New York: Harper Bros. 1950).

3 For some recent publications on women and globalization see, for example, Beneria 1989, Mitter 1986b, and Peterson and Runyan 1993.

4 The Canada-U.S. FTA went into effect 1 January 1989; the NAFTA on 1 January 1994. The current round of GATT began in 1986, was completed late in 1993, and went into effect in January 1995.

5 Poorer countries had long been saddled with this method of development through the policies of the IMF and the World Bank.

6 The FTA, for example, was the first significant international trade agreement to include trade in services. The NAFTA goes further than GATT on issues such as intellectual property rights, resources, and constraints on the public sector.

7 The exceptions to this in the NAFTA agreement are the agencies established to deal with the labour and environmental supplemental agreements. But these supplemental agreements merely require the enforcement of existing laws within each nation, and so do not represent new constraints on market action at the international level.

8 For a discussion of the conditioning process see Grinspun and Kreklewich 1994.

9 NAFTA, for example, is a 2000-page document that requires changes in about 4000 laws in Canada at the federal level alone.

10 In the U.S. Pacific Northwest the damming of rivers for hydro-electric generation has had such a devastating effect on the fish habitat that the salmon-fishing industry in Washington and Oregon was closed in 1994 for the first time in history.

11 Hydro-electric generation is mainly in the public sector in Canada.

12 For a more complete discussion of the effects of NAFTA on the public sector see my article 'Democracy and Trade Agreements' (1995).

13 See *The North American Free Trade Agreement* (Chicago: CCH, 1994), chap. 11, art. 1108, 1 (a).

14 NAFTA, chap. 20, annex 202; chap. 11, art. 1110.

15 Ibid., chap. 15, art. 1502: 3(b).

16 This is a quote from Julius Katz, former Deputy U.S. Trade Representative, who is now a partner of former U.S. Trade Representative Carla Hills in a Washington consulting firm working for the cigarette companies. Hills and Katz, while in office, were the two most powerful officials behind U.S. attempts to open Thailand and other developing nations for the U.S. tobacco industries. 'U.S. Tobacco Companies Challenge Canadian Plain Packaging Proposal,' *NAFTA WATCH* 1 (9) (26 May 1994).

17 This was the New Democratic Party in Ontario during the election of 1990.

18 For a discussion of the progressive possibilities of pluralism see Phillips 1993.

19 The main objections were to the Trade-Related Aspects of Intellectual Property Rights (TRIPs) included in the final draft of the GATT. The patent protection of life-forms granted to giant international pharmaceutical and seed companies would have terrible repercussions for poor nations. For farmers in India it would involve paying royalties to international corporations for the right to use the seeds from their own harvests.

20 Indian farmers also took direct action against international corporations by burning down a Cargill seed plant under construction. See Khor 1993.

21 'Death toll rises in Mexico battle,' *Toronto Star*, 3 January 1994.

22 'Former judges warn against Dunkel package,' *Indian Express*, Kochi, 16 December 1993.

23 For an assessment of the implications of this activity on Canadian feminism see Bashevkin 1989.

24 My writing dealing with the effects of free trade on women includes: *Free Trade and the Future of Women's Work* (1987); 'Americanizing Services' (1988); and 'Women and Free Trade' (1986).

10

Behind Closed Doors: Homework Policy and Lost Possibilities for Change

BELINDA LEACH

Both private business and, more recently, government are increasingly turning to the use of homeworkers as part of a cost-decreasing and efficiency strategy. Yet homework policies are by no means gender neutral. They have a differential impact on men and women, first, because it is mainly women who adopt homework as an income strategy, and second, because men and women adopt homework for very different reasons and under different circumstances. Thus, this policy trend on the one hand reinforces the gendered labour market, while on the other it has the potential to reconstitute the domestic gender division of labour in a regressive fashion. On both counts, the shift to homework represents a step backwards in terms of gains made by the women's movement for women as women and as workers. In many cases, particularly for white-collar workers, it returns women who have experienced working outside the home to a situation of performing all of their work, paid and unpaid, inside the home.

This chapter explores some issues raised by recent trends that indicate that increasing amounts of paid work are being located inside the household.[1] It argues that the consequences of the increasingly popular homework policies are far reaching, going beyond the problem of organizing homeworkers to improve their work conditions, and are of particular concern for feminists. While homework policies are intended to improve worker productivity, the social conditions that propel women into returning to the private sphere and into taking homework are likely to lead to their effective seclusion inside the household, making exposure to and consciousness of different political ideas extremely difficult.

Working at Home: The Economic Context

Homework has been a 'traditional' form of work in the garment industry in Canada for at least a century (Johnson 1982), and the effects of trade liberalization on that industry (Mytelka 1991) together with the constant search for cheaper labour have been responsible for the loss of factory jobs in that industry and the increasing use of subcontracted homeworkers. Homework is now common in newer industries such as electronics, as well as being turned to in numerous other labour-intensive areas such as toy and novelty manufacture, chandelier making, packaging, and labelling. A relatively new, but prospering, area for homework is in the area of telemarketing and as an alternative to centralized call centres for companies dependent upon telephone ordering (such as Pizza Pizza and the Canadian Automobile Association, among numerous smaller and less well known examples). Thus, homework reflects the shift from goods production towards the provision of services, although it remains one of the most cost-effective forms of labour for the production of certain goods. Homework is well documented to be increasing on a global scale (Mitter 1986a; Lipsig-Mumme 1983; West Yorkshire Homeworking Unit 1992; International Labour Organization 1990) as part of several restructuring measures that help companies gain a competitive edge by off-loading many of their costs to subcontracted enterprises and workers. It is well documented that the vast majority of garment homeworkers, in Canada and elsewhere, are women (Johnson 1982; Phizacklea 1990; Fernández-Kelly and Garcia 1985; Phizacklea and Wolkowitz 1995), and initial reports indicate that newer opportunities for working at home, in white-collar and 'sunrise' industries, are both targeted towards and attractive to women (Christensen 1989; Dangler 1989).

Public-Sector Homeworking

Traditionally, homeworking has been a private-sector strategy, but recent ideological shifts in the perceived role of the state, as a result of fiscal constraints, have led to the introduction of homework as a new public-sector strategy. In linking the expectations of white-collar homeworkers with the experiences of industrial homeworkers, I do not wish to diminish the considerable differences between the mainly immigrant, low-paid homeworkers in the garment industry and the relatively high-paid, public-sector homeworkers who continue to receive good public-sector benefits and who, unlike the industrial homeworkers, have so far retained their status as employees, which provides them with protective labour legislation and eligibility for unemployment insurance. It is useful perhaps to visualize a spectrum of homework, where, under present conditions, public-sector homeworkers fall at one, privileged extreme, while garment-industry homeworkers fall at the other. Over time, however, we may well see an erosion of the privilege of public-sector homeworkers and a shift for them in the direction of the less-privileged end of the spectrum.[2]

In 1991 the Government of Canada announced its own 'telework' policy, following from the examples of several major corporations that had experimented with home-based work in the 1980s (Christensen 1992). This policy is significant since it represents the public-sector promotion and institutionalization of a more generalized private-sector trend towards using home-based workers. It is also significant because for several decades the public-sector has provided relatively secure and well paid jobs for women with reasonable working conditions.

It is informative to look a little more closely at the federal government's telework policy because, unlike its private-sector counterparts, the government has to be at least to some extent transparent and accountable in its policy making. Thus, accompanying the policy is an implementation document that sets out some of the 'practical considerations' concerning telework. The government is offering the possibility to work at home to some workers on an optional basis as part of a three-year pilot project the intent of which is to allow workers increased flexibility, while at the same time increasing worker productivity, reducing overhead costs, and reducing traffic congestion and pollution (Treasury Board 1992: 13–15). When the policy was first announced, a Treasury Board spokesperson declared that as much as 10 per cent of the federal public service could be telecommuting in five years (PSAC 1992). The union representing many of the workers potentially affected, the Public Service Alliance of Canada (PSAC), views homework with some caution, warning workers that at present there is no contract language that definitively protects them when they choose to work at home, and that shifting the responsibility for their safety from the employer to the employee may make Workers' Compensation claims extremely difficult to prove (ibid.). Some federal-government workers are enthusiastic about the possibility of working at home, and it is interesting to note some of the advantages they predict will come from it. These include saving time travelling to and from work, the ability to concentrate without regular office distractions, avoiding office 'politics,' and, for many of them, being able to cope better with heavy work loads and not enough office hours (ibid.). These reasons clearly result in advantages to the employer in terms of improved productivity from a home-based employee, and are consistent with the desire for a more flexible and efficient public-sector labour force.

Social Context

Public-sector workers cite several other advantages, such as being able to balance work and family life better, saving money on child care, and being able to stay close to elderly parents as other advantages (PSAC 1992). These are a different, more personal set of reasons, which are more consistent with those cited by garment and other industrial home-workers. They suggest a direct relationship between home-based work and domestic labour and, as well, an assumption that working at home will ameliorate the stress of the double day of paid and unpaid work expected of women. If, however, the earlier-stated advantage of improved concentration and ability to squeeze more work into the work day is linked to this anticipated advantage of being better able to care for family members, there would seem to be a contradiction, a disjuncture, between expectations regarding homework and the actual experience of it. The experience of industrial homeworkers is that increased productivity is an objective inconsistent with the care of family members. Indeed, the garment homeworkers I knew found that instead of being able to weave paid and unpaid work into an effective pattern allowing them to fulfil their goals in both areas, the demands of domestic labour, and in particular child care, frequently forced them to push their paid work into parts of the day and night when children would be sleeping or cared for by other adults after their return from work.[3]

Other writers have also concluded that attempting to combine child care and homework is in fact not only difficult but extremely stressful (Allen 1983; Boris and Daniels 1989). It seems that women who choose the homework solution rather than going out to work and seeking child care have not in fact resolved the problem of juggling paid work and child care. Moreover, if a homework policy is a step towards eradicating the need for a day-care policy, it is a troubling and inadequate solution. Garment homeworkers have struggled with the competing demands of work and children, sometimes believing they had found a satisfactory solution to their difficulty. Yet the daughters of one homeworker told me directly, 'She never has time for us,' and another homeworker related how the birth of her baby had forced her to change her work patterns: 'Now I work whenever I can. Because if I try to work, she just cries and cries. During the day I do maybe one or two hours. Then when my husband arrives, I give him the baby to look after. Then I work. During the day I don't work much' (Tuyet). A Canadian federal-public-service teleworker quoted in the recent study conducted by the Public Service Alliance of Canada supports these experiences: 'I can't work at home if my child is sick. She had chicken pox and I couldn't work and look after her. People have suggested that with small children you can look after them and work at home, but I can't. People don't understand the care and attention children need. I have to concentrate on my work and it is very difficult to do when she is around' (PSAC 1993: 10). In fact, Treasury Board's draft policy is not silent on this issue, and presents the following advice: 'Telework should not be viewed as a substitute for child or elder care. Based on experience in the private and public-sectors, combining a telework arrangement with the full-time care of young children or elders may jeopardize the success of both, and accordingly, these types of arrangements should be discouraged ... Experience in the private sector indicates that work at home employees with young children should consider a reduced hours schedule: working less than thirty hours a week is advisable' (Treasury Board 1992: 19, 43). At the same time the Board policy recognizes that the majority of those who choose to work at home are young parents (ibid.: 43). Not only does this approach decrease women's earning power, its overall thrust is to turn back decades of women's struggles to cast off their status as secondary wage earners.

Cuts in government spending have led to a decline in the level of social-services assistance available, services that impinge directly on the household. Not only has there been a failure to provide an accessible day-care program, but government assistance with child care, in the form of a tax deduction, is far behind the actual cost of having a child cared for during the working day. This discrepancy has a direct effect on women's access to paid work outside the home, since it makes child care prohibitively costly or at least not cost effective for women with lower incomes or with several children. Similarly, those state benefits paid in addition to other household income, such as child allowances and old-age pensions, are not keeping up with the cost of living, while cuts in medical and long-term-care budgets also directly affect women's lives. Much of the responsibility for coping with decreased social-services spending devolves to women. As well as being forced to budget and spend more carefully, they are more likely to be required to care in the home for the young, the sick, the disabled, and the elderly. Threats to kindergarten programs because of shrinking education budgets, which have been carried out by some school boards, are another example of the additional pressure on women's ability to work outside the home.

Working-class women in Britain have been experiencing this squeeze – the need for income combined with the additional responsibility for dependents forced by government cutbacks – longer than their Canadian counterparts. Studies of homeworkers in the north of England revealed this to be a common problem (West Yorkshire Homeworking Unit 1992: 36):

At one time, as well as my young son, I had both my father and mother to look after. That's why I started outwork. (Shirley)

I started mainly for the money and to look after the children. But also my husband was at home, poorly with a heart condition. So it was good that I could stay at home and look after him. (Jean)

As I have argued elsewhere (Leach 1993), the social construction of women's work renders women ideal flexible workers who readily respond to work options that seem to permit them to carry out their domestic responsibilities more easily than a regular job would. We now know that a sexual division of labour that assigns domestic work to women and absolves men from that responsibility dies hard (Luxton 1990), even under the extreme pressure of restructuring. Unemployed working-class men tend to continue their practice of not performing domestic tasks (Campbell 1984), or at most take on only the minimal tasks, even when their wives are employed outside the home (Burman 1988: 174).

Another factor that affects opportunities in the labour market is racism, and this will become an issue of increasing importance where large numbers of people in Canada remain unemployed and there is fierce debate over immigration policy. It is no accident that most of the industrial homeworkers I knew in Southern Ontario were not Canadian-born women, since the way immigrant women are inserted into the Canadian labour force reflects the global dynamics of uneven capitalist development (as Gabriel and Macdonald argue in this volume). As well, systemic discrimination in the labour market limits the work opportunities for visible-minority[4] women. Although I asked no direct questions about these homeworkers' experiences of racism, it would sometimes emerge in conversation, though usually only after long discussions of other topics. Several women spoke sadly of the differences between life in Canada and life in their home countries, especially with regard to their social isolation. One said that in her home country (Vietnam) everyone in the neighbourhood would know each other, whereas in London, Ontario, she had no contact even with her immediate neighbours. In Canada, she said, 'no-one needs each other,' but as we talked further she began to articulate her feeling that part of people's unfriendliness was based in their attitude towards her as a member of a visible-minority group.

It was only with gentle probing that people would talk about racism, it was not an issue they raised voluntarily, particularly with a researcher identified with the dominant culture. One worker described how she had been passed over for promotion inside the factory without mentioning the issue of race, though it was clearly a factor in a company where members of management were predominantly white and Canadian-born, and the homeworkers and shop-floor workers were not. When I eventually asked whether the woman who had been promoted (and who had been her assistant) was Vietnamese, she said that she was not, and added, 'They probably didn't want an Oriental supervisor.' Clearly, these are painful issues to talk about, and not ones that people want to discuss freely. Workers involved in the settlement of Vietnamese immigrants in the London, Ontario, area reported that Vietnamese workers who are laid off from their jobs consistently feel that they have been discriminated against. In the local London press, several racist incidents aimed at Vietnamese were reported in the winter of 1990, indicating an undercurrent of racism in the local community that erupts under certain circumstances. This latent and sometimes overt racism inevitably shapes the local labour market and work culture into which recent visible-minority immigrants are thrust.

Several studies of immigrant and visible-minority workers have suggested that racism at the workplace is a major factor that leads people to take homework or to work in ethnic businesses; in both situations they can evade direct contact with members of the dominant group in a work setting. Although the experience of racism may be quite different for white-collar, public-sector workers, we cannot assume that it is not as strong a factor for a number of them in their work choices as it is for industrial homeworkers. Racism in the labour market and in the work-place has historically been a factor affecting the work choices of black women in the United States, who took homework even when it was illegal to do so (Boris 1989: 38). Mitter (1986b: 130) points to racial incidents in Britain that she says are no longer reported in the media and are subject to only perfunctory investigation by the police, indicating the high level of racism operating in British society. One of the Asian women Swasti Mitter interviewed in London was more blunt than any of the women I talked to: 'The police are no help. They would not admit the attacks on Asian homes are from the racists. How can I look for jobs outside the home in such a situation? *I want to remain invisible, literally* ... At the moment my uncle brings machining work home. It works out to be 50 pence an hour, not great! But I earn and I feed my children somehow. Most of all, I do not have to deal with the fear of racist abuse in this white world' (1986b: 18; my emphasis). Under such conditions, when many have already experienced racism at a formal workplace (Arnopoulos 1979; Bishton 1984), it is not surprising that people try to avoid putting themselves into the position of being a potential target for racist attacks, be they blatant or subtle. While at first glance this might not seem to be an issue affecting public-sector workers who choose to work at home, it may indeed be an additional underlying factor in making such a choice.

Working at home is one way to avoid the racism of the wider society; working for other people of the same ethnic group is another. In London, Ontario, a subcontractor was likely to use immigrants from her own ethnic group to work in her workshop and in their homes, while in Toronto a Latin-American woman employed Latin-American women in her workshop, but recruited whomever she could to work as homeworkers. These examples indicate that the importance and utilization of ethnic networks varies, probably at least partly in response to the specific characteristics of the local labour market. Networks of South-East Asian sewers in London, Ontario, had operated for several years, allocating homework directly from a factory, and were later involved in the development of quasi-independent subcontracting firms. In Toronto ethnic networks may operate around other common interests, but since the immigrant population has a longer history there and employment opportunities in Toronto are far more varied, such networks seem to be relied on less by subcontractors, who tend to advertise for workers when work is available.

The Isolation of Working at Home

The physical separation of homeworkers from their co-workers, as well as the intensity of the work required to keep up with the demand for productivity and make a living, leads to a high degree of isolation. Many of the homeworkers I knew had worked at one time in garment factories, where they had enjoyed the sociability of contact with fellow workers. Often they had given up factory work and turned to home-work when they became pregnant. They found they quickly lost contact with the people they had previously worked alongside, and when their only remaining work experience was homework they became isolated from other workers. Their most significant work relationship was that with the supplier, usually a subcontractor, and they had no peer group with whom to share experiences. Although some writers have argued that ethnic networks (Mitter 1986a; Benson 1989) or kin networks (Beach 1989) operate in the distribution of homework, and that women often carry out their work together (Boris and Daniels 1989), from my research in Ontario I found very few examples of women from different households getting together to carry out the work. Although homework was often distributed to new immigrants through networks of more established immigrants from the same country, the people I knew who had been doing the work for several years described themselves as increasingly isolated – from members of their own ethnic community as much as from members of the broader local community.

A major reason for this isolation is that homework 'permits the worker to overwork, and to extend her working day well past what is considered reasonable and healthy' (Pennington and Westover 1989: 164). The potential for intensification in homework (because of the pres-sure of the piece-rate and the absence of fixed work hours) and the need for intensification in order to make any money, combined with the care of young children, makes it difficult for the workers to find time for other pursuits. A Vietnamese homeworker in London described her day, fairly typically, as follows: 'I get up around 6 am, sometimes ear-lier, work until 7.30 when get children up, get breakfast, etc., and see everyone out of the house. Work from 9 until 11.30, get lunch for chil-dren, work from 1 to 4 when children come home from school, and start supper. Start work again around 7 and work until 9, or 10 or 11' (Trinh).

Frequently homeworkers said that they 'have no weekends,' since every hour counts to get the work done. Given this type of schedule, it is not surprising that homeworkers find themselves with little time for outside activities and friendships. One sewer said all her women friends worked at homework (often, like herself, in addition to having full-time jobs elsewhere), and so were too busy to see one another socially. Another described the situation she faced: 'I don't have friends. I know people who work [for the company]. But I never see them, we don't see each other. I don't see them. I work and I just go shopping, or to the market every weekend, and I go to the company, I don't visit the other people. It's very seldom I see people' (Van). A Toronto homeworker was expected to return her finished shoes to the factory on Fridays. She described her work day as follows: 'I wake up at 5 o'clock in the morning and work until 7.30, then I call the kids, make something for them to go to school, and start the shoes again at 9. I fix something in the house [housework], but not every day because I don't have time. If I fix the house I don't fix the shoes. Then I have to finish at 11.30 because my kids come home for lunch. Then I start the shoes again at 1 and finish at 5, then cook for the family, eat, then at 7.30 or 8 I start again and finish at 10 or 11. It depends if I work more or less, but on Wednesday or Thursday, if the shoes are very hard, maybe no sleep, maybe one hour' (Grace). One of the Yorkshire women described her day like this: 'I'm up at six in the morning. I've always got up early with five kids. You have to be organised. I start some work, counting or stapling. Then I get the kids up and ready for school, and start again, unless it's Monday. That's my shopping day. I carry on till the kids come home from school. Then I make their tea and carry on. Unless it's stapling. The noise drives my husband mad. But if it's sorting and bagging, I carry on. If it's the weekend I often work till twelve or one in the morning. But by then, I've usually had enough any way. There's only a certain amount you can do' (Barbara) (WYHG 1990: 19–20). Another observed: 'Homeworking is very isolating. You have no-one to discuss work with, nor anyone to have a laugh with' (Mary) (YHLPU 1991: 44). Canadian federal-public-service teleworkers echo these kinds of experiences in the context of white-collar homework: 'It's an enormous imposition on my time and it imposes on my family. I tend to do it after 9 pm when the kids are in bed. By 9 pm I'm pooped. This really extends the workday and affects my leisure time. And in some ways it's not great psychologically. There are distractions at home – thinking I should do those dishes or clean up. I don't think I'd do this amount of overtime without the laptop' (PSAC 1993: 4). These kinds of workdays indicate the harsh but common reality that links homeworkers in different parts of the world.

Another feature of homework is that the amount of paid work required to be done, especially when quotas exist, is frequently so great that women call on other members of their family to do it. One home-worker explained her rationale for this: 'They [women homeworkers] have children so they don't go out to work. When they work at home many people can help with the clothes so the whole family is helping with the sewing. That way they can make more money. If she goes out to work she can't make so much money' (Trinh). The availability of only low-pay jobs outside the home seems to be another possible factor that leads people to opt for homework. In general, however, the intensifica-tion of labour through the use of family members results less from the need to make more money and improve the family's standard of living than from the pressure to meet unrealistic quotas and ensure a meagre minimum wage. There are several negative consequences resulting from the involvement of family members, aside from concern over the tacit use of child labour. The use of family labour contributes also to obscuring the amount of work that is going on, and in particular obscures the specific work conditions of women.

Behind Closed Doors

The impact of social-service cutbacks that increase domestic labour, together with a growing number of employer policies that locate paid work in the home, leads to a situation where more and more work is becoming located in the home. Yet we need to be especially aware of and concerned about the impact of popular homework policies on the gender and work relations developing behind closed doors. There are some very close links between homework and the conditions and vul-nerability of the work of domestic workers, and the invisible yet vast volume of work expected of them. There is a tendency to view the homework trend primarily as a challenge for collective organizing and for developing the protections that can be brought about through orga-nization. While this is indeed an important area for concern, there are additional benefits that derive from collective work that are under-mined by sending work back into the home.

Bringing about a change in the domestic division of labour has long been a goal of feminism. From the earliest days of scholarly treatment by feminists of domestic labour, the domestic division of labour has been identified as a crucial underpinning of women's oppression more generally (Barrett 1980). It has been asserted that only through change here can the groundwork begin to be laid for change towards equity for women in other respects. Working outside the home then opens up space for shifting the balance of power between men and women inside the household and in the woman's primary identification of herself as a housewife (Luxton 1990: 41). As well, as working women in Canada join unions that have been influenced by feminism, they are encouraged to assert themselves in the home and to challenge the unequal domestic division of labour. As Luxton (1990) reports for working-class women, and Arat-Koc (1990) for middle-class and professional women, this situation creates a crisis in the domestic arena for many couples. Yet we are clearly far from a situation where work outside the home necessarily brings about the kind of change that feminists have sought. For example, the solution of using a paid domestic worker may solve the immediate intra-household crisis, but it simply passes off the responsibility for domestic labour to another, less advantaged woman. Of course, to a large extent, it is the failure to change the domestic division of labour in any significant sense, or to socialize the care of sick, elderly, or young dependents rather than relying on women to do this work, that attracts women to homework in the first place. However, where work opportunities are presented that make it no longer necessary for women to work outside the home while at the same time sustaining the ongoing struggle inside, there is less and less chance that a shift will take place, since inside-the-home domestic labour and paid labour become mutually obscuring. Instead, more and more work can be absorbed into an endless day of continuous work. Linked to this tendency is the likelihood that any progress that has been achieved in improving women's conditions of paid work vis-à-vis men in the workplace can very easily be lost as women's work is hidden once again in the household, and each woman is left to fight or not fight her own individual battle over the conditions of both paid and unpaid work.

The link between home-based work and violence against women in their own home is rarely made, yet it would seem that working at home helps to create an environment conducive to its continuation. We know well enough that domestic violence is a frequently invisible, yet also common, part of women's lives, regardless of class. Pushing work back into the private sphere leaves women without external personal support, and as well restricts their exposure to alternative courses of action that could help them to extricate themselves from a dangerous or potentially dangerous situation. The clues to this fall-out from homework policies already exist. If homework is isolating because there is no one to laugh with, then there is no one to cry with either. An already pressured husband may be pushed over the brink by the apparently incessant sound of a staple gun or a sewing machine in the early hours of the morning. But beyond the classic relations of domestic violence, there is a new twist to contend with, one that again links these women to domestic workers: the increased vulnerability of women whose only meetings with their 'boss' take place in their own private homes, often in the absence of other household members.

The sexual exploitation of women factory workers in situations where work is scarce and labour cheap and plentiful has been reported from around the world (Elson and Pearson 1981). Homework provides similar conditions, with the added advantage that all of this takes place in complete privacy, behind closed doors. I accompanied Pierre, a subcontractor in Toronto, on a round of visits to 'his' homeworkers. In the car he joked about how he liked visiting the women in their homes, and much preferred to do so during the day when their husbands would not be home. With several of the homeworkers he initiated sexual bantering, and although it was difficult to determine to what extent his behaviour was affected by my presence.

Conclusion

New opportunities for women to work at home are emerging, as homework becomes an increasingly popular efficiency strategy for employers seeking lowered costs and improved flexibility. This strategy represents a change in the conditions of work, one that has the potential to be particularly dramatic for public-sector workers. In spite of assurances from the government that the workers' union contracts and existing working conditions continue to pertain while they work at home, there is no assurance that this will not change as the next generation of public-sector homeworkers is recruited from outside. Critics of labour flexibility theories have been quick to point out that the success of homework is predicated upon structural inequalities in the labour market, which include gender, age, citizenship, and race (Pollert 1988). Homework presents patent examples of how flexible workers can be exploited through the very characteristics of inequality that have been the basis for equality struggles in the workplace. Homework policies have the effect of reinforcing and strengthening unequal power relations between men and women, between whites and people of colour, and between workers and those who supply work. The sexual exploitation of women workers, whether in Canada or in Third World factories, is a stark manifestation of the capitalist system of domination, and reveals the exploitative nature of the labour-capital relation in all its ugliness. There is a kind of vicious circle operating here. Persistent manifestations of sexism and racism in all facets of peoples' lives lead them to be more interested in forms of work that do not require them to leave their homes (or, for some, the relative safety of their own ethnic community), while at the same time more and more of these informal kinds of jobs are being thrown up. Yet neither in the home nor in ethnic-enclave businesses are the ideological principles behind conventional gender relations likely to be challenged, and white society is absolved of the responsibility for confronting structural racism. Not only do homework policies undermine the basis for collective action; the implications of that loss are perhaps more wide-ranging than has hitherto been acknowledged.

NOTES

1 I am grateful to Isa Bakker and Jane Stinson for their thoughtful and helpful comments on a previous draft of this paper. The data on industrial homeworkers in Ontario that forms part of this chapter was gathered through field research carried out for a doctoral degree in social anthropology at the University of Toronto and was supported in part by the Social Sciences and Humanities Research Council of Canada. The field research was carried out between 1987 and 1989 in and around Toronto and London, Ontario. It comprised extended interviews and participant observation with about forty industrial homeworkers and their families, as well as with factory managers and owners, subcontractors, union officials, and immigrant-services workers.

2 My thanks to Jane Stinson for helping me to link these very different kinds of homework.

3 It is worth noting that all the homeworkers I knew, except one who also worked full time outside the home, were in nuclear or extended families, and I attribute this fact to the impossibility of their making sufficient income from homework alone; thus it has to be combined with other kinds of income derived from other household members.

4 Even for those who were not 'visible' in racial terms, their construction as 'immigrant women' (Ng 1986) rendered them distinct from women of Northern European origin.

11

Structural Adjustment, Citizenship, and Foreign Domestic Labour: The Canadian Case

ABIGAIL B. BAKAN AND
DAIVA K. STASIULIS

Among critics of global debt and adjustment policies, the recognition that structural-adjustment policies operate to the detriment of the majority of the residents of underdeveloped countries is increasingly common. The literature in this vein is extensive, documenting the alarming growth in unemployment, underemployment, consumer prices, and disparities in wealth, and the nosedive taken in incomes, basic government services, and the status of women and children.[1] In this chapter, we examine only one aspect of the detrimental effects of structural-adjustment policies – that is, the increasing pressure felt by women of Third World origins to emigrate abroad to take up positions as nannies and maids in First World households.

A brief summary can identify the parameters of the conditions underlying and shaping this migration process. Within developing countries, dislocated rural labour is inadequately absorbed in the factories of the export processing zones. The World Bank and the International Monetary Fund (IMF) have insisted that in return for international service of debts, Third World governments pursue policies that induce their citizens to seek jobs and money elsewhere.[2] Foreign-currency earnings are critical to debt repayment policies, so that overseas employment and remittances to families 'back home' are important means of procuring foreign exchange. These changes have had a considerable impact on migratory flows, especially, though not exclusively, from less developed to more developed states. The governments of developed countries, in turn, have accepted the cheap and exploitable labour of these migrants, for both political and economic reasons.

The acceptance of migrants from the South, however, has occurred within fairly strict terms. Third World migrants have filled labour shortages during periods of expansion from the 1950s to 1970s, at times despite considerable opposition and anti-immigrant hostility from the more established populations of these countries. Even during periods of recession, however, non-white immigrants have been recruited to fill occupations spurned for their degraded conditions by workers with other employment options.

The global implications of structural adjustment have also influenced recent debates on the politics of citizenship. First World countries, drawing upon long historical practices of racial/ethnic exclusion, and beleaguered since the mid-1970s by growing deficits, have increased the policing of Third World migrants' access to the rights normally associated with First World citizenship. Referring to Europe, Balibar (1991: 18) points out how complex the mapping of citizenship and citizenship rights has become. Some 'fundamental social rights' have been extended to 'guest workers' and their families both through 'national law, and even Community law,' yet national laws in most 'advanced'[3] societies are decidedly discriminatory. As Balibar further notes, discrimination 'written into the very nature of the European Community [EC] ... led to the definition of two categories of foreigners with unequal rights' (1991: 6). Emergent EC policies point to the construction of new distinctions between 'insiders' and 'outsiders,' between 'citizens' and 'subjects' (ibid.: 19). In First World states, citizenship, and access to rights traditionally associated with citizenship, are withheld even to long-term residents and their 'native-born' children of races and/or ethnicities viewed as alien, unassimilable, and undesirable. While this is not a new phenomenon, since the return in the mid-1970s of an era of long-term economic crisis and instability, nationalist policies that are increasingly protective of borders have reversed an earlier trend of relaxation of border controls (R. Cohen 1987).

The implications of these recent shifts in global labour allocation and the politics of citizenship have also been gendered. Despite considerable debate regarding the relative merits of the preferential employment or exploitation of women workers in global export processing zones, there is increasing recognition that, on balance, structural-adjustment policies have increased the burden of women's oppression in Third World states.[4] Diane Elson, for example, has identified the dependence of adjustment policies upon the increased provision of women's unpaid labour as a means to compensate for a decline in the level and quality of services and the rise in prices of consumer goods. Women's increased and unpaid work operates as a shock-absorber to promote the apparent 'efficiency' of market-oriented mechanisms.[5]

One major growth area of First World employment for impoverished Third World women that has emerged as a result of this global pattern is that of domestic service, in particular the provision of child care, or nanny service, in the private homes of First World families. Despite the contraction in access to legal migration channels of Third World citizens to First World countries, employment opportunities for immigrant women as domestic workers in Europe and North America are either remaining the same or increasing. The sheer volume of Third World migrants seeking domestic-service jobs in First World countries, as well as in newly industrializing countries, has rendered contemporary domestic work 'an international business with political implications.' The industry has been further augmented by the involvement of the governments of both employers and domestic workers, the IMF, and a host of intermediaries such as recruiting and placement agencies (Enloe 1989: 177). The increased 'supply' of women to work in this occupation has coincided with a socially and economically constructed 'demand' for in-home care, particularly the provision of child care, in the core zones of the global system.

The demand side of the equation has also resulted from changes in the contemporary world system. The increased participation rate of married women with children in the waged workforce that began after the Second World War has tended to continue over the years of long-term global crisis. Provision for child care in most advanced capitalist states, however, has not kept up with the increased demand for it. The prohibitive costs of public child care ensure that there is an economic incentive to opt for live-in care rather than child care organized in the public sphere.[6] The unabated demand for live-in child care is, however, not only the result of economic pressures that have led to cuts in the provision of state-regulated and/or -subsidized child care, but also the product of an explicitly ideological argument. A tendency to discredit public child care has been characteristic of a general backlash against feminism and women's rights that has taken place particularly in North America. The increasing legitimacy of the idea that private in-home child care is the best-quality care available is an important element in the growth of demand for in-home child care in advanced societies.[7]

The following discussion focuses on the impact of poverty and underdevelopment in producing an increasingly large pool of women workers in search of First World citizenship rights. The migration of Third World women to Canada through the foreign-domestic-worker policy (currently the Live-in Caregiver Program, or LCP) is analysed as a clear instance of the link between the global debt crisis and the international migration of Third World women. Our argument is twofold. First, we argue that structural forces, that is, generalized conditions of global unevenness exacerbated and amplified by imperialist structures and policies, tend to create conditions that force female citizens of poor states to seek citizenship on virtually any terms in richer states. Second, we maintain that First World states, such as Canada, are both able and willing to exploit this increased supply in order to advance their own policies of structural adjustment. The example of domestic-worker policy is illustrative of how policies that are damaging to the interests of women as a whole, such as the reduction or elimination of public day care, are rendered palatable, and even beneficial, to women of selectively high income and status within the boundaries defined by First World citizenship.

Central to this argument is the claim that the Canadian example is, in its general contours, typical of global state policy in the construction of the non-citizenship rights of foreign domestic workers. Such a claim could be contested insofar as Canada's foreign- domestic-worker policy is often identified as one of the least abusive among the many countries across the globe employing foreign domestic workers. Thus, in January 1988, the Aquino government in the Philippines responded to public protest of the abuse of overseas domestic workers by announcing a blanket ban on Filipina domestic workers going abroad. Within a few months of the announced ban, however, Canada was exempted from the Philippine government's restriction on the grounds that the domestic workers employed there were not subject to objectionable conditions (Kwitko 1993: 1, 21).[8] Similarly, in Bridget Anderson's impressive comparative analysis of the conditions of domestic workers on an international scale, Canada's LCP is described as a policy that goes 'a long way to regulating the situation'[9] of abusive conditions for domestic workers.

The argument presented here takes exception to this pride of place for Canada's domestic-worker policy. We contend that the LCP appears as a favourable policy only because the conditions of domestic workers on a world scale are so universally oppressive. Yet the measure of abuse considered to be 'acceptable' for domestic workers is itself subject to specialized criteria. Such criteria are a feature of several factors: the generally degraded status of women's work in the home, the absence of comprehensive public support for child care, the denial of citizenship rights to immigrant labour, racist assumptions about women of colour, and the resultant social construction of class divisions among women that arise with the private employment of domestic workers. Thus, we argue that Canada's foreign-domestic policy is more typical than atypical on an international scale, a case that will be elaborated below.

Poverty, Underdevelopment, and Domestic Workers

The process of recruitment of migrant women workers to perform paid domestic labour in developed capitalist states is structurally linked to the uneven pattern of international economic development, to international migration patterns and regulations, as well as to racially and ethnically specific ideological discourses. In post-colonial conditions, the legacy of imperialism has combined with modern conditions of indebtedness to generate large pools of female migrant labour in most Third World states to fill the demand in the domestic-care industry of industrially advanced states.

The historic policies and practices of First World countries, and the international organizations these countries dominate, have served to exacerbate the conditions of poverty that migrant women hope to escape. Structural-adjustment policies, readily advocated by the International Monetary Fund and the World Bank in particular, entail government cuts in social-service budgets and public-sector employment, economic controls that favour the export of commodities over local market expansion, and tax incentives to transnational corporations. Cheryl Payer puts the case starkly: 'The poorer consumers and wage-earners are the real losers ... It is an explicit and basic aim of IMF programmes to discourage local consumption in order to free resources for export.'[10] One result of escalating poverty, income inequality, and unemployment is increased pressure to migrate in search of employment. Migration often occurs first from rural to urban areas and to export processing zones, but much of it is directed to newly industrializing countries and developed economies of the North. As opportunities for migration are directly tied to occupational demand in the receiving countries, however, the gendered and racialized ghettoization of the labour markets of prospective countries of destination limits, conditions, and moulds the character of prospective applicants. Those who wish to migrate can do so legally only if they can prove that they are specifically suited to meet the employment profiles in demand: enter the female Third World immigrant domestic. Before turning to the specific case of foreign domestic workers in Canada, and the conditions in the primary-source regions of the Caribbean and the Philippines from which they originate, a brief consideration of the more general place of paid domestic labour within conditions of modern capitalism is in order.

Domestic Service and Third World Immigrant Women

Domestic service in the home long predated contemporary capitalist global relations. In fact, pre-capitalist economies were largely based on the provision of family labour.[11] With the emergence of modern capitalism came a contraction in family size and a reduction in the amount of labour performed in the private home relative to the amount performed in socialized industrial and service production units. Changes in this direction have been particularly rapid and pronounced since the large-scale participation of married women in the paid workforce, characteristic of the most advanced sections of the global economy. As Mary Romero summarizes: 'The transformation of homemaking activity from production to consumption became more complete and led to new developments for homemakers after World War II ... Both working- and middle-class women's entrance into the work force contributed to the general upward trend of women's employment in the twentieth century ... [However, the] double-day syndrome originated from the social expectation that employed women would fulfil their families' needs through daily activity in the work force and in the home' (1992: 64–5). As new employment opportunities for women workers have developed, those able to gain alternative employment to domestic labour have continually elected to do so. In advanced Western countries in Europe and North America, women moved out of private domestic service and into the growing industries and services in ever-increasing numbers. A situation of chronic labour shortage has therefore come to characterize domestic service under conditions of modern capitalism. The so-called servant problem emerged as the number of women willing to work as the private servants of other women declined. By the 1950s, even the anthropologist Margaret Mead offered suggestions on 'how to survive' without a maid (Martin and Segrave 1985: 69).

Commercial enterprises also took advantage of the market opportunities that became available. As economic boom conditions continued in the 1950s and 1960s, household appliances were advertised in North America as a means of automating housework and technologically 'solving' the 'servant problem.' The single most demanding arena of private household labour, however, the provision of child care, particularly for children of preschool age, has proved to be the most difficult to automate. Under conditions of a chronic labour shortage, classical economics would predict an increase in wages and an improvement in the quality of working conditions as the means of attracting labourers. Domestic labour, however, has proved to be remarkably 'immune to the regulatory infection'[12] of the market. Generated by conditions of chronic poverty in the Third World, large numbers of workers highly motivated to achieve secure employment for themselves and their families have served to offset pressures for improvements in the conditions of domestic care. The existence of this labour pool has thus mitigated against the operation of a pure market model of supply and demand with reference to domestic labour. The denial of citizenship rights to immigrant workers and the racialized image of the Third World domestic worker, who is considered uniquely and 'naturally' suited to serve the needs of First World women and their families, have tended to ensure that what one author has called 'the despised calling' has become identified with the labour of women of 'the despised race.' [13]

The restrictive conditions of employment to which non-citizens in search of gaining the anticipated security of citizenship are prone have ensured that domestic service in the context of the current global process of restructuring has taken on contradictory dimensions. At the same time as it is the most spurned of occupations for those who are entitled to the right of labour mobility, it is one of the most coveted for those who are otherwise refused mobility rights. The notion in the United States, of 'housekeeping for the Green Card,'[14] for example, is paralleled in the Canadian context by the practice of 'doing domestic to get landed' (Macklin 1992). Moreover, racial and gendered barriers to labour mobility also restrict the alternative-employment options of domestic workers, even once formal citizenship is obtained. Phyllis Palmer points out, for example, that in the United States, black southern women who had migrated north in the 1930s to work as domestics found that unlike earlier generations of Euro-American immigrants, they had no access to alternative sources of employment (1989: 67ff.).

Migration and paid domestic service are thus elements of a global process of linkages in which gendered and racialized ideologies play a central part. The particular legislative restrictions and conditions governing foreign domestic labour vary from country to country. None the less, there is clearly an overall pattern in which domestic labour is subject to greater and more exceptional levels of restriction relative to other forms of employment. Hence, in countries where labour rights in general are minimal, foreign domestic workers will be subject to the greatest level of oppression and abuse, when measured on an international scale; where labour rights in general are relatively broad, as in the Canadian context, the conditions of foreign domestic workers may indeed be less abusive compared with those of domestics in other countries, but they remain at a level considered unacceptable in virtually every other occupation within the norms of nation-specific labour-force conditions.

A few examples of the conditions of domestic workers internationally indicate this pattern. The Gulf states,[15] for example, have been identified by domestic-rights advocates as among those countries with the most oppressive conditions for domestic workers.[16] There are an estimated 1.2 million domestic workers in the Gulf states, who have commonly reported 'cases of abuse and extreme exploitation, of rape and beatings, non-payment of wages, physical and mental torture' (Anderson 1993: 14). Domestic workers make up approximately 20 per cent of an estimated 6 million migrant workers, who are entirely dependent for their livelihood on their employers. Their nominal wages vary with their country of origin: according to the International Labour Organization, Filipino workers are entitled to earn US$300 per month; Sri Lankans and Bangladeshis, at the bottom end of the scale, are entitled to US$170 per month.[17] In practice, non-payment of wages, often in return for debts incurred for travel without the knowledge of the worker herself, is common.

Labour laws in the Gulf region are extremely restrictive, and generally serve to increase the control of employers. Exacerbating the situation is the fact that foreign domestic workers often suffer by being considered part of their employers' families, rather than workers entitled to some amount of autonomy or some rights. Even if a worker is under a legal contract, therefore, conditions of virtual slavery may ensue. In one example of a contract between a Bahrain employer and a Filipino domestic, for example, one clause reads: 'Female domestic (housemaids) duty hours will be unlimited as she will be treated as one of the family household. She will not be allowed to go out of the house alone or on her own.' Another clause reads: 'There is no holiday for the House Maids, and it is not allowed for the Christian House Maid to ask her employer to give permission for her to go to Church.'[18]

Hong Kong is commonly also identified as a particularly abusive domain for foreign domestic workers.[19] There are estimated to be more overseas domestic workers in Hong Kong than in any other Asian country, most of them Filipino. In 1990, of 57,971 domestic workers in Hong Kong, 52,868 were from the Philippines.[20] All foreign domestic workers must register and sign a contract governed by the Hong Kong Employment Ordinance. This contractual system is ostensibly in place to ensure a minimum standard of protection, such as a minimum wage, one day off per week, annual paid holidays, food and accommodation, and free passage to and from Hong Kong. However, daily and weekly hours of work are not covered in the terms of the law. According to an August 1991 survey on the conditions of overseas domestic workers conducted by the Asian Migrant Centre in Hong Kong, over 80 per cent of the 2000 workers in the sample worked fourteen or more hours per day.[21] Moreover, since 1987, legislation entitled the New Conditions of Stay for Foreign Domestic Helpers (FDH) – more commonly known as the 'two-week rule' – has been in force. Under this law, if a domestic worker leaves her employer for any reason, including physical or sexual abuse, or if she is fired by her employer, she is required to leave the colony within fourteen days. This regulation applies only to foreign domestic workers, and applies even if her employer retains her passport, return fare, and her earned wages for the time she has been employed.

Canada's Foreign-Domestic-Worker Policy: Institutionalized Abuse

Given the experiences of domestics in countries such as Saudi Arabia, Bahrain, and Hong Kong, Canada's foreign-domestic-worker policy may appear to offer some protection and security for the employees involved. The argument presented here departs from this sanguine or laudatory view of the Canadian policy. We maintain that, rather than preventing or ameliorating the threat of abuse, Canada's Live-in Caregiver Program (LCP) actually only serves to institutionalize such a threat. Moreover, the LCP has been structured by various federal governments over decades with the full knowledge of a highly vulnerable pool of foreign-worker applicants, upon whom exceptionally restrictive conditions are imposed.

In Canada, the federal policy governing the recruitment of in-home domestic care, the Live-in Caregiver Program, was formulated to facilitate and regulate the recruitment of migrant workers. To be eligible by Canadian law to hire a domestic through the LCP, the prospective employing family must indicate its ability to provide a room in the family home, for which rent would be deducted from wages earned, and to meet a minimum combined annual income. As of April 1992, that minimum in Ontario was $65,000 per year, about $20,000 above the national combined average annual family income (Oziewicz 1992).

The policy itself is constructed as a 'special' or separate piece of immigration legislation, applying only to those foreign workers seeking work in Canada as live-in domestics as a temporary means to obtain permanent immigration status. This fact alone indicates the unique conditions to which foreign domestic workers are subject, separated out from the normal pool of immigrant applicants to Canada. Moreover, the distinctive immigration policy, administered at the federal level, also exempts foreign domestic workers from the generalized regulation of labour legislation, which is administered at the provincial level. The regulations of work for domestic workers vary from province to province. Moreover, where foreign domestic workers are covered by specific provincial labour legislation, this has tended to be the result of domestic advocacy movements organizing to ensure coverage, not the largesse of any particular provincial government.[22]

From the legislation of mid-1950s, which was enacted specifically to recruit Caribbean women workers to Canada as live-in domestics, to the present policy enacted in 1992, the federal government has insisted upon maintaining a distinct and exceptional institutional mechanism to govern the migration and work lives of foreign domestic workers. Another notable characteristic of the foreign-domestic legislation is that there has been a secular trend towards the increasing and tightening of restrictions rather than towards their liberalization, despite public lobbying and documented studies calling for equalizing the rights of foreign domestics with those of other workers.[23]

With the 1973 introduction by the Canadian federal government of the Temporary Employment Authorization Program, for example, domestic workers received short-term work permits rather than the previous scheme's provision of permanent resident status upon arrival. These women were permitted to stay in Canada conditionally upon the performance of domestic work for a designated employer, thus transforming 'domestic workers into ... disposable migrant labourers, not unlike European "guest workers"' (Macklin 1992: 691). During the 1970s, the citizenship rights of foreign, and especially Caribbean, domestics thus deteriorated further. While many European domestics continued to enter Canada as landed immigrants, Caribbean domestics increasingly entered on temporary-employment visas, which gave maximum control to the state and employers over the conditions of work and residence of women of colour domestics.[24] Migrant domestics were compelled to endure restrictions in freedoms generally considered unacceptable under liberal democracies, and were spurned by other workers, including those performing the same type of work outside private households.[25]

The Canadian government's objective of bringing in domestic workers under temporary work permits effectively created an indentured or captive labour force. Moreover, it was cost effective from the perspective of the Canadian government: the costs of original production (nurturance, education, and so on) had been borne elsewhere, and workers were unlikely to quit regardless of how exploited or intolerable their work and living situations were. The motivation for administering foreign domestics through the temporary-employment-visa system with no recourse to the previous option of applying for landed-immigrant status from within Canada was clearly stated in 1976 by the government: the aim was to impede the turnover of foreign workers out of compulsory live-in domestic service (Daenzer 1993: 87–108).

In 1981, a revised policy, titled the Foreign Domestic Movement (FDM), was introduced that further institutionalized this objective. Under this program, a foreign domestic worker was eligible to apply for landed-immigrant status after two years of live-in service with a designated employer. Employers could only be changed with the approval of a federal immigration officer. If the worker successfully achieved landed status, all of the restrictions associated with the FDM ceased to apply, providing access to all the formal citizenship rights open to permanent residents. The right to apply for permanent status after two years from inside Canada was heralded as a victory by domestic-worker advocates, and it was indeed a concession to the demands of domestic workers themselves. Nevertheless, the 1981 policy included several regulations that continued the pattern of exceptional, and discriminatory, treatment for foreign domestic workers. It institutionalized the potential for employer abuse, including the threat of deportation, while the worker remained effectively imprisoned by temporary national-residential, and compulsory live-in, status. If after three assessments the domestic worker had not been accepted for permanent-resident status, she would legally have to return to her country of origin. The alternative would be to remain illegally in Canada and to work in the shadow economy.

Other criteria, such as the requirement of educational upgrading to prove 'self-sufficiency' as a condition of achieving landed-immigrant status, were also imposed on those who entered Canada through the FDM. These restrictions were challenged by domestics and their advocates, who criticized the use of criteria not employed to assess the suitability for landing of any other group of immigrants whose occupations, like those of domestic workers, were in high demand in Canada. Notwithstanding these protests, the government's policy remained in place for a decade. Only when the government came under a legal challenge was the policy altered. The government's failure to withstand a 1990 legal challenge to the FDM policy was pivotal in prompting the raising of formal qualifications for entry into Canada of foreign domestic applicants.[26]

Once again, the changed policy did not decrease the considerable restrictions imposed on the rights of foreign domestic workers. Under the 1992 Live-in Caregiver Program guidelines, the upgrading requirements were eliminated in assessments for landed status for foreign domestics, who were now called 'caregivers.' To offset this apparent liberalization in the policy, however, eligibility criteria for entry into Canada by migrant caregivers became *more* restrictive. In other words, the exceptional criteria for eligibility for permanent residential status under the FDM were simply off-loaded to the point of application for admission into the LCP program.

Criteria for entry into the Live-in Caregiver Program originally called for the equivalent of a Canadian grade 12 education, plus six months of full-time formal training in a field or occupation related to the caregiver job sought in Canada. Within months of the program's inception, the latter training requirement was amended to allow for experience in lieu of training. Once again, however, this amendment did not occur without considerable public outcry from domestic workers and worried potential employers (Young 1994: 20–1). The official reasons given by the Immigration Department for upgrading the admissions criteria for foreign domestics were the perceived needs, first, to upgrade the quality of child care and, second, to facilitate the entry into the larger labour market of those domestics who have attained landed status. According to the federal government, without adequate educational backgrounds, domestic workers who have obtained permanent-resident status after completing the required two years of live-in service continue to find employment in only the most poorly remunerated jobs.

The two most repressive aspects of the Foreign Domestic Movement regulations have been retained under the Live-in Caregiver Program, in spite of the government's attempt to sell the new program through the rhetoric of 'reform' resulting from 'widespread consultation.'[27] These are (1) the temporary migrant or 'visitor' status and (2) the compulsory live-in requirement for foreign domestic workers. Accordingly, it is recognized that this 'program is unique' (Young 1994: 20), as it applies specific restrictions on the rights of foreign domestic workers that apply to no other category of workers, regardless of their immigration status. The two restrictions of compulsory live-in labour and temporary immigration status go hand in hand. According to the most recent governmental review of the policy, Canada's shortage of waged domestic labour exists only within the live-in market. Were it not for this labour shortage, foreign labour would not be in demand. Moreover, upon receipt of landed-immigrant status, there is a nearly universal pattern of departure from live-in domestic service to other types of work, including live-out, or day, labour, within the domestic-service industry (Daenzer 1993: 126–9). These two features of the program have also been identified as those that allow for the most abusive and unsafe working conditions, and thus have been consistently opposed by leading domestic workers' rights advocates in Canada.[28] Studies of paid domestic service in the United States have repeatedly identified the single most effective change in domestic labour leading to improved working conditions as the move away from live-in to live-out service.[29] The continued imposition of the compulsory live-in and temporary-residential-status requirements is therefore notable for its exceptional treatment of an identifiable group of women workers, usually of Third World origins, brought in for the sole purpose of private domestic service. Effectively, the Canadian government's insistence on retaining temporary-residence status for foreign domestics as a precondition for their eligibility for formal Canadian citizenship 'established a class of people good enough to do their dirty work, but not good enough to be permanent residents' (Martin and Segrave 1985: 121).

Canada's foreign-domestic-worker policy thus shares in common with the policies of other countries the imposition of exceptionally harsh restrictions, considered unacceptable for workers in other industries or for those (such as full citizens) who have the option of seeking alternative sources of employment. In research on domestic labour internationally, the terms used to describe situations normally considered to be illegal, archaic, and barbaric include 'precapitalist,' 'premodern,' and 'slavery.'[30] Canada's institutionalization of compulsory live-in status, combined with the threat of denial of permanent residence, amounts to a condition of indentured labour. The fact that the condition of indenture is temporary does not in any way mitigate the susceptibility of the employee to abuse. The temporary condition is rendered effective in regulating domestic workers precisely because it holds the promise of increased citizenship rights at the end of the two-year term. In other words, the stick would not be effective without the promise of a carrot.

There is extensive documentation of conditions of abuse commonly experienced by foreign domestic workers in Canada. Since such abuse takes place within the confines of a private home, however, the enforcement and regulation of procedures to correct such abuses are both rare and extremely difficult to carry out. The overriding threat of deportation to conditions of poverty and chronic unemployment in the Third World ensures a structural pattern of intimidation, where the citizen-employer and the non-citizen-employee do not face each other on equal terms. Beginning in the 1950s, Canada has drawn upon, as recruitment areas for foreign domestic workers, two major Third World source regions to which the threat of deportation is sufficiently harsh that even the most oppressive employment options within Canada seem to offer a more secure alternative. It is to the conditions in these regions that we now turn our discussion.

Filipino and Caribbean Domestic Workers in Canada

The conditions of underdevelopment within the Philippines and the English Caribbean are central to the historic role of these regions as the major Third World source areas for the recruitment of foreign domestics in Canada. How Canadian domestic-worker policy has been constructed to take advantage of these conditions, and has adapted its regulations accordingly, is critical to situating Canada's foreign-domestic policy in the context of global restructuring.

While the English Caribbean region as a whole incorporates a wide variety of nations and is influenced by a complexity of economic, social, and political factors, internal migration was negligible in general until the nineteenth century, and external migration involved only a fraction of the population. Those who did migrate were usually of middle- or upper-class background, hoping to advance their prospects by obtaining permanent residence in Europe or North America.[31]

During the 1960s and 1970s, this pattern started to change, with large numbers of residents from the Commonwealth Caribbean seeking migration abroad. Most of the major studies of Caribbean migration for this period maintain that the increase was not necessarily a response to unemployment, but of increased opportunities elsewhere for well-educated, relatively high-status professionals.[32] This is not to say that unemployment did not exist. On the contrary, the British West Indies have seen chronic rates of unemployment ranging between 20 and 30 per cent of the workforce. Restrictive immigration laws in some of the most favoured destination countries, however, ensured that only the most skilled workers were permitted to enter.[33]

The period of the 1960s and 1970s saw an increase in emigration outlets for Caribbean workers at the same time as political independence was being negotiated with the British imperial state.[34] Newly independent Caribbean governments hoped to offset chronic unemployment and secure sources of foreign currency in the form of remittances by encouraging migration abroad. By 1973, Jamaica, the largest of the British Caribbean nations with a population of about two million, registered more than one-half million citizens living off the island.[35] Remittances are now a critical component for family survival in the region. Estimates of the value of remittances to the British West Indies are difficult to verify, given the variations among the islands and poor statistical records. One study provides a 1978 estimate of US$23 billion, roughly equivalent to 10 per cent of the region's merchandise exports; a 1982 study suggests that remittances were the principal source of hard currency in several of the small islands in the region.[36]

Evidence suggests that the early years of this emigration wave favoured the exodus of male workers. This trend coincided with the internal migration of female workers from the rural areas into the cities, particularly to work as domestic servants for private homes and in the burgeoning tourist and hotel industries.[37] This pattern reinforced another: the historically large percentage of households headed by sole-support mothers. According to Momsen, though the percentage of female household heads varies greatly across the region, in general 'women have had to accept responsibility for the financial support of their children since emancipation because of both male migration and male economic marginality' (Henshall Momsen 1988: 147). In 1970, the Commonwealth Caribbean recorded 35 per cent of all households headed by women; a 1986 study confirmed this figure, finding a ratio of one in three households to be under female headship.[38] This factor, and the decline of agriculture as a source of profitable employment, compelled women to seek new sectors of work.[39] Domestic labour in Canada was one such avenue.

Before 1962, Canada had an explicitly racist governmental policy restricting West Indian immigration to Canada. According to the 1958 director of the Immigration Branch of the Department of Citizenship, 'It is not by accident that coloured British subjects other than negligible numbers from the United Kingdom are excluded from Canada ... They do not assimilate readily and pretty much vegetate to a low standard of living. Despite what has been said to the contrary, many cannot adapt themselves to our climatic conditions.'[40] In 1955, this policy was amended slightly to permit a limited number of West Indian women workers to enter Canada on condition that they remain in domestic service with a contractually designated employer for one year; after this time they were permitted to obtain other employment. This policy, like those that were to follow, was distinctly discriminatory. Unlike domestic workers from Europe, the West Indian workers received no government assistance in the cost of passage. Moreover, although permanent-resident status was obtained upon arrival, Caribbean domestics were subject to special conditions of compulsory live-in domestic labour and the threat of deportation. Such restrictions did not apply to domestics from European source countries.[41]

Between 1973 and 1981, West Indian women workers were admitted as domestic workers on temporary employment visas. Others entered as skilled workers, particularly in nursing when there were periodic labour shortages, or as sponsored relatives. The numbers as a whole, however, were relatively small, and since that period have been declining relative to other source countries. Between 1973 and 1978, of all those who obtained landed-immigrant status in Canada, those from all Caribbean source countries totalled only 10 per cent; by 1980, that figure was 6 per cent.[42] Conversely, one of the most rapidly increasing alternative source regions of immigration to Canada overall, as well as in the migration of foreign domestics, is the Philippines. Thus, in the year from July 1975 to June 1976, 44.8 per cent of all entrants to Canada on temporary employment visas assigned to in-home domestic work were from the Caribbean, and only 0.3 per cent were from all countries in Asia; by 1990, only 5 per cent of entrants on the Foreign Domestic Movement program were from the Caribbean, while over 58 per cent were from the Philippines.[43]

Canada, however, is only one destination country for Filipino migrants. Indeed, the vast majority of Filipino migrant domestics abroad work in Asia (particularly Hong Kong and Singapore) and the Gulf states. Between 1982 and 1990, the total number of contract workers processed by the Philippines had almost doubled.[44] In 1990, the estimated size of the total Filipino workforce abroad, comprising both temporary contract migrants and those who had settled permanently abroad, was about 1.8 million (Abella 1992: 27). The 1980s also witnessed an increasing exodus of female migrant labour, so that by the end of that decade women composed between 40 and 50 per cent of all Filipino migrants (Kwitko, 1993: 2; Vickers 1991: 90). This increase was in part a response to high levels of demand for nurses, office workers, domestic workers, and other types of service workers, as well as entertainers, sex-trade workers, and mail-order brides in Asia, the Middle East, Europe, and North America (Carino 1992: 13). By 1991, domestic workers constituted the majority of Filipino women workers registered with the central government's Philippine Overseas Employment Administration (POEA).[45]

The unprecedented rise of Filipino emigration reflects both the growing internationalization of labour markets and the persistence of underdevelopment in the Philippine economy.[46] Development in the Philippines has been hampered by colonization by the Spanish and, since the turn of the century, by colonial and neocolonial policies led by the United States. A pervasive legacy of the Philippine neocolonial status vis-à-vis the United States has been the latter's right to maintain over twenty bases and military installations in the country. The withdrawal of the U.S. military in 1992, however, has only further exposed the Philippines' development problems insofar as it coincided with a significant reduction in American aid (Kwitko 1993: 8).

Several structural factors linked to underdevelopment have triggered the large volume of labour flows from the country. These include the increasing scarcity of land, urban growth without sufficient expansion in urban employment to meet the supply of dislocated and landless agricultural workers, and general poor performance of a predominantly foreign-owned economy. Regarding the latter, it is beyond the scope of this discussion to account for why the Philippines, unlike South Korea and Taiwan, with whom it shares many characteristics, did not become a Newly Industrializing Country. Angeles's account, however, is persuasive, suggesting that the role of the state, burdened by the presence of a strong landlord class, has served to block the enactment of progressive land reform and the emergence of a strong indigenous entrepreneurial class (1991/92: 91). Before the Philippines acquired formal independence from the United States in 1946, the semi-feudal landlord-tenant system was heavily promoted by the ruling élite at the expense of the freeholding sectors of the peasantry (Kwitko 1993: 8).

Critical development problems in the Philippines have been exacerbated by political instability. Between 1972 and 1981, Philippine president Ferdinand Marcos sought to suppress civil unrest in the form of peasant, worker, and student militancy, through the imposition of martial law (Carino 1992: 18). Marcos's economic policies virtually provided an open invitation for foreign investors to freely enter and control any area of the economy through 'service contracts' entered into with Filipino citizens and domestic corporations (Pomeroy 1992: 235–6). In 1984, following the assassination of Senator Benigno Aquino, leader of the opposition to the Marcos régime, some 86,000 workers were laid off by various corporations, and more than 50 per cent of families were living below the officially defined poverty threshold. The removal of Marcos and the installation of the Aquino government in 1986 through a popularly supported military revolt coincided, however, with further economic instability. The policies of the Aquino and, since 1992, the Ramos governments have not significantly alleviated the economic distress felt by almost all Filipinos, with the exception of an élite subservient to U.S. imperialist wishes.

Key to understanding the unstable nature of the Philippine economy have been the debt crisis and structural-adjustment policies whose effects are aptly summed up by Pomeroy: 'A relentless chaining of the Filipino people into a helpless debt situation constituted part of the coldly planned process of reorganizing and reorienting the Philippine economy to suit the needs and operations of U.S. big corporations' (1992: 239). The Philippine experience with IMF–World Bank lending policies began in 1958, and has resulted in enormous and escalating international financial debt, amounting to $28.6 billion in 1986. Augmenting the size of international debt for the non-oil-producing country were the 1973–4 and 1979–80 increases in world oil prices, which plunged the trade balance of the Philippines into ever-steeper deficit (ibid. 238). U.S.-dictated demands by the World Bank for 'structural adjustment' of the Philippine economy included a sharp curtailment of imports, wage restraints, no-strike measures, and further concessions for foreign investors (Vickers 1992: 89; Pomeroy 1992: 239). 'Unofficial figures suggest that combined under and unemployment run as high as 40–50%' (Kwitko 1993: 9). Women have suffered disproportionately from job loss involved in the retrenchments and shutdowns in manufacturing that have formed part of the structural-adjustment process in the Philippines. In spite of high and rising levels of education, they also experience gender discrimination and stereotyping at all levels of the occupational structure (ibid. 10; Vickers 1992: 90).

Since 1974, with the formulation of the Philippine Labour Code,[47] the Philippine government has vigorously pursued overseas employment as a means of alleviating chronic unemployment and balance-of-payments problems.[48] Overseas employment has also been pursued by individuals and households as a means of improving economic stability and opportunities for Filipino families. According to data from the Philippine Overseas Employment Administration, the country recorded the highest share of overseas land-based contract workers in the world for the period between 1984 and 1988.[49] Further, a 1988 household-income-and-expenditures survey revealed that fully 15.5 per cent of families in the Philippines receive income from abroad, making up about 30 per cent of their total incomes (Abella 1992: 30). One common family strategy is to subsidize the higher education of one family member, who is then sent abroad to earn wages that are comparatively much higher than in the Philippines.

Indeed, Filipino migrant workers tend to have higher than average education. According to a 1980 study, over 50 per cent of Filipino migrant workers surveyed had completed some college education, in comparison with only 12.5 per cent of the Philippine labour force (Carino 1992: 13–14). In the context of a 40 per cent unemployment rate among nurses in the Philippines, nursing degrees are deliberately acquired as passports to work abroad, and thereby increase family living standards. What is calculated less frequently than the economic impact of overseas employment, both for the individual migrant worker and for the Philippine economy, are the social consequences of long-term separation of family members entailed in contract migration, as well as widespread abuse and exploitation of migrant workers abroad.[50]

Conclusion: Implications for the Study of Gender, Race, Class, and Citizenship

Poverty and underdevelopment, exacerbated by structural-adjustment policies that serve the interests of foreign commercial banks and corporations, are responsible for producing the pool of migrant female labour available to work as maids and nannies abroad. None the less, foreign-domestic-worker policies of states such as Canada, and the gatekeeping mechanisms that serve to enforce such policies, do fashion the terms and conditions of access for Third World migrant women into developed states as a means of escaping such extreme poverty. Control of citizenship rights is thus central to the regulatory process that compels –

to put the case crudely – poor women from Third World countries to work for rich women in First World countries as domestic employees.

Feminist critiques of the assumption of the universal or impartial character of citizenship have linked women's exclusion from citizenship to the dichotomy between public and private spheres, where the former is associated with a world accessible only or mainly to men, and the latter with the world of women.[51] Other analyses that view citizenship in terms of the articulation of different power relations – based upon race and ethnic, as well as gender and class, divisions – offer further insight into the circumstances of those excluded from the boundaries of citizenship and citizenship rights. Moreover, such analyses are suggestive of an alternative approach that can reveal the material and ideological underpinnings of citizenship itself.

Such an approach, suggested in the foregoing discussion, includes a consideration of rights constituted and denied through citizenship policies of nation-states. While migrant domestic workers lack many basic citizenship rights (including the choice of employer and domicile), their employers, in contrast, generally enjoy full citizenship rights. For citizen-women with economic and social means, the in-home employment of migrant domestic workers provides an outlet for a partial alleviation of the conditions of women's oppression. Despite individual relief of the burdens of private home care, however, the generalized condition of women's oppression is perpetuated. Rather than women employers and private domestic employees experiencing a commonality of oppression based on gender, the result is a division of interests, where class, racial, and citizenship distinctions become paramount.

The international circulation of Third World female domestics is but one of several major flows in contemporary global migration. There is, however, a systematic reproduction of foreign domestic workers that is legally separate from, and structurally subordinate to, 'normal' immigration flows internationally. In this chapter we have argued that, despite Canada's less abusive foreign-domestic-worker policy relative to the policies of some other countries, Canada is inextricably linked to this global pattern, both benefiting from and contributing to the structural exploitation of Third World women endemic in the industry.

This global pattern of structural exploitation suggests the need for a critique of contemporary policies of structural adjustment in both national and global state contexts that, to paraphrase the subtitle of Cynthia Enloe's book (1989), makes class, gender, and antiracist sense of international politics. Feminist strategies that fail to incorporate a critique of these internationally exploitive conditions have fallen prey to a complicit support for their continuation. One *Village Voice* feminist columnist recently summarized such an ill-advised approach as follows: 'Should it occur to you that nursing a baby, supporting one or two more other children, continuing your career, shopping, cooking, cleaning, and otherwise single-handedly maintaining a family are incompatible activities, I will save you hours of anguish by saying definitively that a cleaning woman is the first form of help with which to start.' The author cautions further against hiring unionized maids through the yellow pages, which would only 'liberate your savings account,' and suggests instead that her readers 'hire an illegal alien from either Mexico, Central America or the Caribbean' (Viva 1992: 98). This advice, clearly pitched to affluent women, secure in their citizenship status and rights, fails to recognize that 'every time the housewife or working woman buys freedom for herself with a domestic, that very same freedom is denied to the domestic, for the maid must go home and do her own housework' (Martin and Segrave 1985: 32–3). The restriction of freedom for private maids and nannies is even more severe when there are state-imposed conditions of bonded servitude to particular employers for a specific period of time and compulsory live-in status, and when the migrant worker is separated in time and space from her home and family. Strategies that seek to eliminate the oppression of women – all women – must therefore incorporate an analysis of the ways in which global-restructuring processes have constructed 'both hierarchy and interdependence' (Glenn 1992: 3) among women differentiated by race/ethnicity, class, and citizenship.

NOTES

1 See, for example, George 1992; Ward 1990; Harrison 1993: esp. 448–85; and Sander 1992.
2 For a theoretical and empirical context to this phenomenon, see Sassen-Koob 1983.
3 Our use of such terms as 'advanced,' 'developed,' 'hegemonic,' and so on to designate the economic status of given states in the global economy in no way accepts that these states can be ranked according to ethical or cultural criteria. Nor do we accept a static evolutionary schema of development with 'developed' or 'advanced' states at the pinnacle. While we recognize some of the problems of interpretation in retaining these terms, we continue to employ them given the absence of ready alternatives, and with the understanding that the development of developing states has been blocked as a

result of their economic relations with developed, imperialist states. There are, of course, obvious limitations to a narrowly dualistic framework, which is not intended to be implied by this cursory global division. Rather, the global system of hegemonic and non-hegemonic states is taken to be a spectrum of intersecting relationships in an international division of labour.

4 See, for example, Anker and Hein 1986; Chant 1991; Nash and Fernández-Kelly 1983; L. Lim 1990; and Sparr 1994.

5 Elson 1991. On the specific implications of gender with respect to the international division of labour and the global process of capital accumulation, see Ward 1990; Mitter 1986b; Truong 1990; and Vickers 1991.

6 In some areas, such as Metropolitan Toronto, it is not uncommon for infant day care to cost $1000 per month per child.

7 See Faludi 1991; French 1992: 137–8; Mitchell 1992a and 1992b. One company, Brown-McComas Child Care Management Resources, based in Duncanville, Texas, markets a 'Child Care Screening System' to domestic placement agencies that includes a software program called the Child Abuse Inventory Potential (CAP). The system is advertised to measure 'an applicant's attitudes that exhaustive research and theory have proven to be associated with physical abuse.' Brochure produced by Brown-McComas Child Care Management Resources, n.d.

8 The blanket ban was later removed.

9 Anderson 1993.

10 George 1992; Payer 1974: 42. See also Madrid 1992; and, on the relationship between imperialism and the structural construction of migrant labour on a world scale, R. Cohen 1987.

11 There are several comprehensive historical accounts of the relationship between the changes in production and the role of domestic service in the family. See, for example, Rapoport and Rapoport 1969: 385–408; Tilly and Scott 1978; and Romero 1992: 47–70.

12 This phrase, taken from a somewhat different context, belongs to Phyllis Palmer. See Palmer 1987: 180.

13 Clark-Lewis 1987: 197.

14 Colen 1990: 93.

15 'Gulf states' is used here to refer to the member countries of the Gulf Cooperation Council (GCC), comprising Bahrain, Kuwait, Oman, Qatar, Saudi Arabia, and the United Arab Emirates.

16 See Anderson 1993: 13–27; Fely Villasin (co-ordinator, INTERCEDE) 1990: 5–6; and Middle East Watch Women's Rights Project, 'Punishing the Victim: Rape and Mistreatment of Asian Maids in Kuwait,' *Human Rights Watch* 4(8), August 1992.

17 Weinert 1991, cited in Anderson 1993: 14.

18 Cited in Anderson 1993: 21.

19 See Anderson 1993: 87–8; and Villasin 1990: 2. Statistics and information on domestics in Hong Kong in this section are drawn from these sources.

20 Others were from Indonesia, Thailand, India, and Sri Lanka, with considerably smaller numbers from Burma, Malaysia, Nepal, Pakistan, and Singapore.

21 As cited in Anderson 1993: 88.

22 The regulations regarding foreign domestic workers' hours of work, overtime pay, minimum-wage laws, and the right to organize in trade unions vary among the provinces. Ontario has the widest range of protective legislation for domestic workers. Not coincidentally, it is also the province where the largest and most effective domestic-rights organization in the country, INTERCEDE, has been actively campaigning for domestic workers to be treated on an equal basis with other workers in the province since 1979.

23 This pattern is analysed in more detail in Bakan and Stasiulis 1994: 7–33. See also Daenzer 1993.

24 Overall, in 1974, four times more domestics arrived in Canada on employment visas than as immigrants (Daenzer 1993: 92).

25 In making the distinction between private domestic-service jobs and service jobs performed in restaurants, hotels, hospitals, etc., we are not glorifying the latter. Indeed, as Evelyn Nakano Glenn (1992: 22–3) points out, low-level service jobs, like domestic service, offer poor wages, few or limited benefits, low rates of unionization, and in general 'subject workers to arbitrary supervision.' Nevertheless, service workers 'appreciate not being personally subordinate to an employer and not having to do "their" dirty work on "their" property"' (23). Further, while 'relations with supervisors and clients are hierarchical, ... they are embedded in an impersonal structure governed by more explicit contractual obligations and limits' (23).

26 The 'Pinto case,' heard by the Federal Court Trial Division, involved the appeal by a prospective Ontario employer (Pinto) concerning a woman from Delhi, India who had been refused entry into Canada under the FDM by a Canadian visa officer (Federal Court of Canada, 27 Nov. 1990). The reason given for the refusal was that the woman had insufficient experience under the policy guideline calling for one year of previous 'relevant experience.' The applicant's claim was based on the prospective employee's experience as a single mother and as a school teacher with 16 years of practice.

27 It should be noted that the issue of what constitutes government 'consultation' with concerned constituencies regarding this policy is a subject of considerable debate. In a letter dated 3 March 1992, for example, Glenda P.

Simms, the president of the Canadian Advisory Council on the Status of
Women (CACSW), wrote to Bernard Valcourt, the minister of employment
and immigration responsible for the FDM review process, that she was 'most
disappointed' that a senior governmental official meeting with the CACSW
'for the most part could not provide adequate information on your consultation review process. The group was advised that employers' letters to the
Minister and employment agencies' complaints about domestic workers
had been the basis for the department's consultation.' Valcourt's response
(26 August 1992) was: 'Those consulted include domestic worker advocacy
groups, other federal government departments, provincial government officials, national and municipal day care associations, employer and employment agency representatives, academics and other concerned individuals ...
In making the changes, we have aimed for a balance between the needs of
domestic workers and employers.'

28 See, for example, Khosa 1993: 16–17; and Villasin 1992: 77–80.
29 Romero (1992: 139–62), provides a valuable summary of these studies and an
analysis of their findings and theoretical conclusions.
30 See Warner and Henderson 1990, cited in Romero 1992: 190–1 n.29; Nakano
Glenn 1986; and Anderson 1993.
31 Following British conquest in the mid-seventeenth century, the Caribbean
was exploited as a region rich in land and capital-generating plantation agricultural conditions. In contrast, however, it was an area short in the supply
of labour, particularly following the near-genocide suffered by the indigenous Amerindian population. After the early failure of a movement favouring white European indentured labour, the African slave trade soared and
fuelled the profits of the colonial planters, primarily through the export of
sugar and related products. With emancipation in 1838, an extensive peasantry emerged as freed slaves turned to private land cultivation, and resisted
field labour in protest against the legacy of slavery. Women played a central
role in agricultural marketing, first during the plantation period for the sale
of slave-grown produce, and then after emancipation. While other employment options have opened for women, this tradition has continued until the
present time. See Williams 1944, which, despite volumes of contemporary
debate, remains the best single concise historical source on this period for the
Caribbean region. See also Momsen 1988: 141–58; Despradel 1984: 93–109;
and Bakan 1990: 18–67.
32 See, for example, Peach 1968.
33 See, for example, Satzewich 1989.
34 For an insightful account of this process, focusing on the Jamaican experience, see Trevor Munroe 1972.

35 European Economic Commission (1973) as cited in Despradel 1984: 97.

36 The first figure is drawn from Swamy 1981; the second is from Hymie Rubenstein 1982. For a discussion of remittances to the region in general, and a review of the literature, see Bascom 1991: 71–99.

37 Despradel 1984: 101; Momsen 1988: 151; Housewives Association of Trinidad and Tobago 1975.

38 Cited in Momsen 1988: 147; and Powell 1986.

39 By 1970, women's paid participation rate in the Caribbean labour force over-all had been increased by work in the expanding service sector, largely fuelled by tourism and the hotel industry. See Antrobus 1986 and Gordon 1986.

40 Cited in Satzewich 1989: 77.

41 The policy was implemented on a limited quota basis, with 100 Caribbean women admitted in the first year, and subsequent increases up to 280 per year. The plan was explicitly enacted, and then extended into the 1960s, to assuage the demands of Caribbean governments. For its part, the Canadian government expressed explicit concern that, upon achieving permanent status, the women would sponsor relatives from the Caribbean who would enter Canada and alter the racial complexion of Canadian society. However, Canada's economic interests in the English Caribbean, ranking third in the world in importance to Canada after the United States and Britain, compelled concern that some accommodation to the region's political leaders on the immigration front were in order. See Satzewich (1989) and Daenzer (1993) on the rise and fall of the West Indian Domestic Scheme; see also Calliste 1991; and Henry 1968. On Canada's historic economic interests in the region, see Tennyson 1990; Chodos 1977; and Bakan, Cox and Leys 1993.

42 The largest single source country was Jamaica, followed by Guyana, Haiti, and Trinidad. Richmond 1989: 3.

43 After 1973 and before to 1981, live-in domestic workers arrived on temporary employment visas with no special provision for the attainment of permanent-resident status. Task Force on Immigration Practices and Procedures 1981a: 49; Arnopoulous 1979: 61; Task Force on Immigration Practices and Procedures 1981b: 48–50; and 'Foreign Domestic Workers in Canada,' 5. See also Employment and Immigration Canada 1990: table 2, 3.

44 In 1982, the number of processed contract workers from the Philippines was 314,284, compared with 598,769 in 1990. Moreover, the number of processed Filipino contract workers increased twenty-fold over a 16-year period, from just over 36,000 in 1975 to almost 700,000 in 1991. See Carino 1992: 7, 6.

45 Palma-Bertran 1991.

46 The emergence of massive overseas employment of Filipinos coincided with the opening of the Middle East labour market. Asis 1992: 69.

47 The signing into law of the May 1974 Philippine Labour Code 'signalled earnest government involvement with overseas employment.' The Code provided for the creation of the Overseas Employment Development Board (OEDB) to undertake a systematic program for the overseas employment of land-based workers, banned direct hiring, and made mandatory remittance of overseas workers' earnings. While the 1974 Code was intended to block out participation of the private sector in recruitment and placement, these tasks proved too onerous for the government to handle. Thus, in 1978, the government relegated to the private sector control over recruitment and placement of Filipino workers. Asis 1992: 71–2.

48 Economists acknowledge the substantial contribution of overseas migrants' remittances in offsetting the oil bill and improving the balance of payments, especially during the mid-1980s, a period marked by massive foreign-exchange problems and foreign-capital flight. However, they differ in their assessments of the impact of migration on economic development in the Philippines. The most persuasive accounts conclude that overseas employment is only palliative in character, and that more-lasting solutions to the country's critical development problems must address deeper structural factors. For further discussion of the impact of overseas employment on development in the Philippines, see Abella 1992; Vasquez 1992; Batistella 1992; and Carino 1992: 19.

49 Palma-Beltran 1991: 46. These figures are considered to be conservative, as they do not incorporate those who depart as tourists and are therefore not registered as official overseas workers. Macklin 1992: 695 n.66.

50 See Vasquez 1992: 60–2 for a discussion of the impact of overseas migration on migrants' families and communities.

51 See Pateman 1988; Yuval-Davis 1991; and Young 1990.

12

Transnational Resistance: Strategies to Alleviate the Impacts of Restructuring on Women

JOANNA KERR

Since the 1980s, profound changes in trading relations between countries, in manufacturing processes, and in the role of transnational corporations have created an extremely interconnected, and yet unevenly developed and volatile, international economic system. This economic restructuring has transformed the social, economic, and cultural lives of people around the world. For many women, in particular, restructuring has signified greater insecurity and hardship.

In the past several years, the feminist economics literature and the gender and development literature have provided a critical analysis of the impact of these macro reforms on gender relations and women's empowerment. Several studies have shown that restructuring has reinforced a gender-segregated labour market where women face fewer opportunities than men. Further, where there have been cutbacks in public expenditures, women have been forced to make up for the shortfall. Although it is true that women do not all experience the current economic crisis in the same way, this volume clearly illustrates that the livelihoods of women in the North as in the South are being profoundly affected (see also Beneria and Feldman 1992; Afshar and Dennis 1992; Elson 1991; Bakker 1994a; and Commonwealth Expert Group 1989).

Given this understanding of how restructuring has reinforced gender hierarchies (as well as race, ethnic, and increasingly disparate income hierarchies), the difficult question resurfaces: what should be done? This chapter attempts to provide some strategies to alleviate the burdens borne by women in the process of restructuring. Owing to the extreme unevenness of restructuring, strategies need to be developed in the context of a specific region, country, or sector of workers. Since there is not one universal problem, there is not one universal solution. Nevertheless, there are some trends that require a 'transnational' response. The forces of globalization that are integrating national and regional economies are also making communities around the world more integrated and more interdependent. We need to understand, therefore, that any changes we effect in one region will have an impact on communities elsewhere. For example, policies to protect female textile workers in Canada through trade restrictions may work against the interests of textile workers in Bangladesh.

My intention in this paper is to stimulate further discussion about ideas and strategies to alleviate the problems that global economic restructuring has created for the advancement of women in all parts of the world. The responsibility to remove the burden placed on women as a result of economic reform should ultimately be shared by the international community, by women's groups, the human-rights movement, trade unions, local and national governments, as well as international institutions and transnational corporations.

I will organize my discussion of strategies under five different, but interrelated, sections. First, for all the strategies outlined in this chapter to be effective, there needs to be a significant amount of work done to improve strategic alliances. Second, an important area that requires concrete solutions is the protection of workers under the new economic paradigm. Third, there must be a commitment to investing in social programs. Fourth, policy analysis and reform is integral to alleviating the gender bias in economics. And, finally, the viability of the current economic system needs to be reconsidered in order to shift development objectives towards human ends as opposed to profit.

1. Strategic Alliances

Because global economic restructuring is a competitive led strategy that redistributes jobs, incomes, and unemployment, it has a tendency to create tension between different communities on both a local and global level. This effect is particularly evident when jobs are lost in one area and created in another area of the world. As a result, there is a propensity for some individuals and groups to concern themselves with local problems, insulating themselves from the macro economic situation.

Such a strategy of insulation and protectionism, however, is not appropriate given the interdependency of our lives, regardless of what we do. There are common interests and common problems that can be recognized and resolved through working together. In other words, even within the growing competitive system there is potential to work for the same ends. In order to work towards this result, however, women need to find ways in which to confront and recognize their differences. As Gabriel and Macdonald (this volume) note, 'feminist organizing must confront the differences and tensions that exist between women arising from race, class, and imperialism, particularly as these cleavages are implicated in the processes of hemispheric restructuring.'

When women confront and recognize their differences, it will be possible for them to inform and lobby policy makers to regulate the negative impacts of restructuring policies in ways that benefit all women. For example, in Canada, middle-class women working outside the home have benefited from the hiring of women immigrants as domestic workers. The latter do live-in work for extremely low wages, are denied landed-immigrant status upon arrival in Canada, and are exposed to many forms of exploitation.[2] Perhaps a more appropriate solution for all would be to lobby for national day care, minimum wages for domestic workers, and/or fairer conditions and immigration policies for domestic workers. In other words, if the women's movement develops a greater consciousness of the different realities in which women are struggling, they will be better able to work together to advocate for appropriate policy changes. The importance of this is outlined by Rowbotham and Mitter (1994) when they suggest: 'Alliances are crucial aspects of poor women's organizing efforts. Women workers have rarely been able to exert influence over state policies alone. In contrast, middle class social reformers have often been able to have a more direct impact on the state. Historically the alliance between middle class women and working class women has proved effective when the former have been responsive to the actual demands expressed by the workers' (1994: 219).

The women's movement is, to a greater extent, working at the international level far more effectively and strategically. Those who are familiar with the successes of the women's caucus at the World Conference on Human Rights, the International Population and Development Conference, and the 1995 Women's Conference in Beijing will know that strategic 'transnational resistance' is being mobilized.

More work needs to be done to improve linkages between academics and community-level activists and between researchers, activists, and policy makers. These types of alliances are fundamental to the creation of solutions. Responsibilities need to be shared by these different constituencies and recommendations need to be negotiated. Numerous organizations provide valuable examples for the kind of work I mean. The following are particularly noteworthy:

- ALT-WID (Alternative Women in Development) is an international coalition of women researchers and policy advocates. They work on developing alternative policies to empower women in the United States and the South, especially those living in poverty.
- DAWN (Development Alternatives with Women for a New Era) is an international network of Third World activists, researchers, and policy makers. Through their analysis and activities, DAWN is committed to developing alternative frameworks and methods to attain goals of economic and social justice, peace, and development, free from all forms of oppression by gender, class, race, and nation.
- Freedom from Debt Coalition is a broad-based network of church groups, academic and professional bodies, and community organizations that studies the social and environmental impact of debt in order to find solutions to the crisis that will ease poverty and suffering in the Philippines.

2. Protection of Workers

An integral component of global economic restructuring has been the emergence of new flexible production processes. In order to respond to highly competitive markets, business and governments have adjusted in a variety of ways. First, in some cases workers have been laid off. Second, production has been decentralized, in other words, factories have been relocated to free-trade zones of less-developed countries or subcontracted out to small firms. Finally, there has been a push towards a cheaper and more flexible workforce. In this section I will elaborate on each of these processes, then outline three strategies to deal with the changes entailed by the emergence of this new flexible production system.

Redeployment

The current changes in the organization of work have decreased the availability of jobs in the formal sector. Canadians are all too familiar with the epidemic of plant closures or public-sector down-sizing. These changes have had a differential impact on women in Canada. Between 1990 and 1992, as Armstrong shows in this volume, 'more women than men lost jobs in the manufacturing industries (171,000 women, compared with 149,000 men), even though women accounted for less than a third of those employed in these industries.' Most of the jobs lost belonged to immigrant women in Canada. Similarly, reports from China suggest that approximately 20 million workers have been laid off in recent years, 14 million of whom were women.[3]

Employers see female employment, which comes with the added costs of maternity leaves and days absent to care for sick family members, as too cumbersome for an efficient and low-cost labour force. In OECD countries, employers still perceive women as less readily available, less productive, and less motivated on account of their reproductive functions (Coré 1994). According to Skrypnek and Fast (1993), employers who perceive women to be less committed to work are often themselves less committed to their female employees, granting them fewer advancement opportunities and lower salaries. In China, women are discouraged from entering management positions because of their assumed inherent preoccupation with family responsibilities, which is believed to adversely affect their ability to take on managerial roles.[4] Given that in OECD countries the fertility rate has declined steadily and in China women are officially able to have only one child, these restrictions are clearly based on archaic and sexist notions of women's appropriate roles.

Decentralization

The 1980s witnessed the emergence of export processing zones, also known as free-trade zones or *maquiladoras*. Within these zones, corporations are invited to set up factories that manufacture exported goods. The workers in these industrial zones are mostly female, often from rural areas and engaging in waged work for the first time in their lives (Rosa 1993). Wages are low, working conditions are poor, and workers are not permitted to unionize.[5]

Given the overriding imperative to attract foreign exchange and create jobs, host governments of many developing countries have turned a blind eye to companies or their local subcontracted firms who disobey international and national labour standards. For example, in Honduras, young women workers were allegedly forced to take stimulants so they could work longer hours (Populi 1994). Further, women factory workers said that if they didn't perform their tasks to the satisfaction of their supervisors, they were made to stand holding a chair above their heads for an hour as punishment. Other workers reported that any woman suspected of being pregnant was made to drink excessive amounts of coffee to induce miscarriage. In China last year, eighty-four female workers were killed in a Hong Kong-owned toy factory when a fire broke out. The employer had locked the exit doors for fear that workers would steal the toys (*Wall Street Journal*, 29 June 1994).

Flexibilization

Global competition has compelled corporations to seek flexible production processes that allow them to respond immediately to changes in the market, including those in fashion or design. This strategy, often referred to as Just-in-Time, has had a conspicuous impact on the quantity and quality of jobs for people around the globe. Flexible workers – that is, workers who are temporary, casual, part-time, subcontracted, or home-based – are now used as needed. As a result, the labour force is being polarized into two kinds of workers – those with high salaries, secure positions, and benefits, and those with insecure employment, no benefits, and extremely low wages (Mitter 1993; Barnet and Cavanagh 1994; ILGWU and INTERCEDE 1993). This latter category of 'non-standard' employees constitutes the most rapidly expanding workforce. In 1989, for example, 33 per cent of Canadians were employed in this sector (Economic Council of Canada 1990). The majority of workers in this category are women and, in Canada, particularly women of colour. According to Mitter, 'cultural attitudes combine with social hierarchies; women are often employed because they are regarded as pliable, docile and likely to accept the negative consequences of flexible work' (1993: 16). The report of the Ontario Council of the International Ladies' Garment Workers' Union and INTERCEDE states: 'Domestic workers and homeworkers represent the ultimate form of flexible labour. They are women who perform this work not out of choice, but as a result of economic necessity. They are located at the extreme end of this growing marginal or peripheral workforce. Both homework and domestic work are notoriously low paying, lack status, violate basic employment standards and lack access to unionization' (1993: 5).

Certainly there are positive aspects to these new work patterns in that they may enable more women to balance their family responsibilities. Nevertheless, women are vulnerable to being used as part of a deregulationary strategy by virtue of their segregation into jobs categorized both as separate and inferior.

There are several strategies that could be employed to counteract the negative effects of some of these issues arising from global restructuring. Broadly, these strategies include organizing the unorganized; regulating standards of work; and shifting the burden of family responsibilities.

Organizing the Unorganized
The restructuring of the economy has involved such rapid changes that mainstream unions have been unable to address the needs of the flexible workers. Thus, there is a need to encourage mainstream unions to embrace the changes and also to find alternatives to traditional organizational mechanisms.

(1) Part-time workers: Part-time work has been undervalued by mainstream unions because the interests of full-time workers have always taken priority. Within unions, full-time workers have felt threatened by part-time labour, fearing that their own full-time positions would be jeopardized. While many of the concerns of unions on this issue remain valid, it is necessary for unions to recognize the changes in global economic restructuring that make necessary the increased participation of part-time workers in the labour force. In this light, strategies must be formulated that will address the particular concerns of part-time workers, most of whom are women (Coré 1994).

First, since part-time work is considered inferior, and particular to women, one strategy would be to encourage unions to demand that part-time positions are created across all sectors and levels so that all workers can choose to work the hours they desire, hours that fit into their family and other responsibilities (see Jenson, this volume). In some Nordic countries, for example, all workers have the right to reduce their hours under certain circumstances and for a specific period of time (Coré 1994).

Second, part-time workers need to be given the same benefits as full-time workers. This strategy will prevent companies from hiring part-time workers in order to avoid paying benefits and will also allow workers the freedom to work shorter hours if they choose.

Finally, part-time positions need to be more equitably distributed to both men and women. At the same time, full-time positions should also be more equitably allocated to both men and women (Jenson 1993).

(2) Casual workers: For 'casualized' workers, much of their exploitation

lies in the fact that they are unorganzied and do not have access to collective bargaining. Rowbotham and Mitter's recent anthology *Dignity and Daily Bread: New Forms of Economic Organizing among Poor Women in the Third World and the First* (1994) illustrates the innovative mobilization efforts of marginalized women workers. The Self Employed Women's Association (SEWA) in India has perhaps had the best results. SEWA in India has a membership of over 30,000 mostly illiterate, poor women who derive their income from petty trading, homework, or selling their labour services. It is an association with trade-union status that strives towards a cooperative-based model, to create a spirit of sharing and self-reliance. According to Renana Jhabvala, SEWA's goals are to

- increase income;
- provide assets;
- provide security of work;
- provide access to the social-security services of health, child care, and housing, and to developmental services such as training, communications, and banking;
- build solidarity and cooperation among workers;
- strengthen democracy;
- bring self-employed women into the mainstream of national life; and
- be equal partners and equal beneficiaries in the process of economic development. (1994: 130)

Rowbotham and Mitter (1994) claim that SEWA has been able to make great achievements, where the mainstream (male) trade-union movement could not, because (1) it has been able to make the hidden workers of the industrial sector visible to the national and international policy makers; (2) with a female membership it has been able to address women's specific needs such as child care; (3) as both a trade union and a cooperative, it can lobby government and at the same time receive funds; and (4) it can 'mobilize "casual" workers who are not accustomed to organisation [and who] often become disillusioned when a union fails to accomplish dramatic change' (1994: 221).

The authors qualify that it is not clear how transferable to other communities a model such as SEWA is, given evidence that forms of participatory cooperatives have been successful only where trade unions have been strong. None the less, their book gives ample evidence of the numerous organizations being created around the world that are sustained by flexible women workers. Their innovative ability to provide a vehicle for women workers to improve the lives of their families and themselves should be supported by the international donor community. As Mitter suggests: 'By empowering these community-based organisations, the agencies are therefore likely to reap a high social and economic return on their funds' (Rowbotham and Mitter 1994: 44).

Regulating Standards of Work
Either global standards of work must be raised to some decent minimum or masses of workers everywhere will be dragged down together by the forces of international competition. Guaranteeing minimum labour standards to workers has been a goal of the labour movement for many years. These include the right to participate in decisions related to their employment; the right to collective bargaining; the right to assemble and organize freely; parental and maternity benefits; responsive and flexible workplace supports for families; minimum-wage provisions; equal pay for work of equal value; health and safety standards in the workplace; and remuneration for overtime work.

As has been shown, labour standards for many women workers in export processing zones have been elusive. However, growing international attention and pressure on transnational corporations, as well as the effects of feminist activism, are bringing about positive changes. In Northern Honduras, for example, women working in the *maquiladoras* have launched a struggle for better working conditions. In February 1994, more than 4000 workers from a textile factory organized a strike that paralysed production; they organised demonstrations and blocked traffic and, for several days, sat in factory premises. The factory owners eventually agreed to allow the women to form unions. Within the government, however, there was considerable concern that the actions of the women would scare off foreign investors (Populi June 1994).

In China, the national government recently announced that all foreign-owned companies will have to unionize (*Wall Street Journal*, 29 June 1994). This move is also likely the result of both international pressure and a strong trade-union movement within China.

Regulating conditions for casual workers in Canada: Increased publicity about unfair working conditions, as well as new technological innovations, has made foreign direct investment less important to transnational corporations. Subcontracting 'invisible' and flexible workers therefore has become preferable.

In terms of providing labour regulation for these workers, the International Ladies' Garment Workers and INTERCEDE have produced a report with numerous recommendations, which include the following:

Labour standards for each sector would be set by a tri-partite committee, chaired by a governmental official and with equal employer and employee participation. This committee would also be responsible for such matters as the administration of the relevant portions of the Act and regulations, and the enforcement of standards ...

Central Registries would be established for homeworkers and domestic workers. Registration would be mandatory for all homeworkers and domestic workers. The registry's list of workers for each sector would be used to monitor and enforce standards. Furthermore, each worker on the registry would be provided with a copy of the legal standards in effect for her sector. Unions and/or advocacy groups would be given access to the registries, to further ensure that minimum standards are being adhered to ...

The employer of a domestic worker would be equally obliged to register her employment with the central registry. Canada Immigration and the Ministry of Labour would also submit the names of employers of domestic workers under the LCP to the central registry. The central registry would be entitled to contact domestic workers to inform them of the registry's purpose and the relevant laws. Domestic workers would be entitled to be represented by the registry in disputes with their employers. The central registry would also provide counselling services to domestic workers and establish group insurance plans ...

The tri-partate committees established for each sector would be responsible for the investigation and prosecution of standards and registry violations. Inspectors would be appointed with the same powers as those available to officers under the *Employment Standards Act*. (ILGWU, INTERCEDE 1993: 77–8)

International standards: On an international level, consideration has been given to the notion of including social clauses in trading agreements. This would mean, for example, the inclusion of international labour standards in the rules of the GATT (or its successor, the World Trading Organization). This strategy has not been embraced by labour or women's groups in less-developed countries. For one reason, workers would rather have employment that did not satisfy international labour standards than no work at all. Further, putting social clauses into trade policies could favour richer countries with existing standards, acting almost as a protective barrier against imports from poor countries (*Financial Times*, 14 April 1994). None the less, there are minimum standards, such as the prohibition of child labour, that could be written into trading agreements.

Social clauses of trade agreements are applicable only to governments, not to transnational corporations. Given the greater significance of TNCs in the global economy, their regulation has become all the more important.[6] At present, institutions acting to ensure corporate accountability at the local, national, and international levels are extremely weak. In the absence of an effective international regulatory framework, TNCs should be expected to report publicly to national governments and appropriate international organizations on their corporate practices (North-South Institute 1994). Alternatively, TNCs should be offered the option of subscribing to codes of conduct that would be rewarded by a 'social label,' thereby enhancing their corporate image (ILO 1994).

Consumers as regulators: A further strategy for ensuring that standards of work are regulated is to educate the public in developed countries to exercise their power as ethical consumers. The environmental movement has been very successful in its campaign to encourage consumers to 'buy green,' environmentally responsible, products. Consumers have also rallied to stop supporting corporations, such as Nestlé, for their involvement in the unethical marketing of breast-milk substitutes in developed and developing countries. In the same way, consumers can be encouraged to reject products that have been produced by women who work in unsafe conditions or are paid a wage that is inconsistent with the realities of their lives. Bridgehead is one example of a Canadian alternative trading organization that sells 'fairly traded' clothes, crafts, and food.

As corporations become aware that there is a demand for products that are produced under safe and ethical conditions, they will be encouraged to become socially responsible. The coalition for Fair Wage and Working Conditions for Homeworkers, based in Toronto, has launched the Clean Clothes Campaign to educate consumers about the production practices of retailers and to expose the wage and working conditions in the garment industry. It is beginning to explore the possibility of a Clean Clothes line of clothing.

Indeed, there needs to be greater consultation and communication between feminist organizations and the private sector. There are already in place groups that have an established relationship with the private sector and could foster this kind of program. For example, the Canadian Women's Foundation, which works towards equality for women and girls, works with corporate sponsors to allow them to invest in women's organizations across the country. The connections forged with such donors may result in their being more accountable to women in their corporate practices.

Sharing of Family Responsibilities

A further strategy in the struggle to mitigate the costs of restructuring for women is to create a consensus on the need for family responsibilities to be shared by various members of the family and by society so that the burden of this work does not fall disproportionately, as it has, on women. Women's concentration in child care and domestic work influences the extent and nature of their participation in paid production, giving them a weaker bargaining position within the household and in the market. Until these responsibilities and the costs associated with them are shared by men, employers, and society as a whole, women will continue to bear the costs of restructuring. Government and employers must develop and successfully implement family-responsive polices that appreciate the reciprocal relationship between work and family. Corporations need to be shown that family-related initiatives pay off financially for the company (Skrypnek and Fast 1993). For instance, a study by the United States Department of Labor showed that child-care-related absences of employees cost industry an estimated US$3 billion annually. Far-sighted employers are recognizing that employee assistance to meet family obligations is a sound business investment that comes with the reward of less absenteeism, lower staff turn-over, and an enhanced corporate reputation (International Institute for Labour Studies 1994).

There is in fact an ILO Convention on Workers with Family Responsibilities that calls for the development of support services and other arrangements to relieve tension between family and work for both men and women. Only twenty countries have ratified this convention, Canada not among them. According to the 1994 ILO Labour Report, several countries have cited current severe economic difficulties as one reason for not having done so.

Household duties are a socially ascribed responsibility given to women. An important strategy therefore involves the (culturally specific) intervention in the socialization process of men and women and boys and girls. This intervention might involve adapting school curricula and influencing the media so that both genders are educated into understanding that they must share household duties – this was not the birthright of women.

Any strategies that alleviate the burden of work for women will allow them to have more bargaining power to effectively battle the current realities they face when working both inside and outside the home. National governments also need to be convinced that this is a critical issue for the effective achievement of national development goals. According to Elson (1995), 'if women are too overburdened with the "double-day", they have less time and energy to maintain and reproduce community structures; to create neighbourhoods and networks of reciprocity through informal, everyday contacts to sustain and police social norms. An important bulwark against social disintegration and despair is thus undermined – with implications for both the quality of life and amount of public expenditure devoted to police forces and law courts.'

While this argument, based on an efficiency approach, is important to present, it is also imperative that feminist organizations remain aware of the potential dangers of an argument that continues to present women in their traditional roles. Changes in this area need to be informed by feminist discourse in order to avoid reinforcing traditional stereotypes of women while recognizing the real work that women do perform in this area.

3. Investment in Social Programs

In most parts of the world, including Canada, the scope of national governments to design and implement independent social and economic polices has been reduced. Further, there has been a significant decline in the ability of those same governments to access or to generate adequate resources for social services. A well-documented result of the contraction in social services has been the increase in the responsibility of women. With fewer services provided by the public sector, women have had to make up for the shortfall (Antrobus 1993; Baden 1994; Elson 1991; Mayatech Corporation 1991; Feldman 1992). For example, women under structural-adjustment programs in Africa have been shock-absorbers in the process of adjustment, curtailing their own consumption and increasing their workload to compensate for the loss in household income. In Central and Eastern Europe, there has been a total collapse of the highly developed systems of social protection that have existed for many years. For women this is particularly threatening, since social programs allowed women to participate in the formal economy (Moghadam 1993). In Canada, the decline in health-care services has meant greater hardship for women. Women are receiving less health care for themselves and are called upon to care for those who are released early from hospital or require home care that would previously have been provided in the health-care system. In other words, when governments remove the resources for social services, women are called on to perform their traditional roles as the nurturers and carers of the community in a way that increases their already staggering burden of work.

When thinking about strategies for alleviating the problems women have faced under economic restructuring, it is crucial that we reconsider the value of the social sphere in human life. As Brodie (1994) suggests, 'Perhaps we have been too quick to accept the determinism and unrestrained economism of restructuring discourse.' In other words, does restructuring necessarily imply a cutback in social services? Do all societies have to restructure according to market criteria?

Thus, in countries where social programs are being eroded, there needs to be a recommitment to health, education, and social security for the citizens. This commitment needs to be made not only by the government, but by the collective members and organizations within any society.

From such an understanding of the importance of the social sphere, it follows that benefits and security need to be provided to all, not just to those affiliated with a place of employment. These include the self-employed, elderly, disabled, home-based workers, domestic workers, and women who do not work outside of the home (that is, work done at home needs to be recognized explicitly for some benefits). In Benin, Cyprus, and Morocco, women previously in formal employment are allowed to continue to make benefit contributions (International Institute for Labour Studies 1994). The Canadian government has shown some sensitivity in this area by allowing women in the public sector to take maternity leave for up to five years. These women continue to make benefit contributions and are guaranteed a position at the same level at the end of their leave. Unfortunately, many women feel unable to take this time with their children because they cannot afford to make the contributions. Ultimately, this benefit needs to be offered equally to men.

Any strategy that is developed to confront this situation must be based on the context of the existing social and economic system. For example, the overwhelming imperative of fiscal restraint in Canada makes it clear that simply demanding that governments stop cutting back on social services is not an adequate strategy. Rather, policy makers need to be convinced that health care, education, and social security are absolutely necessary to long-run national economic-development objectives (because the labour force will be unhealthy, unskilled, or overburdened with family obligations). Where the political will does not exist to pursue policies based on human-development objectives, then it is necessary to rely on efficiency arguments. For example, it is efficient to educate girls, who as mothers will have a better understanding of the importance of good nutrition and will therefore raise healthier children, who will be more productive members of society. Women's groups and feminist researchers must be able to produce viable policy and program options, rather than relying on a critique of bad choices. Further, it is important to recognize that there are allies within governments (that is, those working for similar objectives) who need to be supported by activists on the outside. Groups need to be strategic and informed in their interactions with policy makers. Activists and researchers need to create their own fora to consult and negotiate with policy makers, as opposed to waiting for whatever opportunity is presented.

While governments cannot be allowed to abrogate their duty to provide social services by burdening non-governmental organizations and women with those tasks, it is also the obligation of communities – of both men and women – to take on these responsibilities. Since restructuring has also involved the shift from an emphasis on the collective needs of a community to individual needs, people have stopped looking out for one another.

Where collective responsibility is concerned, activists in the North have much to learn from the kind of strategies that groups have developed in the South. In the absence of government-provided social assistance and services, innovative methods of mobilization and collective organizing have emerged. For instance, the case of the Self-Employed Women's Association of India (SEWA), which was discussed earlier in this chapter, provides an example of the kind of group that takes on the responsibility for the community when the government is unable to act in that capacity.

4. Policy Analysis

A major barrier to the adoption of strategies to alleviate the burdens of restructuring on women is that policy makers and mainstream economists have yet to believe that macroeconomic reform is indeed gender biased. Diane Elson, a pioneer of gender analysis of development economics, states: 'It is not that macro policy reforms are deliberately designed to favour men. Nor is the key issue that male biased social traditions prevent women from taking advantage of macropolicy reforms that could work in their favour. The key issue is that macro economics has a one-sided view of the macro economy: it only considers the monetary aggregates of the "productive economy". It ignores the human resource aggregates of the "reproductive economy", the indicators of population, health, nutrition, education, skills' (Elson 1994).

A crucial strategy, therefore, in addressing the negative impacts of restructuring involves a systematic gender analysis of economics and economic policy. It is here that feminist economics has made and can make a significant contribution. The goal of this school of economics is to make women more visible as workers and farmers; to value as integral to the economy the non-market activities and unpaid work of women; to document and explain the economic inequalities that exist by gender (such as the occupational segregation and gender wage differentials); to modify the theory, methods, and practice of the discipline (in order to better understand intra-household dynamics and non-market activity); and to reinterpret received wisdom through a more inclusive approach by integrating all of these aspects into economics (MacDonald, 1993).

It is of particular importance that the goals of feminist economics be encouraged and that these goals be shared by mainstream economists, policy makers and ministers of trade and finance. There are several strategies that would facilitate the adoption of these goals into policy.

First, there must be a concerted effort by academic institutions to ensure that feminist economics is given legitimacy within university curricula and academia in general.

Second, feminist economics needs to better inform the activism that is going on at the grass-roots level. The benefits of this kind of communications can be seen in the women's human-rights movement, where lawyers and legal scholars have provided critical legal analysis of the weakness of the human-rights system and offered viable strategies by which to guarantee rights for women through international law. This same kind of information sharing between feminist economists and activists could prove equally fruitful.

Third, governments need to do a systematic analysis of the ways in which their economic policies are affecting men and women. This work should not be marginalized into a women's department or become the responsibility of a junior female civil servant. It should be a regular function of the trade and finance departments. It is, therefore, fundamental that feminist economists are hired into these influential ministries.

Finally, women's groups and other social activists need to adopt the language of neoclassical economics in order to influence ministers of finance. For example, Ingrid Palmer (1994) argues that women should use 'hard-nosed' economic arguments about the opportunity costs to women and to the whole economy resulting from their additional burden for social reproduction. It is this kind of economic argument, she claims, that will have the greatest impact on policy makers.

5. Towards a New Value System

This chapter has attempted to offer strategies to address the negative impacts of the current market-oriented economic system. Currently, however, many women's groups are questioning whether women's equality could ever be achieved through a system driven by profit and measured by GNP growth. Although the market economy has become the universally accepted model (ILO 1994), the question remains whether women's subordination and class and race oppression are manifestations of an outdated capitalist, patriarchal system.

To strive for an entirely new economic system is a dubious solution. None the less, a transformation of our value system is within our means. A value system where people are valued before money and human beings are seen as ends rather than means would come closer to meeting the development goals of improving economic growth, the sustainable livelihoods of people, and the environment. As Diane Elson suggests: 'More fundamental changes are needed, including international agreements, regulations and norms that support the right of every member of society, women and girls as well as men and boys, to be valued for themselves, as irreplaceable and unique; and to strengthen the entitlements of those who provide the unpaid care that makes such valuation possible' (Elson, 1995).

Feminist organizations need to support initiatives that do not use

GNP as a yardstick for economic development, but instead rely on indicators such as life expectancy, political freedom, and health. The UN Human Development report (the annual report of the United Nations Development Programme) which uses different categories of development, has contributed significantly to a greater acceptance of human-development priorities and should be supported.

Conclusion

Restructuring of the global economy has created new challenges to the advancement of women in Canada and around the world. Feminist struggles in the past have focused on changes to the workplace and the nation-state. However, the changes brought about by restructuring are changing the terrain on which the struggle for women's equality should be fought. Feminist activists in alliance with other social movements, academics, and policy makers must now pursue women's equality beyond the parameters of the nation-state, since transnational dynamics are having such a profound impact on women's lives. At the same time, it is necessary to develop strategies to deal with the new invisible workplaces brought on by the flexibilization of labour. Transnational resistance will be essential if women are to benefit from this new world order.

NOTES

1 I would like to thank Lynne Hately fo her contribution and assistance. I would also like to acknowledge Julie Delahanty for her generous support.
2 See Bakan and Stasiulis, this volume.
3 Interview with Wang Xing Juan, president of the Women's Research Institute, Beijing, December 1993.
4 Interview with Women's Committee of the Trade Union Association of China, Beijing, December 1993.
5 I want to emphasize the lack of labour rights of these workers. It is important, however, to keep in mind that these factories have provided important jobs for women, who as a result of their employment have experienced new economic freedom and solidarity with other women. See Rosa 1993.
6 The ILO director general, in his 1994 report, 'Social Justice in a Global Economy: An ILO Agenda,' stated that transnationals control approximately one-third of the private sector's productive assets worldwide.

Bibliography

Aaron, Henry J., and Alicia H. Munnell. 1992. 'Reassessing the Role for Wealth Transfer Taxes.' *National Tax Journal* 45(2): 119.

Abella, Manolo. 1982. 'International Migration and Development.' In G. Batistella and A. Paganoni, eds, *Philippine Labor Migration: Impact and Policy.* Quezon City: Scalabrini Migration Center.

Adelstein, R.P. 1991. 'The Nation as an Economic Unit: Keynes, Roosevelt, and the Managerial Ideal.' *Journal of American History* 19: 161–87.

Afshar, Haleh, and Carolyn Dennis, eds. 1992. *Women, Recession and Adjustment in the Third World.* London: Macmillan

Akyeampong, E., and Jo Winters. 1993. 'International Employment Trends by Industry.' *Perspectives on Labour and Income* 5(2): 33–7.

Allen, Sheila. 1983. 'Production and Reproduction: The Lives of Women Homeworkers.' *Sociological Review* 31(4): 649–65.

Amariglio, Jack. 1988. 'The Body, Economic Discourse, and Power: An Economist's Introduction to Foucault.' *History of Political Economy* 20: 583–613.

– 1990. 'Economics as a Postmodern Discourse.' In Warren Samuels, ed., *Economics as Discourse.* Norwell, MA: Kluwer.

Amariglio, Jack, S. Resnick, and R. Wolff. 1990. 'Division and Difference in the "Discipline" of Economics.' *Critical Inquiry* 17: 108–39.

Anderson, Benedict. 1991. *Imagined Communities.* London: Verso.

Anderson, Bridget. 1993. *Britain's Secret Slaves: An Investigation into the Plight of Overseas Domestic Workers.* United Kingdom: Anti-Slavery International and Kalayaan.

Angeles, Leonora. 1991/92. 'Why the Philippines Did Not Become a Newly Industrializing Country.' *Kasarinlan* 7 (2 and 3).

Anker, Richard, and Catherine Hein. 1986. *Sex Inequalities in Urban Employment in the Third World.* New York: Tavistock Publications.

Antrobus, Peggy. 1986. 'Employment of Women Workers in the Caribbean.' In
   Pat Ellis, ed., *Women of the Caribbean*, 31–2. London: Zed Books.
– 1993. 'Structural Adjustment: Cure or Curse? Implications for Caribbean
   Development.' in *Focus on Gender: Perspectives on Women and Development*. Vol.
   1, Women and Economic Policy, no. 3, October.
Arat-Koc, S. 1990. 'Importing Housewives: Non-Citizen Domestic Workers and
   the Crisis of the Domestic Sphere in Canada.' In M. Luxton, H. Rosenberg,
   and S. Arat-Koc, eds, *Through the Kitchen Window: The Politics of Home and Family*. Toronto: Garamond.
Armstrong, P. 1989. 'Is There Still a Chairman of the Board?' *Journal of Management and Development* 8(6): 118–35.
– 1993. 'The Feminization of the Labour Force: Harmonizing Down in a Global
   Economy.' Paper presented to the North-South Conference on Structural
   Change and Gender Relations in the Era of Globalization, Toronto.
Armstrong, P., and H. Armstrong. 1992. 'Sex and the Professions in Canada.'
   Journal of Canadian Studies 27(1): 118–35.
– 1994. *The Double Ghetto: Canadian Women and Their Segregated Work*. Toronto:
   McClelland and Stewart.
– 1995. 'Wasting Away.' Unpublished book manuscript. Toronto.
Armstrong, P., J. Choiniere, and E. Day. 1993. *Vital Signs: Nursing in Transition*.
   Toronto: Garamond Press.
Arizpe, Lourdes, and Carlota Botey. 1987. 'Mexican Agricultural Development
   Policy and Its Impact on Rural Women.' In Carmen Diana Deere and
   Magdalena León, eds, *Rural Women and State Policy: Feminist Perspectives on
   Latin American Agricultural Development*. Boulder: Westview.
Arnopoulos, S. 1979. *Problems of Immigrant Women in the Canadian Labour Force*.
   Ottawa: Canadian Advisory Council on the Status of Women.
Asis, Maruja M.B. 1992. 'The Overseas Employment Program Policy.' In G.
   Batistella and A. Paganoni, eds, *Philippine Labor Migration: Impact and Policy*.
   Quezon City: Scalbrini Migration Center.
Baden, Sally. 1993. 'The Impact of Recession and Structural Adjustment on
   Women's Work in Developing Countries.' Interdepartmental Project for
   Women in Employment, Working paper no. 19. Geneva: ILO.
Badets, J., and N. McLaughlin. 1989. 'Immigrants in Product Manufacturing.'
   Perspectives on Labour and Income 1(3): 39–48.
Bakan, Abigail B. 1990. *Ideology and Class Conflict in Jamaica: The Politics of Rebel-
   lion*. Montreal: McGill-Queen's University Press.
Bakan, Abigail B., David Cox, and Colin Leys, eds, 1993. *Imperial Power and
   Regional Trade: The Caribbean Basin Initiative*. Waterloo, Ont.: Wilfrid Laurier
   University Press.

Bakan, Abigail B., and Daiva Stasiulis. 1994. 'Foreign Domestic Worker Policy in Canada and the Social Boundaries of Modern Citizenship.' *Science and Society* 58(1) (Spring): 7–33.

Bakker, Isabella. 1988. 'Women's Employment in Comparative Perspective.' In Jane Jenson et al., eds, *The Feminisation of the Labour Force: Paradoxes and Promises*. Oxford: Polity.

– 1991. 'Pay Equity and Economic Restructuring.' In J. Fudge and P. McDermott, eds, *Just Wages: A Feminist Reassessment of Pay Equity*. Toronto: University of Toronto Press.

– 1993. 'Gender Relations, Macroeconomics and Structural Change in the OECD in the 1980's.' Paper presented at the conference 'Out of the Margins,' Amsterdam.

– 1994a. *The Strategic Silence: Women and Economic Policy*. London: Zed Books / The North-South Institute.

– 1994b. 'Macroeconomics through a Feminist Lens.' In *Economic Equality*. Ottawa: Status of Women Canada. Also in Brodie 1995.

Bakker, Isabella, and Riel Miller. 1996. 'Escape from Fordism: The Emergence of Alternative Forms of State Administration.' In Robert Boyer and Daniel Drache, eds, *Markets against States: The Limits of Globalization*. London: Routledge.

Bakker, Isabella, and Katherine Scott. 1996. 'From Postwar to Postliberal Keynesian Welfare State.' In Wallace Clement and Glen Williams, eds, *Building on the New Canadian Political Economy*. Montreal: McGill-Queen's Press.

Bale, Gordon. 1989. *Wealth Transfer Taxation: An Important Component of a Good Tax System*. Wellington, NZ: Victoria University Press for the Institute of Policy Studies.

Balibar, Etienne. 1991. 'Es Gibt Keinen Staat in Europa: Racism and Politics in Europe Today.' *New Left Review* no. 186 (March/April): 18.

Balibar, Etienne, and Immanuel Wallerstein. 1991. *Race, Nation, Class: Ambiguous Identities*. London: Verso.

Bannerji, Himani. 1993. 'Popular Images of South Asian Women.' In H. Bannerji, ed., *Returning the Gaze*. Toronto: Sistervision Press.

– 1995. *Thinking Through: Essays on Feminism, Marxism and Anti-Racism*. Toronto: Women's Press.

Banting, Keith. 1991. 'The Politics of Wealth Taxes.' *Canadian Public Policy* 17(3): 351.

Barnet, Richard, and John Cavanagh. 1994. *Global Dreams: Imperial Corporations and the New World Order*. New York: Simon and Schuster.

Barrett, Michele. 1980 and 1988. *Women's Oppression Today: The Marxist/Feminist Encounter*. London and New York: Verso.

Bascom, Wilbert O. 1991. 'Remittance Inflows and Economic Development in Selected Anglophone Caribbean Countries.' In Sergio Dîaz-Briquets and Sidney Weintraub, eds, *Migration, Remittances and Small Business Development: Mexico and Caribbean Basin Countries*. Boulder: Westview Press.

Bashevkin, Sylvia. 1989. 'Free Trade and Canadian Feminism: The Case of the National Action Committee on the Status of Women.' *Canadian Public Policy* 15(4): 363–75.

– 1991. 'NAC's Opposition to Free Trade: The Costs and Benefits.' In S. Bashevkin, *True Patriot Love: The Politics of Canadian Nationalism*. Toronto: Oxford University Press.

Batistella, Graziano. 1992. 'Migration Opportunity or Loss?' In G. Batistella and A. Paganoni, eds, *Economic and Social Impact of Labor Migration*, 113–34. Quezon City: Scalabrini Migration Center.

Beach, Betty. 1989. *Integrating Work and Family Life: The Home-Working Working Family*. Albany: State University of New York Press.

Becker, Gary. 1991. *A Treatise on the Family*. Enlarged ed. Cambridge: Harvard University Press.

Beechey, Veronica. 1987. *Unequal Work*. London: Verso.

– 1988. 'Rethinking the Definition of Work: Gender and Work.' In Jane Jenson et al., eds, *The Feminisation of the Labour Force: Paradoxes and Promises*. Oxford: Polity.

Beilhartz, Peter. 1987. 'Reading Politics: Social Theory and Social Policy.' *Anzjs* 23(3) (November).

Belcourt, Monica, Ronald J. Burke, and Helene Lee-Gosselin. 1991. *The Glass Box: Women Business Owners in Canada*. Ottawa: Canadian Advisory Council on the Status of Women.

Beneria, Lourdes. 1989. 'Gender and the Global Economy.' In Arthur MacEwan and William Tabb, eds, *Instability and Change in the World Economy*. New York: Monthly Review Press.

Beneria, Lourdes, and Shelley Feldman, eds. 1992. *Unequal Burden: Economic Crisis, Persistent Poverty, and Women's Work*. Boulder: Westview Press.

Beneria, L., and M. Roldan. 1987. *The Crossroads of Class and Gender*. Chicago: University of Chicago Press.

Bennett, Fran, Rosa Heys, and Rosalind Coward. 1980. 'The Limits to "Financial and Legal Independence": A Socialist Feminist Perspective on Taxation and Social Security.' In *Politics and Power One*. London: Routledge & Kegan Paul.

Benson, Susan Porter. 1989. 'Women, Work and the Family: Industrial Homework in Rhode Island in 1934.' In E. Boris and C.R. Daniels, eds, *Homework: Historical and Contemporary Perspectives on Paid Labor at Home*. Urbana: University of Illinois Press.

Berman, M. 1988. *All That Is Solid Melts into Air*. New York: Penguin.

Bhabha, Homi K., ed. 1990. *Nation and Narration*. London: Routledge.

Bherer, Harold, Sylvie Gagnon, and Jacinte Roberge. 1990. *Wampum and Letters Patent: Exploratory Study of Native Entrepreneurship*. Halifax: Institute for Research on Public Policy.

Bird, Richard. 1970. 'The Tax Kaleidoscope: Perspectives on Tax Reform in Canada.' *Canadian Tax Journal* 18: 444.

– 1972. 'The Case for Taxing Personal Wealth.' In *Report of the Twenty-third Tax Conference, 1971*: 6–24 Toronto: Canadian Tax Foundation.

– 1978. 'Canada's Vanishing Death Taxes.' *Osgoode Hall Law Journal* 16(1): 133.

Bishton, D. 1984. *The Sweat Shop Report*. Birmingham: AFFOR.

Blau, Francine D., and John W. Graham. 1990. 'Black-White Differences in Wealth and Asset Composition.' *Quarterly Journal of Economics*, May: 321.

Blumberg, Rae Lesser. 1991a. 'The "Triple Overlap" of Gender Stratification, Economy and the Family.' In Rae Lesser Blumberg, ed., *Gender, Family and Economy: The Triple Overlap*. Newbury Park, Calif.: Sage Publications Inc.

– 1991b. 'Income under Female versus Male Control: Hypotheses from a Theory of Gender Stratification and Data from the Third World.' In Blumberg, ed., *Gender, Family and Economy*.

Blumstein, Philip, and Pepper Schwartz. 1991. 'Money and Ideology: Their Impact on Power and the Division of Household Labor.' In Blumberg, ed., *Gender, Family and Economy*.

Bordo, Susan. 1987. *The Flight to Objectivity*. Albany: State University of New York Press.

Boris, Eileen. 1989. 'Black Women and Paid Labor in the Home: Industrial Homework in Chicago in the 1920s.' In E. Boris and C.R. Daniels, eds, *Homework*. Urbana: University of Illinois Press.

Boris, Eileen, and Cynthia R. Daniels, eds, 1989. *Homework: Historical and Contemporary Perspectives on Paid Labor at Home*. Urbana: University of Illinois Press.

Borowy, Jan, et al. 'Are These Clothes Clean? The Campaign for Fair Wages and Working Conditions for Homeworkers.' In Linda Carty, ed., *And Still We Rise*. Toronto: Women's Press.

Bossons, John. 1972. 'Economic Overview of the Tax Reform Legislation.' In *Report of the Twenty-third Tax Conference, 1971*. Toronto: Canadian Tax Foundation.

Boyd, M., M.A. Mulvihill, and J. Myles. 1991. 'Gender, Power and Post Industrialism.' *Canadian Review of Sociology and Anthropology* 28(4): 407–36.

Brand, Dionne. 1993. 'A Working Paper on Black Women in Toronto: Gender, Race and Class.' In H. Bannerji, ed., *Returning the Gaze*. Toronto: Sistervision Press.

Brand, Dionne, et al. 1984. 'A Working Paper on Black Women in Toronto: Gender, Race and Class.' *Fireweed*, no. 19 (Summer/Fall).

British Columbia. 1986. Survey of Women Business Owners in British Columbia: Major Findings and Policy Implications. Victoria: Ministry of Industry and Small Business Development.

– 1991. *Women in Business: Profile of Women Business Owners in British Columbia*. Victoria: Ministry of Economic Development, Small Business and Trade.

Brodie, Janine. 1994. 'Politics on the Boundaries: Restructuring and the Canadian Women's Movement.' Eighth Annual Robarts Lecture, York University, Toronto, 1 March.

– 1995a. *Politics on the Margins: Restructuring and the Canadian Women's Movement*. Halifax: Fernwood Press.

– ed. 1995b. *Women and Canadian Public Policy*. Toronto: Harcourt Brace and Company.

Brooks, Neil. 1990. *Paying for Civilized Society: The Need for Fair and Responsible Tax Reform*. Ottawa: Canadian Centre for Policy Alternatives.

Bulletin sur les Femmes et l'emploi dans la CE. 1993. Published by the Commission of the European Communities. No. 3, October.

Buck-Morss, Susan. 1995. 'Envisioning Capital: Political Economy on Display.' *Critical Inquiry* 21 (Winter): 434–67.

Burman, P. 1988. *Killing Time, Losing Ground: Experiences of Unemployment*. Toronto: Thompson Educational Publishing.

Buss, Terry F., and F. Stevens Redburn. 1983. *Shutdown at Youngstown: Public Policy for Mass Unemployment*. Albany: SUNY Press.

Bustamante, Jorge A. 1983. '*Maquiladoras*: A New Face of International Capitalism on Mexico's Northern Frontier.' In J. Nash and M.P. Fernández-Kelly, eds, *Women, Men, and the International Division of Labour*. New York: State University of New York Press.

Butterwick, Shauna. 1992. 'The Labour Force Development Strategy: Tripartism and the Inclusion/Exclusion of "Equity" Groups.' *Policy Explorations*, Centre for Policy Studies in Education, Occasional Papers, vol. 6, no. 1 (Spring).

Callender, Claire. 1987. 'Women and the Redundancy Process: A Case Study.' In Raymond M. Lee, *Redundancy, Layoffs and Plant Closures: Their Character, Causes and Consequences*. London: Croom Helm.

Calliste, Agnes. 1991. 'Canada's Immigration Policy and Domestics from the Caribbean: The Second Domestic Scheme.' In Jesse Vorst et al., eds, *Race, Class, Gender: Bonds and Barriers*. Toronto: Garamond Press.

Cameron, Barbara, and Teresa Mak. 1991. 'Working Conditions of Chinese Speaking Homeworkers in the Toronto Garment Industry.' Summary of

Results of a Survey conducted by the International Ladies' Garment Workers' Union. Six-page summary.

Campbell, A. 1984. *Wigan Pier Revisited: Poverty and Politics in the 80s*. London: Virago.

Canada. 1994a. *Budget Speech*. Ottawa: Department of Finance.

- 1994b. *Improving Social Security in Canada: A Discussion Paper*. Hull: Human Resources Development Canada.

Canada, Department of Manpower and Immigration. 1971. *Annual Report 1968/69*. Ottawa: Information Canada.

- 1971. *Annual Report 1970/71*. Ottawa: Information Canada.

- 1974. *Annual Report 1972/73*. Ottawa: Information Canada.

- 1975. *Annual Report 1973/74*. Ottawa: Information Canada.

Canada, Employment and Immigration Canada. 1978. *Annual Report 1977/78*. Ottawa: Supply and Services Canada.

- 1980. *Annual Report 1979/80*. Ottawa: Supply and Services Canada.

- 1981a. *Annual Report 1980/81*. Ottawa: Supply and Services Canada.

- 1981b. *Annual Statistical Bulletin 1980–81*. Ottawa: EIC.

- 1983a. *Annual Report 1982/83*. Ottawa: Supply and Services Canada.

- 1983b. *Annual Statistical Bulletin, 1982/83*.Ottawa: EIC.

- 1985. *Annual Statistical Bulletin. National Training Program. 1984/85*. Ottawa: EIC.

- 1987. *Annual Report 1986/87*. Ottawa: Supply and Services Canada.

- 1989. *Success in the Works. A Policy Paper. A Labour Force Development Strategy for Canada*. Ottawa: EIC.

- 1990. 'Statistical Profiles.'Ottawa: EIC, Strategic Planning and Research Directorate.

- 1991. *1991–92 Estimates. Part III. Expenditure Plan*. Ottawa: Supply and Services Canada.

Canada, Human Resources Development Canada. 1994a. *Agenda: Jobs and Growth, Improving Social Security in Canada*. Ottawa: Minister of Supply and Services.

- 1994b. *Evaluation of Employability Initiatives for Social Assistance Recipients (SARS) in CJS*. Program Evaluation Branch, Strategic Policy, April.

Canada, Royal Commission on Equality in Employment. 1984. *Report*. Ottawa: Supply and Services Canada.

Canada, Royal Commission on the Status of Women. 1970. *Report*. Ottawa: Information Canada.

Canada, Secretary of State. 1991. *Canada's Off-Reserve Aboriginal Population: A Statistical Overview*. Ottawa: Secretary of State.

Canadian Advisory Council on the Status of Women. 1974. *What's Been Done? An Assessment of the Federal Government's Implementation of the Recommendations of the Royal Commission on the Status of Women.* Ottawa: The Council.

Canadian Labour Congress (CLC). 1993. 'Women Workers and the Recession.' Ottawa: CLC, June.

Capdevielle, Jacques, Hélène Y. Meynaud, and René Mouriaux. 1990. *Petits boulots et grand marché européen: Le travail démobilisé.* Paris: FNSP.

Carino, Benjamin V. 1992. 'Migrant Workers from the Philippines.' in G. Batistella and A. Paganoni, eds, *Philippine Labor Migration: Impact and Policy.* Quezon City: Scalabrini Migration Center.

Cassels, Jamie, and Lisa Philipps. 1994. 'Why Lawyers Need Statistics about Unpaid Work.' In *Proceedings, Statistics Canada International Conference on the Measurement and Valuation of Unpaid Work.* Cat. no. 89-532E. Ottawa: Statistics Canada.

Cassin, A. Marguerite. 1993. 'Equitable and Fair: Widening the Circle.' In ed., Allan M. Maslove, *Fairness in Taxation.* Toronto: University of Toronto Press.

Chant, Sylvia. 1991. *Women and Survival in Mexican Cities: Perspectives on Gender, Labor Markets and Low-income Households.* New York: Manchester University Press.

Chatterjee, Partha. 1986. *Nationalist Thought in the Colonial World: A Derivative Discourse.* Tokyo: United Nations University.

Chawla, Raj K. 1990. 'The Distribution of Wealth in Canada and the United States.' *Canadian Economic Observer*, April.

Chodos, Robert. 1977. *The Caribbean Connection.* Toronto: James Lorimer.

Christensen, K. 1989. 'Homebased Clerical Work: No Simple Truth, No Single Reality.' In E. Boris and C.R. Daniels, eds, *Homework.* Urbana: University of Illinois Press.

– 1992. Untitled paper presented at conference on homeworking. Toronto, November.

Clark-Lewis, Elizabeth. 1987. 'This Work Had an End ...' In C. Groneman and M.B. Norton, eds, *'To Toil the Livelong Day': America's Women at Work 1780–1980.* Ithaca: Cornell University Press.

Clarke, Tony. 1992. 'Afterword.' In Ronnie Leah, 'Taking a Stand: Strategies and Tactics of Organizing the Popular Movement in Canada.' Ottawa: Canadian Centre for Policy Alternatives, June.

Cockburn, Cynthia. 1985. *Brothers: Male Dominance and Technological Change.* London: Pluto.

Cohen, J. 1988. *Enterprising Canadians.* Ottawa: Supply and Services Canada.

– 1992. 'Hard at Work.' *Perspectives on Labour and Income* 4(1): 8–14.

Cohen, Marjorie G. 1982. 'The Problem of Studying Economic Man.' In Angela

R. Miles and Geraldine Finn, eds, *Feminism in Canada: From Pressure to Politics*. Montreal: Black Rose Books.

– 1986. 'Women and Free Trade.' In Duncan Cameron, ed., *The Free Trade Debates*. Toronto: Lorimer.

– 1987. *Free Trade and the Future of Women's Work: Manufacturing and Service Industries*. Toronto: Garamond.

– 1988. 'Americanizing Services.' In Ed Finn, ed., *The Facts on Free Trade*. Toronto: Lorimer.

– 1996. 'Democracy and Trade Agreements: Challenges for Disadvantaged Women, Minorities and States.' In R. Boyer and D. Drache, eds, *Markets against States: The Limits of Globalization*. London: Routledge.

Cohen, Robin. 1987. *The New Helots: Migrants and the International Division of Labor*. Vermont: Gower Publishing Co.

Colen, Shellee. 1990. '"Housekeeping" for the Green Card: West Indian Household Workers, the State and Stratified Reproduction in New York.' In Roger Sanjek and Shellee Colen, eds, *At Work in Homes: Household Workers in World Perspective*. Washington: American Ethnological Society Monograph Series.

Commission des Communautés Européennes. 1991. *La place des femmes sur le marché du travail: Tendances et évolutions dans les douze pays de la CE, 1983–90*. Cahiers de Femmes d'Europe, 36.

Commonwealth Expert Group on Women and Structural Adjustment. 1989. *Engendering Adjustment for the 1990's*. London: Commonwealth Secretariat.

Connelly, M.P. 1994. 'Gender Matters: Restructuring and Adjustment, South and North.' Paper presented to the Gender and Development Research Network, Centre for Human Settlements, University of British Columbia, Vancouver, May.

Connelly, Patricia, and Martha MacDonald 1990. *Women and the Labour Force*. Ottawa: Supply and Services.

– 1992. 'State Policy, the Household and Women's Work in the Atlantic Fishery.' *Journal of Canadian Studies* 26(4) (Winter).

Cooper, Brian. 1992. 'Disciplining Economics: The Case of Gender.' Paper presented at the ASSA meetings, New Orleans.

Coré, Francoise. 1994. 'Women and the Restructuring of Employment.' *The OECD Observer*, no 186, February/March.

Correspondencia 14 (Winter), 1992.

Crawford, W.E. 1993. 'Provincial Wealth Taxes? The Numbers Just Don't Justify Them.' *Canadian Tax Journal* 41(1): 150.

Crompton, S. 1993. 'The Renaissance of Self-Employment.' *Perspectives on Labour and Income* 5(2): 23–6.

Crotty, James. 1990. 'Keynes and the Stages of Development of the Capitalist Economy: The Institutional Foundation of Keynes' Methodology.' *Journal of Economic Issues* 24 (September): 761–80.

Cullenberg, Stephen. 1992. 'The Political Economy of Marxist Theories of the Falling Rate of Profit: Methodological Considerations.' *Methodus* 4(1): 44–54.

Cullity, Maurice C. 1972. 'Historical Background to the Succession Duty Act R.S.O. 1970, ch.449.' Prepared for Provincial Advisory Committee on Succession Duties. Osgoode Hall Law School, York University.

Daenzer, Patricia. 1993. *Regulating Class Privilege: Immigrant Servants in Canada 1940s–1990s*. Toronto: Canadian Scholars' Press.

Dale, Patricia. 1980. *Women and Jobs: The Impact of Federal Government Employment Strategies on Women*. Ottawa: Canadian Advisory Council on the Status of Women.

Dance, Terry, and Susan Witter. 1988. 'The Privatization of Training: Women Pay the Cost.' *Women's Education des Femmes* 6(1) (Winter): 11.

Dangler, J. 1989. 'Electronic Subassemblers in Central New York: Nontraditional Homeworkers in a Nontraditional Homework Industry.' In E. Boris and C.R. Daniels, eds, *Homework*. Urbana: University of Illinois Press.

Das Gupta, Tania. 1986. *Learning from Our History: Community Development by Immigrant Women in Ontario. 1958–1986*. Toronto: Cross Cultural Communication Centre.

Davies, James B. 1991. 'The Distributive Effects of Wealth Taxes.' *Canadian Public Policy* 17(3) 279.

Dehli, Kari. 1993. 'Subject to the New Global Economy: Power and Positioning in Ontario Labour Market Policy Formation.' *Studies in Political Economy* 41 (Summer).

Despradel, Lil. 1984. 'Internal Migration of Rural Women in the Caribbean and Its Effects on Their Status.' In UNESCO, *Women on the Move: Contemporary Changes in Family and Society*. New York: UNESCO.

Donner, A.W. 1991. 'Recession, Recovery and Redistribution: The Three R's of Canadian State Macro Policy in the 1980's.' In D. Drache and M.S. Gertler, eds, *The New Era of Global Competition: State Policy and Market Power*. Montreal and Kingston: McGill-Queen's University Press.

Dowler, J.M., D.A. Jordan, and O. Adams. 1992. 'Gender Inequalities in Care-Giving in Canada.' *Health Reports* 4(2) Statistics Canada, Cat. 82-003.

Drache, Daniel. 1992. 'Conclusion.' In Daniel Drache, ed., *Getting on Track: Social Democratic Strategies for Ontario*. Kingston: McGill-Queen's University Press.

Duff, David G. 1993. 'Taxing Inherited Wealth: A Philosophical Argument.' *Canadian Journal of Law and Jurisprudence* 6(1).

Duffy, Ann, and Norene Pupo. 1992. *Part-Time Paradox: Connecting Gender, Work and Family*. Toronto: McClelland and Stewart.

Eagleton, Terry, F. Jameson, and E. Said. 1990. *Nationalism, Colonialism and Literature*. Minneapolis: University of Minnesota Press.

Economic Council of Canada. 1965. *First Annual Review*. Ottawa: Queen's Printer.

– 1984. *Towards Equity*. Ottawa: Supply and Services.

– 1990. *Good Jobs, Bad Jobs: Employment in the Service Economy*. Ottawa: Economic Council of Canada.

– 1991. *Employment in a Service Economy*. Ottawa: Economic Council of Canada.

Edwards, Meredith. 1980. *Financial Arrangements within Families*. Canberra, Aust.: National Council of Women.

Eichler, Margrit. 1990–1. 'The Limits of Family Law Reform or, The Privatization of Female and Child Poverty.' *Canadian Family Law Quarterly* 7: 59–84.

Elson, Diane. 1991. 'Male Bias in Macro-economics: The Case of Structural Adjustment.' In Diane Elson, ed., *Male Bias in the Development Process*. Manchester: Manchester University Press.

– 1994. 'Micro, Meso, Macro: Gender and Economic Analysis in the Context of Policy Reform.' In I. Bakker, *The Strategic Silence*. London: Zed Books / The North-South Institute 1994.

– 1995. 'Rethinking Strategies for Development: From Male-Biased to Human Centered Development.' In D. Elson, ed., *Male Bias in the Development Process*. 2nd edition. Manchester: Manchester University Press.

Elson, D., and R. Pearson. 1981. 'Nimble Fingers Make Cheap Workers: An Analysis of Women's Employment in Third World Export Manufacturing.' *Feminist Review* 7: 87–105.

England, Paula. 1989. 'A Feminist Critique of Rational Choice Theories: Implications for Sociology.' *American Sociologist* 20: 14–28.

– 1993. 'The Separative Self: Androcentric Bias in Neoclassical Assumptions.' In Marianne Ferber and Julie Nelson, eds, *Beyond Economic Man: Feminist Theory and Economics*. Chicago: University of Chicago Press.

England, Paula, and Barbara Kilbourne. 1990. 'Markets, Marriages and Other Mates: The Problem of Power.' In R. Friedland and A.F. Robertson, eds, *Beyond the Marketplace: Rethinking Economy and Society*. New York: Aldine de Gruyter.

Enloe, Cynthia. 1989. *Bananas, Beaches and Bases: Making Feminist Sense of International Politics*. Berkeley: University of California Press.

Esping-Anderson, Gosta. 1990. *The Three Worlds of Welfare Capitalism*. Princeton: Princeton University Press.

Evans, Patricia. 1995. 'Ontario's Welfare Policy: Restructuring the Debate.' In Janine Brodie, ed., *Women and Canadian Public Policy*. Toronto: Harcourt Brace and Company.

Fagnani, Jeanne. 1992. 'Travail et fécondité en France et en Allemagne de l'Oeust.' *Revue Française des Affaires Sociales* 2.

Faludi, Susan. 1991. *Backlash: The Undeclared War against American Women*. New York: Crown Publishers.

Feldman, Shelley. 1992. 'Crises, Poverty, and Gender Inequality: Current Themes and Issues.' In Beneria and Feldman, eds, *Unequal Burden*. Boulder: Westview Press 1992.

Ferber, Marianne, and Julie A. Nelson. 1993. *Beyond Economic Man: Feminist Theory and Economics*. Chicago: University of Chicago Press.

Fernández-Kelly, María Patricia. 1983. *For We Are Sold, I and My People: Women and Industry in Mexico's Frontier*. Albany: State University of New York Press.

Fernández-Kelly, María Patricia, and Anna M. Garcia. 1985. 'The Making of an Underground Economy: Hispanic Women, Home Work, and the Advanced Capitalist State.' *Urban Anthropology* 14 (1–3): 59–90.

Finch, J. 1983. *Married to the Job: Wives' Incorporation in Men's Work*. London, Boston: Allen & Unwin.

Finnie, Ross. 1993. 'Women, Men and the Economic Consequences of Divorce: Evidence from Canadian Longitudinal Data.' *Canadian Review of Sociology & Anthropology* 30(2): 205.

Folbre, Nancy. 1986. 'Cleaning House: New Perspectives on Households and Economic Development.' *Journal of Development Economics* 22.

– 1994. *Who Pays for the Kids? Gender and the Structure of Constraint*. London: Routledge.

Folbre, Nancy, and Heidi Hartmann. 1988. 'The Rhetoric of Self-Interest: Ideology and Gender in Economic Theory.' In A. Klamer, D. McCloskey, and R. Solow, eds, *The Consequences of Economic Rhetoric*. Cambridge: Cambridge University Press.

'Foreign Domestic Workers in Canada – Where Do They Come From? How Has That Changed over Time?' 1991. *The Moment* 2 (5).

'Former judges warn against Dunkel package.' 1993. *Indian Express*, Kochi, 16 December.

Foster, John. 1993. 'The Canadian Case: A Participant's Reflections.' Draft paper presented to research seminar 'Redefining Governance: The Transnationalization of Civic Participation in North America,' Center for U.S.-Mexican Studies, University of California, San Diego, 17 March.

Foucault, Michel. 1973a. *Madness and Civilization: A History of Insanity in the Age of Reason*. Translated by R. Howard. New York: Random House.

– 1973b. *The Order of Things: An Archeology of the Human Sciences*. New York: Harper and Row.

– 1979. *Discipline and Punish*. New York: Vintage.

– 1980. 'The Eye of Power.' In *Power/Knowledge*. New York: Pantheon.

Fraser, Nancy. 1989. *Unruly Practices*. Minneapolis: University of Minnesota Press.

– 1993. 'Clintonism, Welfare, and the Antisocial Wage.' *Rethinking Marxism* 6(1): 9–23.

Fraser, Nancy, and Linda Gordon. 1994. 'A Geneology of Dependency: Tracing a Keyword of the US Welfare State.' *Signs* 19(2) (Winter).

French, Marilyn. 1992. *The War against Women*. New York: Summit Books.

Fudge, Judy. 1989. 'The Privatization of the Costs of Social Reproduction: Some Recent Charter Cases.' *Canadian Journal of Women and the Law* 3: 246–55.

– 1991. *Labour Law's Little Sister: The Employment Standards Act and the Feminization of Labour*. Ottawa: Canadian Centre for Policy Alternatives.

– 1992. 'The Gendered Dimension of Labour Law: Why Women Need Inclusive Unionism and Broader-Based Bargaining.' Paper presented at the conference of the Centre for Research on Work and Society on Broadening Bargaining Structures in the New Social Order, York University, North York, Ontario, 7–8 May.

Fudge, Judy, and Patricia McDermott. 1991. *Just Wages: A Feminist Assessment of Pay Equity*. Toronto: University of Toronto Press.

Gabriel, Christina, and Laura Macdonald. 1994. 'NAFTA, Women and Organizing in Canada and Mexico: Forging a Feminist Internationality.' In *Millennium* 23(3) (Winter).

Gardner, Robert. 1981. 'Tax Reform and Class Interests: The Fate of Progressive Reform.' *Canadian Taxation*, Winter.

Gavigan, Shelley A.M. 1988. 'Law, Gender and Ideology.' In A. Bayesfsky, ed., *Legal Theory Meets Legal Practice*. Edmonton: Academic Printers & Publishing.

– 1993. 'Paradise Lost, Paradox Revisited: The Implications of Familial Ideology for Feminist, Lesbian, and Gay Engagement to Law.' *Osgoode Hall Law Journal* 31.

Gee, Ellen, and Meredith Kimball. 1987. *Women and Aging*. Toronto: Butterworths.

Gellner, Ernest. 1983. *Nations and Nationalism*. Oxford: Blackwell.

George, Susan. 1992. *The Debt Boomerang: How Third World Debt Hurts Us All*. Boulder: Westview Press.

Gereffi, Gary. 1992. 'Mexico's Maquiladora Industries and North American Integration.' In Stephen J. Randall, ed., *North America without Borders? Integrating Canada, the United States, and Mexico*. Calgary: University of Calgary Press.

Gillespie, W.I. 1966. *The Incidence of Taxes and Public Expenditures in the Canadian Economy*. Ottawa: Royal Commission on Taxation. Study no. 2.

Glenn, Evelyn Nakano. 1992. 'From Servitude to Service Work: Historical Continuities in the Racial Division of Paid Reproductive Work.' *Signs* 18(11).

Gordon, Lorna. 1986. 'Women in Caribbean Agriculture.' In Pat Ellis, ed., *Women of the Caribbean*, 35–40. London: Zed Books.

Grappard, Ulla. 1993. 'Robinson Crusoe: The Quintessential Economic Man?' Unpublished manuscript.

Gray, Gratton. 1990. 'Social Policy by Stealth.' *Policy Options* 11(2).

Grayson, J. Paul. 1986. 'Plant Closures and Political Despair.' *Canadian Review of Sociology and Anthropology* 23(3): 331–49.

Grbich, Judith. 1987. 'The Position of Women in Family Dealing: The Australian Case.' *International Journal of the Sociology of Law* 15: 309–32.

Grewal, Inderpal, and Caren Kaplan. 1994. *Scattered Hegemonies: Postmodernity and Transnational Feminist Practices*. Minneapolis: University of Minnesota Press.

Grinspun, Ricardo, and Robert Krinklewich. 1994. 'Consolidating Neoliberal Reforms: 'Free Trade' as a Conditioning Framework.' *Studies in Political Economy* 43 (Spring).

Hacking, Ian. 1990. *The Taming of Chance*. Cambridge: Cambridge University Press.

Hadley, K. 1994. 'Working Lean and Mean: A Gendered Experience of Restructuring in an Electronics Plant.' Doctor of Education dissertation, Graduate Department of Education, University of Toronto.

Hagen, Elisabeth, and Jane Jenson. 1988. 'Paradoxes and Promises: Work and Politics in the Postwar Years.' In Jane Jenson et al., eds, *The Feminisation of the Labour Force: Paradoxes and Promises*. Oxford: Polity.

Hall, Peter. 1989. *The Political Power of Economic Ideas: Keynesianism across Nations*. Princeton: Princeton University Press.

Hansen, Gary B. 1988. 'Layoffs, Plant Closings, and Worker Displacement in America: Serious Problems That Need a National Solution.' *Journal of Social Issues* 44(4): 153–71.

Haraway, Donna. 1991. *Simians, Cyborgs and Women: The Reinvention of Nature*. New York: Routledge.

Harder, Sandra. 1992. *Economic Restructuring in Canada: Developing a Gender-Sensitive Analytic Framework*. Ottawa: Status of Women Canada.

Harding, Sandra. 1986. *The Science Question in Feminism*. Ithaca: Cornell University Press.

Harrison, Paul. 1993. *Inside the Third World*. Harmondsworth: Penguin Books.

Hartle, Douglas. 1988. 'Some Analytical, Political and Normative Lessons from Carter.' In Neil Brooks, ed., *The Quest for Tax Reform*. Toronto: Carswell.

Hartmann, Heidi, and Nancy Folbre. 1988. 'The Rhetoric of Self-Interest and the Ideology of Gender.' In Klamer, McCloskey, and Solow, eds, *The Consequences of Economic Rhetoric*, 184–206. Cambridge: Cambridge University Press.

Harvey, David. 1989. *The Condition of Postmodernity*. London: Basil Blackwell.

Henry, Frances. 1968. 'The West Indian Domestic Scheme in Canada.' *Social and Economic Studies* 17(1).

Hernández Navarro, Luis. 1993. 'Mexican NGOs in Transition.' *Enfoque* (Center for U.S.-Mexican Studies), (Spring): 4, 10.

Hobsbawm, Eric. 1990. *Nations and Nationalism since 1780*. Cambridge: Cambridge University Press.

Holland, W., and A. Bissett-Johnson, eds. 1980. *Matrimonial Property Law in Canada*. Agincourt, Ont.: Carswell.

hooks, bell. 1984. *Feminist Theory: From Margin to Centre*. Boston: South End Press.

– 1991. 'Sisterhood: Political Solidarity between Women.' In S. Gunew, ed., *A Reader in Feminist Knowledge*. London: Routledge.

Housewives Association of Trinidad and Tobago. 1975. *Report on Employment Status of Household Workers in Trinidad*. Port of Spain: HATT, March.

Hovius, B., and T.G. Youdan. 1991. *The Law of Family Property*. Toronto: Carswell.

INSEE. 1987. *Données Sociales 1987*. Paris: INSEE.

– 1991. *Contours et caractères: Les Femmes*. Paris: INSEE.

International Institute for Labour Studies. 1994. *Women Workers in a Changing Global Environment: Framework for Discussion*. International Forum on Equality for Women in the World of Work (Challenges for the Future), Geneva, 1–3 June 1994.

International Labour Organization. 1990. 'Homeworkers: The Case for Better Protection.' *ILO Information* 26(3).

– 1994. 'Defending Values, Promoting Change: Social Justice in a Global Economy: An ILO Agenda.' Report of the Director General to the International Labour Conference, 81st Session.

International Ladies' Garment Workers' Union (ILGWU). 1993. 'Brief to the Ontario Cabinet Committee on NAFTA.' March.

International Ladies' Garment Workers' Union and INTERCEDE. 1993. *Meeting the Needs of Vulnerable Workers: Proposals for Improved Employment Legislation and Access to Collective Bargaining for Domestic Workers and Industrial Homeworkers*. Toronto: ILGWU.

Jameson, F. 1984. 'Postmodernism, or the Cultural Logic of Late Capitalism.' *New Left Review* 146: 53–92.

Jenson, Jane. 1988. 'The Limits of "and the" Discourse: French Workers as Marginal Workers.' In Jane Jenson et al., eds, *The Feminisation of the Labour Force: Paradoxes and Promises*. Oxford: Polity.

– 1989a. '"Different" but not "Exceptional": Permeable Fordism in Canada.' *Canadian Review of Sociology and Anthropology* 26(1).

- 1989b 'The Talents of Women, the Skills of Men: Flexible Specialization and Women.' In Stephen Wood, *The Transformation of Work*. London: Unwin Hyman.
- 1990. 'Labor Market and Family Policy in France: An Intersecting Complex for Dealing with Poverty.' In Gertrude Goldberg and Eleanor Kremen, eds, *The Feminization of Poverty: Only in America?* Westport, Conn.: Greenwood. With Ruth Kantrow.
- 1993. 'Part-time Employment and Women: A Range of Strategies.' Prepared for the Economic Equality Workshops, Status of Women Canada, Ottawa, 29–30 November.

Jenson, Jane, and Rianne Mahon, eds. 1993a. *The Challenge of Restructuring: North American Labor Movements Respond*. Philadelphia: Temple University Press.

- 1993b. 'Representing Solidarity: Class, Gender and the Crisis in Social-Democratic Sweden.' *New Left Review* 201.

Jenson, Jane, and Mariette Sineau. 1995. *Mitterand et les Françaises. Un rendez-vous manqué*. Paris: Presses de Sciences Po.

Jessop, Bob. 1993. 'Toward a Schumpeterian Workfare State? Preliminary Remarks on Post-Fordist Political Economy.' *Studies in Political Economy* 40 (Spring).

Jhabvala, Renana. 1994. 'Self-Employed Women's Association: Organising Women by Struggle and Development.' In Sheila Rowbotham and Swasti Mitter, eds, *Dignity and Daily Bread: New Forms of Economic Organising among Poor Women in the Third World and the First*. London: Routledge.

Johnson, L.C., and R. Johnson. 1982. *The Seam Allowance: Industrial Home Sewing in Canada*. Toronto: The Women's Press.

Johnson, T. 1992. 'Homework No Solution for Families.' *Technotes* 1: 4–5.

Jones, Kathy, and Valerie Huff. 1989. 'Plant Closure. Its Effect on Immigrant and Women Workers.' *Our Times*, January.

Josling, Tim. 1992. 'NAFTA and Agriculture: A Review of the Economic Impacts.' In N. Lustig et al., eds, *North American Free Trade*, 144–75. Washington: Brookings Institute.

Kabeer, Naila. 1994. *Reversed Realities: Gender Hierarchies in Development Thought*. London: Verso.

Katz, Julius. 1994. *NAFTA WATCH* 1(9) (26 May).

Keller, Evelyn Fox. 1985. *Reflections on Gender and Science*. New Haven: Yale.

Kergoat, Danièle. 1984. *Les femmes et le travail à temps partiel*. Paris: Documentation Française.

Kerr, Richard. 1992. *An Economic Model to Assist in the Determination of Spousal Support*. Ottawa: Department of Justice.

Kessler, Denis, and Pierre Pestieau. 1991. 'The Taxation of Wealth in the EEC: Facts and Trends.' *Canadian Public Policy* 17(3): 309.

Keynes, J.M. 1933. 'National Self-Sufficiency.' *Yale Review* 22 (June): 755–69.

– 1973. *The Collected Writings of John Maynard Keynes*. Ed. Donald Moggridge. London: MacMillan.

Khor, Martin. 1993. *Third World Network Features*, 1 November.

Khosla Punam. 1993. *Review of the Situation of Women in Canada*. Toronto: National Action Committee on the Status of Women, July.

Kline, Melanie. 1994. 'The Colour of Law: Ideological Representations of First Nations in Legal Discourse.' *Social and Legal Studies* 3.

Knight, Russell M. 1988. *Family Business Entrepreneurs in Canada*. London: University of Western Ontario National Centre for Management Research and Development, Working Paper Series no. NC 88-24.

– 1989. *The Role of Female Entrepreneurs in Family Business*. London: University of Western Ontario National Centre for Management Research and Development, Working Paper Series no. 89-05.

Kopinak, Kathryn. 1993. 'The Maquiladorization of the Mexican Economy.' In Ricardo Grinspun and Maxwell A. Cameron, eds, *The Political Economy of North American Free Trade*. Montreal: McGill-Queen's University Press.

Krahn, Harvey. 1991. 'Non-Standard Work Arrangements.' *Perspectives on Labour and Income* 2(4): 36–8.

– 1992. *The Quality of Work in the Service Sector*. Ottawa: Ministry of Industry, Science and Technology.

Kwitko, Ludmilla. 1993. 'Filipina Domestic Workers and the New International Division of Labour.' Paper presented at 'Asia in the 1990s: Making and Meeting a New World' conference, Queen's University, Kingston.

Lahey, Kathleen A. 1985. 'The Tax Unit in Income Tax Theory.' In E. Diane Pask, Kathleen A. Mahoney, and Catherine A. Brown, eds, *Women, the Law and the Economy*. Toronto: Butterworths.

Leach, B. 1993. '"Flexible" Work, Precarious Future: Some Lessons from the Canadian Clothing Industry.' *Canadian Review of Sociology and Anthropology* 30(1).

Leckie, Norm, 1993. 'An International Review of Labour Adjustment Policies and Practices.' Draft paper for Queen's–University of Ottawa Economic Projects.

Le Dressay, Andre. 1993. 'A Brief Tax(on a me) of First Nations Taxation and Economic Development.' In *Sharing the Harvest*, Report of the National Roundtable on Aboriginal Economic Development and Resources. Ottawa: Minister of Supply and Services Canada.

Lemmon, J.C., and J. Kirkpatrick. 1990. *Native Entrepreneurs in Canada*. London,

Ont.: University of Western Ontario, National Center for Management and
Research Development, Working Paper Series no. NC 90-36.

Levy, F., and R. Murnane. 1992. 'U.S. Earnings Levels and Earnings Inequality:
A Review of Recent Trends and Proposed Explanations.' *Journal of Economic
Literature* 30, September.

Li, Peter S. 1988. *Ethnic Inequality in a Class Society*, Toronto: Thompson Educational Publishing.

Lim, L. 1990. 'Women's Work in Export Factories: The Politics of a Cause.' In
I. Tinker, ed., *Persistent Inequalities*. New York: Oxford University Press.

Lindsay, Colin. 1992. *Lone-parent Families in Canada*. Catalogue no.89-522E.
Ottawa: Statistics Canada.

Lipietz, Alain. 1987. *Mirages and Miracles*. London: Verso Books.

Lipsey, Richard G. 1993. 'Globalisation, Technological Change and Economic
Growth.' The Annual Sir Charles Carter Lecture, May.

Lipsig-Mumme, Carla. 1983. 'The Renaissance of Homeworking in Developed
Economies.' *Relations industrielles* 38(3): 545–67.

Little Bear, Leroy. 1976. 'A Concept of Native Title.' *Canadian Association for the
Support of Native Peoples Bulletin* 17(3): 30.

Lustig, Nora, Barry P. Bosworth, and Robert Z. Lawrence, eds. 1992. *North American Free Trade: Assessing the Impact*. Washington: Brookings Institute.

Luxton, M. 1990. 'Two Hands for the Clock: Changing Patterns in the Gendered
Division of Labour in the Home.' In M. Luxton, H. Rosenberg, and S. Arat-
Koc, eds, *Through the Kitchen Window: The Politics of Home and Family*. Toronto:
Garamond.

McBride, Stephen, and John Shields. 1993. *Dismantling a Nation: Canada and the
New World Order*. Halifax: Fernwood.

McCallum, Margaret E. 1986. 'Keeping Women in Their Place: The Minimum
Wage in Canada, 1910–25.' *Labour/Le Travail* 17 (Spring): 29–56.

McCloskey, Donald. 1985. *The Rhetoric of Economics*. Madison: University of
Wisconsin Press.

MacDonald, Leslie. 1985. 'Taxing Comprehensive Income: Power and Participation in Canadian Politics, 1962–1972.' Ph.D. dissertation, Carleton University.

MacDonald, Martha. 1991. 'Post-Fordism and the Flexibility Debate.' *Studies in
Political Economy*, Autumn.

– 1993. 'What Is Feminist Economics?' Paper prepared for Economic Equality
Workhop, Status of Women Canada, 29–30 November.

– 1995. 'Economic Restructuring and Gender in Canada: Feminist Policy Initiatives.' *World Development* 23(11).

MacDonald, Martha, and M. Pat Connelly. 1990. 'From Crisis to Crisis: Restructuring and Work in the Fishing Industry in Atlantic Canada.' Paper presented

at the International Labour Market Segmentation Conference, University of Notre Dame, Indiana.

McDowell, Linda. 1991. 'Life without Father and Ford: The New Gender Order of Post-Fordism.' *Transactions of the Institute of British Geography* 16: 400–19.

McFarland, Joan. 1993. 'Combining Economic and Social Policy through Work and Welfare: The Impact on Women.' Paper presented to the Economic Equity Workshop, Status of Women, Ottawa.

MacKinnon, Catharine. 1987. *Feminism Unmodified.* Cambridge, Mass.: Harvard University Press.

McKeen, Wendy. 1987. *Canadian Jobs Strategy: Current Issues for Women.* Ottawa: Canadian Advisory Council on the Status of Women.

Macklin, Audrey. 1992. 'Foreign Domestic Worker: Surrogate Housewife or Mail Order Servant?' *McGill Law Journal* 37(3).

McLeod Arnopoulous, Shiela. 1979. *Problems of Immigrant Women in the Canadian Labour Force.* Ottawa: Canadian Advisory Council on the Status of Women.

McLuhan, T.C. ed. 1971. *Touch the Earth: A Self-Portrait of Indian Existence.* New York: Simon and Schuster.

Macmillan, Katie, 1987. 'Free Trade and Canadian Women: An Opportunity for a Better Future.' Background paper, Canadian Advisory Council on the Status of Women, September.

McQuaig, Linda. 1987. *Behind Closed Doors: How the Rich Won Control of Canada's Tax System* (Markham: Penguin Books Canada Ltd.).

Madrid, Raul L. 1992. *Over-Exposed: US Banks Confront the Third World Debt Crisis.* Boulder: Westview Press.

Mahon, Rianne. 1987. 'From Fordism to ?: New Technology, Labour Markets and Unions.' *Economic and Industrial Democracy* 8.

– 1991. 'From Solidaristic Wages to Solidaristic Work: A Post-Fordist Historic Compromise for Sweden.' *Economic and Industrial Democracy* 12(3).

Maida, Carl A., Norma S. Gordon, and Norman L. Farberow. 1989. *The Crisis of Competence: Transitional Stress and the Displaced Worker.* New York: Brunner/ Mazel Psychosocial Stress Series no. 16.

Maloney, Maureen. 1988. 'Distributive Justice: That Is the Wealth Tax Issue.' *Ottawa Law Review* 20(3): 601.

– 1989. 'Women and the Income Tax Act: Marriage, Motherhood, and Divorce.' *Canadian Journal of Women and the Law* 3: 182.

– 1994. 'What Is the Appropriate Tax Unit for the 1990s and Beyond' In A.M. Maslove, ed., *Issues in the Taxation of Individuals.* Toronto: University of Toronto Press.

Martin, Linda, and Kelly Segrave. 1985. *The Servant Problem: Domestic Workers in North America.* Jefferson, NC: McFarland.

Maruani, Margaret. 1992. 'Les nouvelles frontières de la division sexuelle du marché du travail.' In Claudine Baudoux and Claude Zaidman, eds, *Égalité entre les sexes : Mixité et démocratie*. Paris: L'Harmattan.

Maruani, Margaret, and Chantal Nicole. 1989. *Au labeur des dames: Métiers masculins, emplois féminins*. Paris: Syros.

Mayatech Corporation. 1991. 'Gender and Structural Adjustment.' Mayatech Corporation, Silver Spring, Md. Series TR 91-1026-02. Case studies: Jamaica, Pakistan, Ghana, and Côte d'Ivoire.

Medjuck, S., M. O'Brien, and C. Tozer. 1992. 'From Private Responsibility to Public Policy: Women and the Cost of Care-Giving to Elderly Kin.' *Atlantis: A Women's Studies Journal* 17(2) (Spring-Summer).

'Memoria Testimonial: Primer Encuentro Trinacional de Trabajadoras ante la Integración Económica y el Tratado de Libre Comercio.' 1992. Unpublished document. Valle de Bravo Toluca, Mexico, 5–9 February.

Michalos, Alex C. 1988. 'A Case for a Progressive Annual Wealth Tax.' *Public Affairs Quarterly* 2(2): 105.

Mintz, Jack. 1991. 'The Role of Wealth Taxation in the Overall Tax System.' *Canadian Public Policy* 17(3): 248.

Mitchell, Allana. 1992a. Toronto *Globe and Mail*, 20 April.

– 1992b. 'Our Families Come First: Why More Mothers Are Choosing to Stay at Home.' *Chatelaine*, February.

Mitter, Swasti. 1986a. 'Industrial Restructuring and Manufacturing Homework: Immigrant Women in the UK Clothing Industry.' *Capital and Class* 27.

– 1986b. *Common Fate, Common Bond: Women in the Global Economy*. London: Pluto.

– 1990. 'The Impact of Flexible Employment on Women's Employment and Women's Lives.' Paper presented to Women's Studies Department, University of Toronto, February.

– 1993. 'On Organising Women in Casualised Work: A Global Overview.' In Sheila Rowbotham and Swasti Mitter, eds, *Dignity and Daily Bread: New Forms of Economic Organising among Poor Women in the Third World and the First*. London: Routledge.

Moghadam, Valentine. 1993. 'Gender Dynamics of Restructuring in the Semi-Periphery.' Paper prepared for conference on Engendering Wealth and Well-being, University of California, San Diego.

Mohanty, Chandra Talpade. 1991a. 'Cartographies of Struggle.' In Chandra Talpade Mohanty et al., eds, *Third World Women and the Politics of Feminism*. Bloomington: Indiana University Press.

– 1991b. 'Under Western Eyes: Feminist Scholarship and Colonial Discourses.' In Mohanty et al., eds, *Third World Women*.

– 1992. 'Feminist Encounters: Locating the Politics of Experience.' In Michele Barrett and Anne Phillips, eds, *Destabilizing Theory*. Cambridge, UK: Polity Press.

Molyneux, Maxine. 1985. 'Mobilization without Emancipation? Women's Interests, State and Revolution in Nicaragua.' *Feminist Studies* 11(2).

Momsen, Janet. 1988. 'Gender Roles in Caribbean Agricultural Labour.' In Malcolm Cross and Gad Hueman, eds, *Labour in the Caribbean*. London: Macmillan Caribbean.

Morton, Mary. 1988. 'Dividing the Wealth, Sharing the Poverty: The (Re)Formation of "Family" Law in Ontario.' *Canadian Review of Sociology and Anthropology* 25(2): 254–75.

Mossman, Mary Jane, and Morag MacLean. 1986. 'Family Law and Social Welfare: Toward a New Equality.' *Canadian Journal of Family Law* 5: 79–110.

Mouffe, Chantal. 1993. *The Return of the Political*. London: Verso.

Munroe, Trevor. 1972. *The Politics of Constitutional Decolonization, 1944–62*. Mona, Jamaica: Institute of Social and Economic Research.

Myles, John. 1991. 'Post-Industrialism and the Service Economy.' In Daniel Drache and Meric Gertler, eds, *The New Era of Global Competition: State Policy and Market Power*. Montreal: McGill-Queen's University Press.

Myles, J., G. Picot, and T. Wannell. 1988. 'The Changing Distribution of Jobs, 1981–86.' *Canadian Economic Observer*, November.

Mytelka, L. 1991. 'Global Shifts in the Textile and Clothing Industries.' *Studies in Political Economy* 37: 177–201.

Nadeau, Denise. 1992. 'Women Fight Back.' In Jim Sinclair, ed., *Crossing the Line*, 152–67. Vancouver: New Star Books.

Nakano Glenn, Evelyn. 1986. *Issei, Nisei, War Bride: Three Generations of Japanese American Women in Domestic Service*. Philadelphia: Temple University Press.

– 1992. 'From Servitude to Service Work: Historical Continuities in the Racial Division of Paid Reproductive Labor.' *Signs: Journal of Women in Culture and Society* 18(1).

Nash, June. 1983. 'The Impact of the Changing International Division of Labor on Different Sectors of the Labor Force.' In June Nash and María Patricia Fernández-Kelly, eds, *Women, Men, and the International Division of Labour*.

Nash, June, and María Patricia Fernández-Kelly, eds. 1983. *Women, Men, and the International Division of Labour*. New York: State University of New York Press.

National Action Committee on the Status of Women. 1985. *Submission to the Minister of Employment and Immigration on the Canadian Jobs Strategy*. Toronto: NAC.

– 1993a. 'Review of the Situation of Women in Canada 1992.'

– 1993b. 'Future of Women's Work: Preliminary Report.' June.

National Association of Women and the Law. 1991. *Background Paper in Support of Tax Resolutions*. Ottawa: NAWL.

National Council of Welfare. 1990. *Women and Poverty Revisited*. Ottawa: NCW.

National Union of Provincial Government Employees. 1989. *Canadian Women at Work: Their Situation, Their Union Status and the Influence on the Public Sector*. Ottawa: NUPGE.

Nelson, Julie. 1992. 'Gender, Metaphor and the Definition of Economics.' *Economics and Philosophy* 8(1): 103–25.

Nesiah, Vasuki. 'Toward a Feminist Internationality: A Critique of US Feminist Legal Scholarship.' *Harvard Women's Law Review* 16.

New Democratic Party (Canada). 1976. *New Democratic Policies, 1961–1976*, ed. Anne Scotton. Ottawa.

– 1993. *Strategy for a Full-Employment Economy*. Ottawa: NDP.

Ng, Roxanna. 1986. 'Social Construction of 'immigrant women' in Canada.' In R. Hamilton and M. Barrett, eds, *The Politics of Diversity*. Montreal: Black Rose Books.

– 1990. 'Immigrant Women: The Construction of a Labour Market Category.' In *Canadian Journal of Women and the Law* 4.

Ng, Winnie. 1993. Excerpt from written brief presented by Coalition of Visible Minority Women of Ontario to Ontario Cabinet Committee on NAFTA, 8 March 1993.

Nicholson, L., ed. 1990. *Feminism/Postmodernism*. New York: Routledge.

North American Free Trade Agreement. 1994. Ottawa: External Affairs Canada.

North-South Institute. 1994. *Expert Group Meeting on Women and Global Economic Restructuring: Final Report*. Prepared by Joanna Kerr.

OCDE. 1991. *Conduire le changement structurel, le rôle des femmes*. Paris: OCDE.

Oja, Gail. 1987. *Changes in the Distribution of Wealth in Canada, 1970–1984*. Cat. no. 13-588. Ottawa: Statistics Canada.

Oja, Gail, and R. Love. 1988. *Pensions and Incomes of the Elderly in Canada, 1971–1985*. Cat. no. 13-548. Ottawa: Statistics Canada.

Oliver, Melvin L., and Thomas M. Shapiro. 1990. 'Wealth of a Nation: A Reassessment of Asset Inequality in America Shows At Least One Third of Households Are Asset-Poor.' *American Journal of Economics and Sociology* 49(2): 129–51.

Olsen, Frances. 1983. 'The Family and the Market: A Study of Ideology and Legal Reform.' *Harvard Law Review* 96(7): 1497.

Ontario. Ministry of Industry, Trade and Technology. 1992. 'An Industrial Policy Framework for Ontario.' July.

Ontario. Ministry of Labour. 1993. *The Displaced Workers of Ontario: How Do They Fare?* Toronto, February.

Ontario Fair Tax Commission. 1992a. *Low Income Tax Relief Working Group Report.* Toronto: OFTC.
– 1992b. *Women and Taxation Working Group Report.* Toronto: OFTC.
– 1993. *Wealth Tax Working Group Report.* Toronto: OFTC.
Ontario Law Reform Commission. 1993a. *Report on Family Property Law.* Toronto: OLRC.
– 1993b. *Report on the Rights and Responsibilities of Cohabitants under the Family Law Act.* Toronto: OLRC.
Ontario Women's Directorate. 1993. 'Racial Minority Women: Women in the Labour Market.' January.
Organization for Economic Co-operation and Development. 1983. *Positive Adjustment Policies: Managing Structural Change.* Paris: OECD.
– 1993. *Women and Structural Change in the 1990s.* Paris: OECD. Report by Gunther Schmid.
Orloff, Ann Shola. 1993. 'Gender and the Social Rights of Citizenship: The Comparative Analysis of Gender Relations and Welfare States.' *American Sociological Review* 58 (June).
Osborne, David, and Ted Gabler. 1993. *Reinventing Government: How the Entrepreneurial Spirit Is Transforming the Public Sector.* New York: Penguin Books.
Oziewicz, Estanislao. 1992. 'Nanny Policy Called Necessary Protection.' Toronto: *Globe and Mail,* 29 April.
Pahl, Jan. 1989. *Money and Marriage.* Great Britain: MacMillan Educations Ltd.
Palma-Beltran, Ruby. 1991. 'Filipino Women Domestic Helpers Overseas: Profile and Implications for Policy.' *Asian Migrant* 4(2) (April–June).
– 1992. 'Gender Equity and Economic Efficiency in Adjustment Programmes.' In H. Afshar and C. Dennis, eds, *Women, Recession and Adjustment in the Third World.* London: Macmillan.
Palmer, Ingrid. 1994. 'Macro-Economics from a Gender Perspective,' Paper prepared for GO-NGO regional meeting: Women, Economics and Sustainable Development, Singapore, 26–29 April.
Palmer, Phyllis. 1987. 'Housewife and Household Worker: Employer-Employee Relationships in the Home, 1928–1941.' In Carol Groneman and Mary Beth Norton, eds, *'To Toil the Livelong Day': America's Women at Work, 1780–1980.* Ithaca: Cornell University Press.
– 1989. *Domesticity and Dirt: Housewives and Domestic Servants in the United States, 1920–1945.* Philadelphia: Temple University Press.
Parker A., M. Russo, D. Sommer, and P. Yaeger, eds. 1992. *Nationalisms and Sexualities.* New York: Routledge.
Pask, E.D., and M.L. McCall, eds. 1989. *How Much and Why? Economic Implica-*

tions of Marriage Breakdown: Spousal and Child Support. Calgary: Canadian Research Institute for Law and the Family, University of Calgary.

Pateman, Carole. 1988. *The Sexual Contract*. Oxford: Polity Press.

– 1989. 'Feminist Critiques of the Public/Private Dichotomy.' In *The Disorder of Women: Democracy, Feminism and Political Theory*. Cambridge: Polity.

Payer, Cheryl. 1974. *The Debt Trap: The International Monetary Fund and the Third World*. New York: Monthly Review.

Peach, C. 1968. *West Indian Migration to Britain: A Social Geography*. London: Oxford University Press.

Pearson, Ruth. 'Latin American Women and the New International Division of Labour: A Reassessment.' *Bulletin of Latin American Research* 5(2).

Pennington, Shelley, and Belinda Westover. 1989. *A Hidden Workforce: Home-workers in England, 1850–1985*. Basingstoke: MacMillan.

Perspectives on Labour and Income. 1993. 'Key Labour and Income Facts.' Vol. 5(1): 64.

Peterson, V. Spike. 1994. 'Women, Households, and the World Economy.' Prepared for the 9th Conference of the European Forum of Left Feminists, November.

– ed. 1992. *Gendered States*. Boulder: Lynne Rienner Publishers.

Peterson, V. Spike, and Anne Sisson Runyan. 1993. *Global Gender Issues*. Boulder: Westview Press.

Philipps, Lisa. 1992. 'Taxing Inherited Wealth: Ideologies about Property and the Family in Canada.' LL.M. thesis, Osgoode Hall Law School, York University.

Phillips, Anne, 1993. *Democracy & Difference*. University Park, Pa.: Pennsylvania State University Press.

Phillips, Paul, and Erin Phillips. 1993. *Women and Work: Inequality in the Canadian Labour Market*. Toronto: Lorimer.

Phipps, P. 1990. 'Industrial and Occupational Change in Pharmacy.' In B. Reskin and P. Roos, eds, *Job Queues, Gender Queues*. Philadelphia: Temple University Press.

Phizacklea, A. 1990. *Unpacking the Fashion Industry: Gender, Racism and Class in Production*. London: Routledge.

Phizacklea, A., and C. Wolkowitz. 1995. *Homeworking Women: Gender, Racism and Class at Work*. London: Sage.

Picot, G., J. Myles, and T. Wannell. 1990. 'Good Jobs / Bad Jobs and the Declining Middle: 1967–1986.' Research paper no. 29. Ottawa: Statistics Canada Analytical Studies Branch.

Pierson, Ruth Roach, and Marjorie Cohen. 1984. 'Educating Women for Work: Government Training Programs for Women before, during and after World

War II.' In Michael S. Cross and Gregory S. Kealey, eds, *Modern Canada 1930–1980's*. Toronto: McClelland and Stewart.

– 1994. *Canadian Women's Issues, volume II; Bold Visions*. Toronto: James Lorimer and Co.

Piore, M., and C. Sabel. 1984. *The Second Industrial Divide*. New York: Basic Books.

Pitrou, Agnès. 1987. 'À la recherche du temps gagné.' *Informations Sociales*, May.

Pollert, A. 1988. 'Dismantling Flexibility.' *Capital and Class* 34.

Pomeroy, William J. 1992. *The Philippines: Colonialism, Collaboration, and Resistance!* New York: International Publishers.

Populi. 1994. 'Industrial Might and Women's Rights.' *The UNFPA Magazine* 21(6) (June).

Porter, Ann. 1993. 'Women and Income Security in the Post-War Period: The Case of Unemployment Insurance, 1945–1962.' *Labour/Le Travail* 31 (Spring): 111–44.

Porter, Ann, and Barbara Cameron. 1987. *Impact of Free Trade on Women in Manufacturing*. Ottawa: Canadian Advisory Council on the Status of Women, September.

Postman, Neil. 1992. *Technopoly: The Surrender of Culture to Technology*. New York: Alfred A. Knopf.

Powell, Dorian. 1986. 'Caribbean Women and Their Response to Familial Experiences.' *Social and Economic Studies* 35(2): 83–127.

Pringle, Rosemary, and Sophie Watson. 1990. 'Fathers, Brothers, and Mates: The Fraternal State in Australia.' In Sophie Watson, ed., *Playing the State: Australian Feminist Interventions*. London: Verso.

Public Service Alliance of Canada. 1992. 'Homework (telework) for Federal Public Workers.' Kit for conference entitled 'From the Double Day to the Endless Day.' Toronto, November.

– 1993. *Go Home ... And Stay There?: A PSAC Response to Telework in the Federal Public Service*. Ottawa: PSAC.

– n.d. 'Homework: Discussion paper.'

Pujol, Michele. 1992. *Feminism and Anti-Feminism in Early Economic Thought*. Aldershot, Eng.: Edward Elgar.

Rapoport, Rhonda, and Robert Rapoport. 1969. 'Work and Family in Contemporary Society.' In John N. Edwards, ed., *The Family and Change*. New York: Knopf.

Rashid, A. 1980. *Characteristics of High Income Families*. Cat. no. 13-584. Ottawa: Statistics Canada.

– 1993. 'Seven Decades of Wages Changes.' *Perspectives on Labour and Income* 5(2): 17–21.

Rebick, Judy. 1993. Interview by Pat Armstrong for *Studies in Political Economy*, Toronto, 12 October.

Red Mexicana de Acción Frente al Libre Comercio (RMALC). 1992. *Memoria de Zacatecas: La opinión Pública y las negociaciones del Tratado de Libre Comercio: Alternativas Ciudadanas.* México, DF: RMALC, February.

Resnick, Steven, Harriet Fraad, and Richard Wolff. 1991. 'For Every Knight in Shining Armor There's a Castle to Be Cleaned: A Marxist/Feminist Analysis of the Household.' *Rethinking Marxism* 2(4): 9–69.

Richmond, Anthony (for Statistics Canada). 1989. *Current Demographic Analysis: Caribbean Immigrants.* Ottawa: Minister of Supply and Services.

Robinson, Joan. 1980. 'Introduction' to V. Walsh and H. Green, *Classical and Neo-classical Theories of General Equilibrium: Historical Origins and Mathematical Structure.* New York: Oxford University Press.

Rogerson, Carol. 1990. 'Women, Money, and Equality: The Background Issues.' In Karen Busby, Lisa Fainstein, and Holly Penner, eds, *Equality Issues in Family Law*, 97–118. Winnipeg: Legal Research Institute, University of Manitoba.

Romero, Mary. 1992. *Maid in the USA.* New York: Routledge.

Rosa, Kumudhini. 1993. 'The Conditions and Organisational Activities of Women in Free Trade Zones: Malaysia, Philippines and Sri Lanka, 1970–1990.' In Sheila Rowbotham and Swasti Mitter, eds, *Dignity and Daily Bread.* London: Routledge.

Rosenthal, Marguerite. 1990. 'Sweden: Promise and Paradox.' In Gertrude Gold-berg and Eleanor Kremen, eds, *The Feminization of Poverty: Only in America?* Westport, Conn.: Greenwood.

Rowbotham, Sheila, and Swasti Mitter. 1994. 'Introduction.' In Rowbotham and Mitter, eds, *Dignity and Daily Bread: New Forms of Economic Organizing among Poor Women in the Third World and the First.* London: Routledge.

Rubenstein, Hymie. 'The Impact of Remittances in the Rural English Speaking Caribbean.' In W.F. Stinner, Klaus de Albuquerque, and R.S. Bryce-Laporte, eds, *Return Migration and Remittances: Developing a Caribbean Perspective.* RILES Occasional Paper, no. 3. Washington: Research Institute and Ethnic Studies.

Rubery, Jill, ed. 1988. *Women and Recession.* London: Routledge and Kegan Paul.

Ruccio, D.F. 1991. 'When Failure Becomes Success: Class and the Debate over Stabilization and Adjustment.' *World Development*

Ruccio, D., S. Resnick, and R. Wolff. 1990. 'Class beyond the Nation State.' *Review of Radical Political Economics*, 22(1): 14–27.

Said, Edward. 1979. *Orientalism.* New York: Vintage Books.

Said, Edward. 1993. *Culture and Imperialism.* New York: Knopf.

Saint Pierre, Céline 1993. 'Recognizing the Working Mother: The Quebec Labour Movement and the Feminization of the Labour Force.' In Jane Jenson and

Rianne Mahon, eds, *The Challenge of Restructuring: North American Labor Movements Respond*. Philadelphia: Temple University Press.

Samuels, W., ed., 1990. *Economics as Discourse*. Boston: Kluwer.

Samuelson, Paul. 1956. 'Social Indifference Curves.' *Quarterly Journal of Economics* 70(1): 1–22.

Sander, Cerstin. 1992. 'Action and Reaction: The Linkages between Structural Adjustment Programmes and the Informal Economy in Jamaica.' Ph.D. dissertation, Queen's University, Department of Political Studies, Kingston, Ontario.

Sassen-Koob, Saskia. 1983. 'Labour Migrations and the New International Division of Labour.' In June Nash and Maria Patricia Fernández-Kelly, eds, *Women, Men and the International Division of Labour*, 175–204. Albany: State University of New York.

Satzewich, Vic. 1989. 'Racism and Canadian Immigration Policy: The Government's View of Caribbean Migration, 1962–66.' *Canadian Ethnic Studies* 21(): 77–97.

Sen, Amartya. 1984. 'Economics and the Family.' In *Resources, Values and Development*. Oxford: Blackwell.

– 1990. 'Gender and Cooperative Conflicts.' In Irene Tinker, ed., *Persistent Inequalities: Women and World Development*. New York: Oxford University Press.

Seward, Shirley, and Tremblay, Marc. 1989. 'Immigrants in the Canadian Labour Force: Their Role in Structural Change.' Ottawa: Studies in Social Policy.

Shackle, G.L.S. 1973. *An Economic Querist*. Cambridge: Cambridge University Press.

Sinclair, Jim. 1992. 'Cheap Labour, Cheap Lives.' In J. Sinclair, ed., *Crossing the Line*, 52–65. Vancouver: New Star Books.

Skrypnek, Berna, and Janet Fast, 1993. 'Trends in Canadian Women's Labour Force Behaviour: Implications for Government and Corporate Policy.' Paper presented at the Economic Equality Workshop, Status of Women Canada, Ottawa, 29–30 November.

Smith, Adam. 1937. *The Wealth of Nations*. Toronto: Random House.

Sparr, Pamela, ed. 1994. *Mortgaging Women's Lives: Feminist Critiques of Structural Adjustment*. London: Zed Books.

Spencer, Herbert. 1891. *Essays: Scientific, Political and Speculative*. New York: Appleton.

Spivak, G. 1988. *In Other Worlds*. New York: Routledge, Chapman and Hall.

Standing, G. 1989. 'Global Feminization through Flexible Labour.' *World Development* 17(7).

Statistics Canada. 1986a. *Income Distribution by Size 1984*. Cat. no. 13-207. Ottawa: Statistics Canada.

– 1986b. *The Distribution of Wealth in Canada 1984*. Cat. no. 13-580. Ottawa: Statistics Canada.

– 1986c. *1986 Census: Profile of Ethnic Groups*. Cat. no. 93-154. Ottawa: Statistics Canada.

– 1988. *Occupational Trends, 1961–1986*. Ottawa: Supply and Services Canada.

– 1990a. *Highlights: Disabled Persons in Canada*. Cat. no. 82-602. Ottawa: Statistics Canada.

– 1990b. *Selected Socio-economic Consequences of Disability for Women in Canada*. Cat. no. 82-615. Ottawa: Statistics Canada.

– 1990c. *Women in Canada. A Statistical Report*. 2nd edition. Ottawa: Statistics Canada.

– 1990d. *Labour Force Annual Averages: 1989*. Ottawa: Minister of Industry, Science and Technology.

– 1991. *Labour Force Annual Averages: 1990*. Ottawa: Minister of Industry, Science and Technology.

– 1992a. *A Closer Look: A Profile of People with Disabilities in British Columbia*. Ottawa: Statistics Canada.

– 1992b. *Dwellings and Households*. Cat. no. 93-311. Ottawa: Statistics Canada.

– 1992c. *Labour Force Annual Averages: 1991*. Ottawa: Minister of Industry, Science and Technology.

– 1992d. *Earnings of Men and Women*. Ottawa: Minister of Industry, Science and Technology.

– 1992e. *Canada's Women: A Profile of Their 1988 Labour Market Experience*. Cat. no. 71-205. Ottawa: Minister of Industry, Science and Technology.

– 1993a. *Families: Social and Economic Characteristics*. Cat. no. 93-320. Ottawa: Statistics Canada.

– 1993b. *Schooling, Work and Related Activities, Income, Expenses and Mobility* (1991 Aboriginal Peoples Survey). Cat. no. 89-534. Ottawa: Statistics Canada.

– 1993c. *Labour Force Annual Averages: 1992*. Cat. no. 71-220. Ottawa: Minister of Industry, Science and Technology.

– 1993d. *1991 Census: Labour Force Activity*. Cat. no. 93-324. Ottawa: Minister of Industry, Science and Technology.

– 1993e. *1991 Census: Employment Income by Occupation*. Ottawa: Minister of Industry, Science and Technology.

– 1993f. *Earnings of Men and Women*. Cat. no. 13-217. Ottawa: Minister of Industry, Science and Technology.

– 1993g. *Family Income: Census Families 1990*. Cat. no. 13-208. Ottawa: Minister of Industry, Science and Technology.

- 1993h. *The Daily.* 13 April.
- 1994. *Disability & Housing* (1991 Aboriginal Peoples Survey). Cat. no. 89-535. Ottawa: Statistics Canada.
Stewart, D., and L. McFadgen. 1992. 'Women and the Economic Consequences of Divorce in Manitoba: An Empirical Study.' *Manitoba Law Journal* 21.
Stiglitz, Joseph. 1989. 'Rational Peasants, Efficient Institutions and a Theory of Rural Organization.' In P. Bardhan, ed., *The Economic Theory of Agrarian Institutions*, 18–29. Oxford: Oxford University Press.
Stoddard, Ellwyn R. *Maquila: Assembly Plants in Northern Mexico.* El Paso: Texas Western Press.
Strassman, Diana, and Lyvia Polanyi. 1992. 'Shifting the Paradigm: Value in Feminist Critiques of Economics.' Paper presented at the First Annual Conference for International Feminist Economics, July.
Sunter, D. 1993. 'Working Shift.' *Perspectives on Labour and Income* 5(1): 18–21.
Sutherland, R., and J. Fulton. 1994. *Spending Smarter and Spending Less: Policies and Partnerships for Health Care in Canada.* Ottawa: The Health Group.
Swamy, Gurushi. 1981. 'International Migrant Workers' Remittances: Issues and Prospects.' World Bank Working Papers, no. 481. Washington: World Bank.
Swedberg, Richard, and Mark Granovetter. 1992. 'Economic Action and Social Structure: The Problem of Embeddedness.' In Richard Swedberg and Mark Granovetter, *The Sociology of Economic Life.* Boulder: Westview Press.
Task Force on Barriers to Women in the Public Service. 1990. *Beneath the Veneer.* Ottawa: Minister of Supply and Services Canada.
- 1981b. *Domestic Workers on Employment Authorizations.* Ottawa: Government of Canada, Office of the Minister of Employment and Immigration, April.
Tennyson, Brian Douglas, ed. 1990. *Canadian-Caribbean Relations: Aspects of a Relationship.* Sydney, NS: Centre for International Studies.
Tiano, Susan. 1990. 'Maquiladora Women: A New Category of Workers?' In Kathryn Ward, ed., *Women Workers and Global Restructuring.* Cornell: ILR Press.
Tilly, L.A., and J.W. Scott. 1978. *Women, Work and Family.* New York: Holt, Rinehart, and Winston.
Tobin, James. 1980. *Asset Accumulation and Economic Activity.* Oxford: Basil Blackwell.
Toronto Star. 1994. 'Death toll rises in Mexico battle.' 3 January.
Toye, J.F.I. 1993. *Dilemmas of Development.* Oxford: Blackwell.
Treasury Board. 1992. *Telework Pilot Program in the Public Service.* Ottawa: Supply and Services.
Truong, Thanh-Dam. 1990. *Sex, Money and Morality: Prostitution and Tourism in South-East Asia.* London: Zed Books.

Tunnicliffe, Ross D. 1993. 'Barriers to Business Financing: The Legal Context.' Presented at 'Financing First Nations' conference (sponsored by Native Investment and Trade Association of BC), Vancouver.

Turpel, Mary Ellen. 1990. 'Aboriginal Peoples and the Canadian Charter: Interpretive Monopolies, Cultural Differences.' *Canadian Human Rights Year Book*, vol. 6.

– 1991. 'Home/Land.' *Canadian Journal of Family Law* 10(1): 17–40.

United Nations Development Programme. 1993. *Human Development Report 1993*. New York: Oxford University Press.

Ursel, Jane. 1992. *Private Lives, Public Policy: 100 Years of State Intervention in the Family*. Toronto: Women's Press.

U.S. Agency for International Development. 1992 'Gender and Adjustment.' Washington: USAID.

Vasquez, Noel. 1992. 'Economic and Social Impact of Labour Migration. In G. Batistella and A. Paganoni, eds, *Philippine Labour Migration: Impact and Policy*, 39–67. Quezon City: Scalabrini Migration Center.

Vickers, Jeanne. 1991. *Women and the World Economic Crisis*. London: Zed Books.

Vickers, Jill, Pauline Rankin, and Christine Appelle. 1992. *Politics As If Women Mattered*. Toronto: University of Toronto Press.

Villasin, Fely. 1990. 'Domestic Workers from the Philippines: One Month Observation Report.' Toronto: INTERCEDE.

– 1992. 'Domestic Workers' Struggle for Equal Rights in Canada.' In Mary Ruby Palma-Bertran and Aurora Javate de Dios, eds, *Filipino Women Overseas Contract Workers: At What Cost?* Manila: Goodwill Trading Co.

Viva, 1992. 'Maid in New York. How to Get and Keep Your Help.' *Village Voice*, n.d., as cited in Romero 1992: 98.

Wagner, Richard E. 1980. 'Sense versus Sensibility in the Taxation of Personal Wealth.' *Canadian Taxation* 2(1), Spring.

Wall Street Journal. 1994. 'China orders foreign firms to unionize: Decree seeks to ease strife at plants, cut accidents – Employer abuses cited.' 29 June, A12.

Ward, David A. 1980. 'The Case against Capital Taxes.' *Canadian Taxation* 2(1), Spring.

Ward, Kathryn, ed. 1990. *Women Workers and Global Restructuring*. Ithaca: Cornell University Press.

Waring, Marilyn. 1988. *If Women Counted: A New Feminist Economics*. San Francisco: Harper and Row.

Warner, Judith Ann, and Helen K. Henderson. 1990. 'Latina Women Immigrants' Waged Domestic Labour: Effects of Immigration Reform on the Link between Private Households and the International Labour Force.' American Sociological Association paper.

Weinert, Patricia. 1991. 'Foreign Female Domestic Workers: Help Wanted!' Geneva: ILO World Employment Programme working paper.

Weintraub, E.R. 1991. *Stabilizing Dynamics*. Cambridge: Cambridge University Press.

Weston, Anne, Ada Piazze-McMahon, and Ed Dosman. 1992. 'Free Trade with a Human Face?' Ottawa: The North-South Institute.

West Yorkshire Homeworking Group. 1990. *A Penny a Bag: Campaigning on Homework*. Batley: Yorkshire and Humberside Low Pay Unit.

West Yorkshire Homeworking Unit. 1992. 'Outwork in Leeds.' Unpublished report.

White, Julie. 1993. 'One Union Responds: The Case of the Canadian Union of Postal Workers.' In Jane Jenson and Rianne Mahon, eds, *The Challenge of Restructuring: North American Labor Movements Respond*. Philadelphia: Temple University Press.

Williams, Eric. 1944. *Capitalism and Slavery*. Chapel Hill: University of North Carolina Press.

Williams, Fiona. 1989. *Social Policy: A Critical Introduction*. London: Polity Press.

Williams, Joan. 1991. 'Gender Wars: Selfless Women in the Republic of Choice.' *New York University Law Review* 66: 1559.

Williams, Mariama. 1994. 'Clintonomics – The New Social Contract: A Gender Perspective.' Paper presented at the International Studies Association Convention, Washington, DC.

Wilson, Gail. 1987. 'Money: Patterns of Responsibility and Irresponsibility in Marriage.' In *Give and Take in Families: Studies in Resource Distribution*. London, Boston: Allen & Unwin.

Wolff, Edward N. 1987. *International Comparisons of the Distribution of Household Wealth*. Oxford: Clarendon Press.

– 1992. 'Changing Inequality of Wealth.' *American Economic Review* 82(2): 552.

Wolfson, Lorne H. 1989. 'The Family Law Act: How Planning for It May Ruin Your Marriage While Not Planning for It May Destroy Your Company.' *Canadian Family Law Quarterly* 4: 322.

Women's Reference Group, Canadian Labour Force Development Board. 1992. 'A Draft Paper: Towards a Women's Agenda on Training.' Toronto: Women's Reference Group.

Woodman, Faye. 1990. 'The Charter and the Taxation of Women.' *Ottawa Law Review* 22(3): 625.

Woodward, Jack. 1989. *Native Law*. Toronto: Carswell.

Wynant, Larry, and James Hatch. 1990. *Banks and Small Business Borrowers*. London: Western Business School, University of Western Ontario.

Yalnizyan, Armine. 1993. 'Defining Social Security, Defining Ourselves: Why We

Need to Change Our Thinking Before It's Too Late.' Monograph. Toronto: Canadian Centre for Policy Alternatives.

Yanz, Linda. 1992. 'Account of NAC's Global Strategies Committee.' Memo to NAC's AGM Participants.

Yeatman, Anna. 1990. *Bureaucrats, Technocrats, Femocrats: Essays on the Contemporary Australian State*. Sydney: Allen and Unwin.

– 1993. 'Voice and Representation in the Politics of Difference.' In S. Gunew and A. Yeatman, eds, *Feminism and the Politics of Difference*. Halifax: Fernwood Publishing.

– 1994. *Postmodern Revisionings of the Political*. New York: Routledge.

York, Geoffrey. 1993. 'Social Programs Called Outdated.' *Globe and Mail*, 17 November, A1.

Yorkshire and Humberside Low Pay Unit. 1991. 'A Survey of Homeworking in Calderdale.' Unpublished report.

Young, C.F.L. 1994a. 'Child Care and the Charter: Privileging the Privileged.' 2 *Review of Constitutional Studies* 20.

– 1994b. 'Taxing Times for Lesbians and Gay Men: Equality at What Cost?' *Dalhousie Law Journal* 17(2).

– 1994c. 'Child Care – A Taxing Issue.' *McGill Law Journal* 39(3).

Young, Iris Marion. 1990. *Justice and the Politics of Difference*. Princeton: Princeton University Press.

Young, Margaret. 1994. 'Canada's Immigration Program: Background Paper.' Ottawa: Minister of Supply and Services.

Yuval-Davis, Nira. 1991. 'The Citizenship Debate: Women, Ethnic Processes and the State.' *Feminist Review* 39: 58–68.

Zier, Joe. 1994. 'The Green Spouse Effect: Asset Syphoning, in Anticipation of Marriage Breakdown Is Becoming a Harsh Fact of Modern Life.' *The National: CBA Magazine*, May.